# Acceptance

# Acceptance

### A MEMOIR

### Emi Nietfeld

PENGUIN PRESS
NEW YORK
2022

PENGUIN PRESS
An imprint of Penguin Random House LLC
penguinrandomhouse.com

Portions of the material on pages 249–50 and 266 appeared in
different form as "Self Portrait as a Human Interest Story" in *Longreads*,
December 19, 2019. Copyright © 2019 by Emi Nietfeld.

LIBRARY OF CONGRESS CATALOGING-IN-PUBLICATION DATA
Names: Nietfeld, Emi, author.
Title: Acceptance: a memoir / Emi Nietfeld.
Description: New York: Penguin Press, 2022.
Identifiers: LCCN 2021046322 (print) | LCCN 2021046323 (ebook) |
ISBN 9780593489475 (hardcover) | ISBN 9780593489482 (ebook)
Subjects: LCSH: Nietfeld, Emi. | Foster children—
United States—Biography.
Child welfare—United States. | Social mobility—United
States—Psychological aspects
Classification: LCC HT612 .N54 2022 (print) | LCC HT612 (ebook) |
DDC 305.5/130973—dc23/eng/20211117
LC record available at https://lccn.loc.gov/2021046322
LC ebook record available at https://lccn.loc.gov/2021046323

Printed in the United States of America
1st Printing

Designed by Amanda Dewey

# Acceptance

# INTRODUCTION

One week before my fiancé's parents met my mom, I paced across my living room, figuring out what to tell them. "Do I have to say anything?" I asked Annette, my mentor from high school, over the phone. I prayed that my mom would show up showered and park far enough away that they wouldn't see the trash piled to the ceiling of her minivan. Maybe then they'd see the parent I loved, who'd snuck me to figure drawing classes while I was in foster care, who'd taken me to the library to study after the residential treatment counselors confiscated my books, who'd driven me from Minneapolis to Washington, DC, just for a photo exhibition.

"What have you told them?" Annette asked.

I bit my lip and stared out at the ginkgo trees outside my apartment in New York's West Village. "I said I went to boarding school. That's what I always say."

"Emi, you're getting married in a month."

"Seven weeks." Even this seemed too soon; I'd hoped the families would introduce themselves at the rehearsal dinner, pose for a picture after the ceremony, and then never see each other again. I wanted my future in-laws to believe that I'd always been destined for an elite university and a *New York Times* wedding announcement, not the truth: that I'd slept in my car while writing my college applications. Perhaps Byron's parents had sensed my deception—they'd bought themselves plane tickets to my hometown the same week we'd be there finalizing details.

"And they never asked about your family, how you grew up, anything like that?" Disapproval leached out of my mentor's voice. I imagined her stern face, pale skin harsh against her dark hair. I felt like a teenager all over again.

But what did Annette think I would have told them? When I vented about my mom's hoarding and about how she'd had me medicated, letting the doctors believe I was dramatic and delusional rather than admitting her own problems, Annette would say, "She's sick, Emi." For years, the idea of having a normal adulthood—let alone the intellectual life I'd craved—had seemed absurd. Yet Annette chided, "Let sleeping dogs lie." Of course I hadn't told my future in-laws anything.

"I think maybe they should just meet her," I offered. "Make their own first impression."

"No. You absolutely cannot do that. You need to call Byron's mother right away. You have to give them time to prepare."

Annette was probably right. What would my in-laws think if they expected someone normal, of modest means, and then met my mom?

Still, once we hung up, I sat on my Moroccan rug and searched for any excuse not to call. Saying anything felt like a betrayal. When I was growing up in Minnesota, my mom was the smartest person I knew, besides a few doctors. It was us against the provincial idiots. When I talked about my family, I described my brilliant half brother who never went to college and my mom who almost got into Stanford, whose life would have been so different if she had. She was the one person who had always believed in me and my Ivy League ambitions, even when that faith seemed untethered from reality. Didn't my in-laws deserve to see that version of my mom?

Did they really need to know that because of her, I knew what it meant to be desperate? I wanted to forget all the places I'd slept, no one knowing where I was, always one step away from tragedy. All I'd wanted growing up was to read books and study, but instead I learned how few acceptable ways there were to need help. You had to be perfect, deserving, hurt in just the right way—even then, adults were so constrained in what they could offer. Everyone who dealt with disadvantaged kids, from therapists to college admissions officers, treated us as if we could overcome any abuse or neglect with sheer force of will. In the present tense, I was sick of pretending to be so "resilient," so I preferred to keep my mouth shut.

But I rarely said no to Annette, the woman who'd signed up to help out a struggling girl a decade ago. Even though I was twenty-five now, not fifteen, I still felt like my survival depended on keeping all the adults happy.

I dialed.

"Hello?" My mother-in-law-to-be's crisp enunciation scared the shit out of me.

"Hi, Christine." I put on the voice I learned in college and made small talk. We talked about her latest run, that weekend's chamber music concert, our upcoming date at the Met Opera.

"I wanted to, um, share some information with you before you meet my mom." I read what Annette told me to say from a Post-it note: "My mom is a compulsive shopper and hoarder. It's put a lot of strain on our relationship. I last lived at home when I was fourteen."

Once I'd said it, I felt crazy that I'd been with her son for four years. Four Thanksgivings, four Christmases skiing in Aspen, four New Year's Eve tins of caviar, and they didn't even have this stripped-down version. But then again, my college friends didn't know. My colleagues assumed I grew up rich, next to a lake. Even Byron, with whom I planned to spend my life, had only the outline.

I'd done everything I could to distance myself from that old world: moved to Manhattan, landed a fancy job, applied Retin-A fastidiously to remove the worry lines etched into my face, and shot my cheeks with Botox to soften my jaw, thickened from clenching. I worked out twice a day until my abs popped and woke up early even on the weekends. I basked in my apparent health and productivity, but I'd organized my life so that I never had more than fifteen minutes free for everything I'd overcome to come back to haunt me.

ONE WEEK LATER, in Minneapolis, forty-five minutes after we'd told my mom to meet us, I saw her and gripped Byron's hand. "Hi, honey!" she said, eyes brightening. She'd cleaned herself up—her greasy hair still had comb marks through it. A billfold bulged out of her pocket, making her slacks stretch across her stomach and then sag over the wrinkled black leather of her men's tennis shoes. When she leaned in to hug me, must filled my nose. "I have some things for you in the car."

Byron's parents appeared outside the restaurant moments later, fifteen minutes early. His mom wore pearl stud earrings, lipstick, and a blouse, eager to make a good impression. After I'd told her about my mom's issues, she'd quizzed me on her hobbies and interests. I felt grateful to be marrying into such a considerate family.

My mom stuck her hand out to shake theirs. I sighed in relief; if they didn't hug her, they might not smell her. As we took our seats, I wasn't sure what worried me more: that my mom would disgust them or that she'd charm them, as she charmed the doctors when I was young.

Once we'd ordered, my mom pushed her glasses up on her nose. "So what do you do?" she asked Byron's father.

"I'm a software engineer," he said, smiling, explaining that his wife and two sons—everyone—were also engineers.

My mom nodded approvingly. "Wow. Smart family. Good genes." She took a sip of water. "I was a crime scene photographer for thirty-one years. People always think it's upsetting, but you get used to it very quickly. Dead people basically all look the same."

When the food came, my mom was explaining her system of shopping for care packages for kids overseas. "Last year, we filled seven hundred shoeboxes, plus had three SUVs' worth of stuff left over!" Byron's parents smiled politely before their eyes drifted to the wall. Operation Christmas Child was a charity meant to teach American children about generosity and compassion, but my mom had turned it into a factory operation. She detailed how much she paid, item by item. Even with her "incredible bargains"—"fifty cents for a pair of scissors!"—these hauls surely ate up most of her pension and Social Security. I clenched Byron's hand until he shook it away.

"Oh, wow, that's amazing!" my fiancé interjected. He kept talking until my mom had lost her train of thought and took a tiny bite.

Once Byron paused to eat, my mom leapt into her favorite topic besides shopping. "I have an amazing memory. Almost photographic," she explained as the waiter boxed up her burger. "Emi's brilliant, too, as I'm sure you noticed. But sometimes she messes things up. She got her birth weight wrong in her college application essay!" My hand flopped under the table, searching for Byron's fingers, something to grip.

I wanted to yell at her, but I knew that wouldn't impress my future in-laws. My mom would probably just think I was premenstrual. Instead I just smiled, my lips tight. "Does that really matter?"

She turned to Byron's parents. "Ask your old mother! I know. I was there."

It was a familiar argument: these outsiders should trust her, not me. But I couldn't say anything more to defend myself. It would be so easy for my mom to sabotage me. She would never do it maliciously; it would be an accident: my beleaguered mother sharing the story of her daughter's troubled teenage years. Her need for validation as a parent would once again trump my need for privacy, my perspective on the facts. It was up to me to keep the peace by saying nothing.

AFTER WE SAID GOODBYE, Byron and I walked my mom back to her car. I kept looking over my shoulder to check that his parents weren't spying. My mom complained to Byron that the police were out to get her because she couldn't see through the back windshield. "That's what rearview mirrors are for!" She opened the door and the stench of rotting bananas drifted out.

"I'm surprised you're getting married in Minneapolis," my mom said as she dug through plastic shopping bags, orphaned shoes, and pet toys that she thought would amuse children in war-torn countries. "Why not the Harvard Club? Byron, isn't your grandfather a member there?"

"He is," Byron said. My fists clenched. He whispered into my ear, "Just take whatever she gives you. We'll throw it away later."

But the stuff wasn't the problem: it was my whole life. How many times had I stood outside my mom's car, waiting for her to clean out the passenger seat, to pick me up from some place that was supposed to take care of me because she couldn't? Each time, she offered me something— seven Mitchum deodorant sticks, four palettes of watercolors, a case of crumpled SlimFast bars—as if it compensated for the fact that the only space we shared was a vehicle loaded with trash.

"We really have to go," I said. "Wedding stuff." She ignored me.

When Byron said we had to leave, my mom turned around, eyes glowing, wet. "I'm so proud of you," she said to me.

I had to get away before I cried or screamed.

I ran back to our rental car. I was supposed to feel relieved: Our parents had met. My wedding was still on. I'd made it through another visit with my mom without a confrontation. The next day, I'd fly back to New York and resume the life I couldn't even fathom ten years prior.

But the détente came at such a high cost. No matter what I achieved, it never got any easier.

## One

Before my first day of prekindergarten, I knelt beside my bed and prayed, "Dear Lord Jesus, please let me learn how to read." Then I cried, filled with the desire to learn and terrified that I'd fail. It became one of my mom's favorite stories about me: how studious I was, how sincere.

By the end of the week, I was tearing through books. All I wanted to do was study. I memorized Bible verses competitively and planned to attend the best college in the world: Moody Bible Institute in Chicago. With God's blessing, anything was possible—I could disprove evolution, become a medical missionary, find a cure for AIDS, *and* perform praise pop to sold-out stadiums. Meanwhile, my teachers called home about my uncombed hair, dirty socks, and shrunken shirts. Every few months, my dad's mother, Grandma Edna, visited and made me cry as she critiqued my grooming, dragging me to the beauty school to get an awful haircut.

"Some of us have to work for a living," my mom huffed as soon as my grandmother left. My mom earned the money; she and I did all the housework. My father had briefly been a nurse but stopped working before I was born. He believed it was the women's job to cook and clean (unless it was warm enough to grill bratwursts).

My mom bemoaned what had become of her life. As a girl, she'd dreamed of attending Stanford. "I almost got in," she told everyone she could. "I think they only rejected me because I was sixteen." Remaining at home was not an option: her parents starved their daughters, allowing each of them a single can of Metrecal diet drink for breakfast and making them do calisthenics while chanting songs in unison. (All four sisters would go on to struggle with their weight, chronic illnesses, and hoarding.) Eager to escape, my mom fled to a rural campus of the University of Minnesota, where she studied art and education and then got a job at the state crime lab.

Apparently, everything would have been different if my mom had gone to Stanford. Especially when things were tense with my father, she rhapsodized about how she could have been living in California, with palm trees and an ocean, instead of scraping ice off her windshield six months out of the year. She would have married a medical student who made good money and helped out at home, instead of marrying two deadbeats, one after the other.

I doubted that things were so simple, an inevitable path from point A to point B. Like when my mom told the story of how she met my dad: she was thirty-eight, with a ten-year-old son from her first marriage, and longed for a blonde daughter to name "Honey." My dad had a hazy backstory involving photography school, a botched surgery, a monastery, lots of LSD, hallucinations of headless chickens falling from trees, and a stint in solitary confinement after throwing baby bottles full of blood at the Pentagon. When my mom met him, he'd been bouncing around for twenty years. He had platinum hair and stonewashed blue eyes but no stable address. Two months later, she married him, even though the son from her first marriage begged her not to. Ten-year-old Noah feared a stepfather and a baby would sabotage his future. My mom told this story with a laugh because Noah's premonition proved true: my father didn't want a stepson and banished Noah downstairs to raise himself. My dad didn't want kids, period. "But he was too lazy to go buy condoms!" my mom told me, chuckling. Just after she turned forty, she gave birth to me.

Luckily, when my father held me, "he fell in love." He nixed the "Honey" idea and named me Margaret Frances. My father was home every day, watching *Jeopardy!* or building computers, our half-Maltese, half-cockapoo mutt, Poochie, sitting beside him. I didn't mind his strict rules: no nail polish (too sexy), no sports (filled with lesbians), no Girl Scouts (filled with lesbians and abortionists). Even when I wasn't allowed to see Noah, it made sense: he was my half brother, not my real brother, according to my father. Both my parents called me an only child. But as the years passed, my mom chafed over my dad's controlling ways and started spending her lunch hours scouring the clearance sections at local stores. She shopped in secret, buying a hundred Winnie-the-Pooh watches for one dollar each at Target, hiding the loot in her office. After piano recitals, she snuck me to McDonald's for ice cream—outings that would become her favorite memories.

I couldn't stand hearing my mom complain, the way she acted as if she had no agency. By the time I was eight, I told her all the time, "If you hate my dad so much, why don't you just get a divorce?"

"Oh, sweetheart," she said in the voice that indicated I was cluelessly naive. After my father lost his job, my grandma had given him a trust fund worth two hundred thousand dollars. It was a lot of money, even to Grandma Edna, the widow of a small-town doctor. My mom, bitterly, called it "a retainer for our marriage." During the boom years of the nineties, the interest my parents withdrew was almost as much as my mom made working full time. The money did its job: my parents stayed together, and we lived in a suburb and rented out the duplex my mom owned in Minneapolis. We were middle class, almost exactly at the median—but if one thing changed, we wouldn't be anymore.

When the dot-com bubble burst, my parents started fighting more: my dad blocking my mom in the doorway, my parents throwing phone books in the kitchen, my mom calling the police, both of them sitting in a squad car, the cop telling them to civilly decide who'd file the tax returns while I hid in the garage.

That same year, I became the state champion in Bible memorization. I walked door-to-door by myself hawking fundraising calendars and sold so many I got to ride in a limo. While my parents yelled at each other downstairs, I lay on my mattress and schemed about how I could hijack the ABBA cover band the A-Teens and rewrite their songs to glorify the Lord. I took for granted that, no matter what happened in my life, I could escape into my ambitions; they would transport me to a future where the way I grew up couldn't matter less.

ONE MORNING, my mom pulled me out of fourth grade and swore me to secrecy. "I'm not going to lie to my father!" I argued. "It's a sin." But then she bribed me with Radio Disney, a rare secular treat. Rain pounded on the windshield and Lil' Bow Wow crooned on AM 1440 as my mom drove me to see my first therapist.

We pulled into an office park. Inside a dumpy building, a lady wearing fancy shoes took me to a room filled with toys. Smiling, she asked me to make a family out of dolls. A one-way observation mirror stretched along the wall.

Immediately, I suspected why my mom had brought me to therapy: she was looking for a confession of abuse, something that would justify leaving and make it easier for her to win custody. I folded my arms and refused to draw a house or play in the sandbox. When the therapist dropped me back off with my mom, she explained, "Sometimes it takes a while for the resistance to wear down."

After that, I didn't trust shrinks, and I didn't trust my mom, who seemed irritated she'd taken time off work to get nothing. "I can't believe you made me miss school," I complained as she drove me back. My mom reached over and flicked off the radio, ". . . Baby One More Time" giving way to the swoosh of windshield wipers.

It almost seemed as if my mom wanted me to have been abused, in some gruesome way she didn't know about, because it would make her life easier. She claimed she took me to therapy because she wanted to help. But nothing was wrong with me, besides that I was a bookworm with a bowl cut dressed in outgrown clothes whose parents hated each other.

Or maybe my mom was sad that I wasn't a "child": I'd been doing all my family's dishes and laundry since I was five. I often shoveled our driveway for hours, my labor cheaper than buying a snowblower. But I was that way because I had to be. In my responsibilities and my grand dreams, I found independence, believing I was the star of God's great saga. Now I felt like a pawn in my mom's plans.

IN THE END, my mom didn't need me to produce a confession: that spring, my dad told me he was changing his name to Michelle. After the "stunning announcement," my mom moved out and into the lower apartment of the duplex she owned in the city. I lived with Michelle while my parents fought over custody.

"How do you feel?" a social worker asked me. I sat on my hands in an office filled with boxes and manila envelopes. The filing cabinets, I was sure, contained the lives of kids like me, locked up for eternity in this windowless bureaucracy with musty carpet that irritated my allergies.

"Fine," I replied, guarded. Like the play therapist, the custody evaluators wanted to extract secrets. They would read whatever they wanted into what I said. One wrong word, I suspected, could destroy my life.

All of them called me "traumatized"—by the divorce, but mostly by the fact that my father was coming out as a woman. It was 2002; there hadn't even been a trans person on *Oprah*. No one would believe me that I was relieved my parents had separated. Once she started transitioning,

Michelle was happier and nicer. She became a Unitarian, and I quickly stopped believing in an Abrahamic God who sent Girl Scouts to hell with their lesbian lovers, the abortionists. If my loss of faith was a loss, I didn't realize it. At my new public school in the suburbs, where I went to fifth grade, I even got to play the drums.

"I want to live with Michelle," I told the social worker and everyone who'd listen.

She nodded empathetically, then reminded me that they didn't consider children's wishes until they turned twelve. I was only ten, so my preference didn't matter. The process infuriated me. Why ask how I felt if it didn't matter what I wanted, as if my desires were completely decoupled from my emotional state? Maybe, as people, the social workers cared. But, to the system, it didn't matter. The entire custody evaluation seemed like a joke. For months, my mom moved boxes of all the junk she'd quickly accumulated into the rental apartment upstairs, which she'd left vacant to use as storage. At the home visit, we wore matching sweaters and showed off our sewing projects. They thought we were so cute; I didn't think to pick a fight with my mom or tell the social workers to look upstairs.

The Friday night before I started sixth grade, Michelle came home from family court and told me to pack. "D's on her way," she said: my mom had won custody.

I was moving in with my mom, changing school districts, leaving my friends without saying goodbye. Michelle was moving away, across the country, saying she couldn't keep dealing with my mom. I'd see her a few more times that month; then, after one phone call, we'd never have another conversation. Bleary-eyed, I shoved my *Yu-Gi-Oh!* cards and library books into a black plastic garbage bag and kissed Poochie goodbye.

My mom's car pulled up in the driveway, headlights blazing, victorious.

———

I KNEW THAT any reasonable parent in my mom's situation would take their kid to therapy if they could. But I resisted: What good did it do to talk about things I couldn't change that were still unfolding?

When we sat down at the first family therapy session a few months after I moved in with my mom, I learned that counseling wasn't about my feelings anyway. "I need to collect evidence," my mom explained to the psychologist as she opened her journal. "In case he"—she used Michelle's old male name, as always—"tries to contest the custody decision."

"*Michelle*," I hissed, hating my mom and hating the shrink for acting like it was normal for a parent to haul a child to his office and ask the kid, baldly, to provide ammunition.

I recognized that, from my mom's vantage point, she had rescued me. Without Michelle to spoil our fun, we could drive ten hours each way to go to the world's number-one amusement park and stay out late on school nights, clearance-shopping until the mall cops escorted us out. We knew how to sing seven different renditions of "Happy Birthday" in harmony. Under the fluorescent lights of Walgreens, we pretended to star in a reality TV show.

My mom had done so much for me, and Michelle had absconded, yet I was completely ungrateful. I missed Poochie. My mom and I were broke, with no more support from my grandma, mired in legal bills and credit card debt, the house full of trash and rustling with mice. At my new underfunded public school in Minneapolis, I was utterly unchallenged and relentlessly bullied. Combining the social skills of a Bible quiz champion with my new provocative secular outfits—including a fishnet-sleeve top and a miniskirt that zipped all the way up, purchased by Michelle for my first day of sixth grade—I was an easy target. Classmates called me a slut and a ho a hundred times a day. Adults told me I needed a thicker skin; there was no way to stop it.

Things went from bad to worse around my eleventh birthday, when an eighth grader started groping me on the bus. When he threatened me and forced me to touch him, I finally told my mom. She'd just come home from work and looked utterly exhausted. "Well, did you tell your teacher?" my mom asked. When I said no, she told me to go tell someone at school: she wasn't there when it happened; there was nothing she could do. I knew better than to go to her when other bad things happened that year. All my friends seemed to have similar experiences, but we had no cultural depictions we could relate to, no way to talk about it except in whispers in the middle of the night. During the afternoons, scared to be alone, I wandered around with the other children who had no one watching them. Unable to sleep in my own bed, I crawled into my mom's.

"I think Emi has ADD," my mom told the psychologist. She explained that she had attention deficit disorder and so did my brother, though he was never diagnosed. (My mom had tried, but the doctor refused.) In our family mythology, that was why my brother never went to college and instead worked as many shifts as he could as a security guard.

My mom laid out the evidence: I was disheveled, disorganized, and chronically late. Most damning: when I read, I became "hyperfocused."

I yelled at her to stop talking about me as if I weren't there. The psychologist took rapt notes on what my mom was saying. Why wouldn't he believe her? She was white and well spoken, with a house, a college degree, and full custody of me. My complaints meant nothing to him because I was a child. So, like a child, I picked up a stuffed animal and threw it at the shrink. Behind her bifocals, my mom raised her eyebrows, as if to say, "You see?"

After one more hour-long appointment and completing a brief questionnaire, I was referred to a pediatrician for medication.

———

ILLNESS GALVANIZED MY MOM. As a government employee, she got excellent benefits. Even though she didn't have the money for special classes or supervision until she got home, she could always take me to the doctor. Whenever I had a stomachache, a headache, or a cough, we went to the urgent care clinic. Usually, by the time I was out of the house, I felt better, but we were already there and had nothing else to do, so we stayed. I loved the waiting room, so clean, with a great collection of magazines.

Even though our HMO had electronic medical records, and my mom knew all the nurses by name, no one seemed to notice that we were there almost every week, sometimes multiple times. It was the way my mom showed her love for me: the doctor, then French fries for dinner after. I tried to drag out our evenings so that we didn't have to go home, where the stench of mouse pee permeated every room.

My mom regretted that Noah never got treated for ADD. The doctor had asked to speak with my brother alone: "Do you have ADD?" My brother said no. To my mom, this was proof of the doctor's incompetence. "Why would you ask an eleven-year-old if he has ADD? How would he know?" Yet for whatever reason, she didn't take him to another doctor.

She seemed to feel guilty about this. She couldn't make Michelle like Noah. My mom was too busy to force her son to do his homework or even ensure that he got to school. When he was seventeen and considering college, she had too much on her plate to give him guidance about financial aid. There were so many things my mom couldn't do for Noah— the least the doctor could have done was prescribe Ritalin.

She wouldn't make the same mistake with me. No one asked me if I had ADD or listened when I protested that I got straight A's and that when I didn't pay attention at school it was because I knew all of the material.

The pediatrician gave me Concerta. When I freaked out, I got Xanax. After a few weeks of Wellbutrin, my mom fed me her leftover Adderall, just as a trial. This didn't seem to bother the physician's assistant I was seeing, who wrote me my own prescription. When the amphetamine made me jittery and sweaty and cry hysterically, he took that as a sign I was depressed.

"Come to the house," I begged the adults, sure that if anyone saw how we lived, they'd understand why I was increasingly miserable.

"Emi is exaggerating," my mom said. "She's spoiled."

The family therapist told me to clean up and assigned me chores. "You can start by washing the dishes."

"We don't have hot water," I shot back. My mom admitted that was true. It was winter and we couldn't shower. The psychologist told her to fix it, but never brought it up again. In the years that followed, lots of professionals became privy to my living situation. Out of the blue, I got a hacking cough. "It's because our house is so dirty," I told the pediatrician. "There are mice everywhere." The doctor prescribed me inhalers. My mom openly speculated that my migraines were because of mold; I was put on anticonvulsants. I stepped on a Christmas ornament walking to the kitchen in July and needed surgery to extract shards of leaded glass from my foot. The doctor seemed unfazed.

No one would listen to me. No one would trust me. No one came.

"I can't take it," I yelled at my mom. "I don't want to live here anymore." When I got "hysterical," my mom put me on the phone with the nurse helpline to talk me down.

Just after I turned thirteen, a kind voice suggested I go to a shelter.

"That's fine if you want to get molested," my mom said. I winced. "You think it will be better than living with your mom, but it won't be." We had this conversation many times: other girls had to live with their moms' boyfriends, men who inevitably raped them.

Along the way, I picked up new coping skills that became more and more central to my life: the calm after I threw up or scratched my arms with safety pins; the thrill of losing weight and edging closer to death, which began to feel like my only way out.

Shortly after the nurse suggested a shelter, I went to the psych ward for the first time. I loved it there. I stopped coughing in the clean air and luxuriated in the endless hot water, the meals that came on trays. As soon as I got home, I wanted to go back. The doctors prescribed more and more intense drugs until I was on antipsychotics. My mom took me to dialectical behavior therapy, where a tableful of teenagers read aloud from worksheets. "Not accepting pain = suffering" a photocopy declared in Comic Sans font, insisting that our misery was a choice. Adults had decided that our problem was emotion regulation; we were there to learn skills to fix our bad behaviors. Shrinks preached the doctrine of radical acceptance, which did not seem like the best fit for my situation.

All I wanted to know was why no one made my mom change. The physician's assistant spent much of our appointments asking my mom about her diagnoses and her treatment. For a few weeks, she took Paxil. Then she quit. She didn't like the way the pills made her feel. Because she was an adult, no one would make her do anything. Because I was a minor, they could make me do whatever they wanted.

"Focus on what you can control," the shrinks preached. But *who* could be controlled seemed more relevant.


Two and a half years after the initial ADD diagnosis, when I was thirteen, I attempted suicide. During the resulting hospitalization, the on-staff psychiatrist decided that my mom was the real issue, so my mom signed me out of the hospital against medical advice. She was the consumer; she could pick clinicians who shared her view of her daughter. As soon as someone challenged her, she took me out of their care. I went back home and resumed my self-destruction.

But the doctor had referred my case to Hennepin County. There was no maltreatment investigation; instead I was assigned to a special social worker who handled troubled teenage girls sick enough to be their own problems. One afternoon, Ingrid showed up on my front porch. I eased the screen door shut behind me.

"Hi, Emi," she said, cheerfully, as if she knew me, or as if I were interchangeable with her other clients. Gray curls framed her wrinkled face—skin worn out from destroying families, I was sure. "Can I come in?"

It was a weekday. My mom was at work. I eyed Ingrid's white government-issue-looking Ford.

Was this the moment I'd been waiting for? For years, I'd begged adults to come to the house. Now here someone was, right in front of me. All I had to do was open the door.

But then what? Ingrid would make phone calls. Child Protective Services would investigate. I'd get in her car and she'd drive me to a holding tank and then I'd go to some house with one room of bunk beds for all the girls and probably get molested just as my mom had warned. My mom's house would most likely be condemned. Then she'd be destitute. And it would all be my fault.

Ingrid couldn't force her way inside—I knew that. Instead, she was leaving me the choice: a warm shower, clean sheets, needing a judge's approval for every little thing. Or this house with my mom, who could sign paperwork and give me money and check me out of places, retelling stories all the while about fourth grade, when I was "reading at a college level!" My mom's one rule was not to let anyone inside, especially not anyone from the government. If I did, I doubted she'd ever forgive me. Even if it was still possible for her to help me after that, I wasn't sure she would.

Maybe *this* was why no one had come to the house: if they knew the truth, they'd be obligated to take action. They didn't want to open a door they couldn't close again, not when it led to such bleak places.

"Sorry, I can't let anyone inside," I told Ingrid, clenching my fists and readying myself for a difficult discussion. "It's the rules."

"Okay," she said, cheerful. My fists clenched tighter. We sat down on the mildewing porch chairs, beside a stack of soggy cardboard boxes. No one would push past my self-protective resistance and come save me. That's when I realized: I was screwed.

THREE MONTHS LATER, just after my fourteenth birthday, I sat in front of my new psychiatrist. I was on my way to the hospital, this time for inpatient eating disorder treatment.

"Look," Dr. Woods said, leveling with me. "You have two options: You can choose to be well and get out in four to six weeks. Or you can choose to be sick and get locked up for a nice long time."

I appreciated Dr. Woods's candor, after all the shrinks who had talked down to me, but I argued nonetheless. "I don't think it works like that. I don't think I can just *choose* to be well."

I was sick of adults insisting that a change of attitude, a dose of positivity, and a regimen of deep-breathing exercises would fix my fucked-up situation. Dr. Woods seemed like yet another voice in that chorus.

She glared at me as if I were missing the point. "You think they won't throw away the key," she said, raising her eyebrows. "But they will."

I sighed and rolled my eyes. The psych ward was always the same: drugged-up kids getting their chemicals adjusted, playing Egyptian Rat Screw while graduate student staff members observed, making sure no one built a shank. Eventually, I got bored and eventually they needed the bed, so the cycle repeated. This time, I'd have to gain weight, which sucked, but how different could it be?

At the end of our hour, Dr. Woods led me to the door. Her hand hovered above the knob. She paused. Graying hair fell around her face as she reminded me, "The choice is yours."

## Two

The Methodist Hospital Eating Disorder Institute smelled like salmon. Branded purple signs smiled from the walls. In the TV room, magenta sofas seated rows of adolescent girls who knitted narrow scarves while comparing Advanced Placement classes. They seemed eager to get better and get out, back to their track meets and mission trips to orphanages in Guatemala. I hated every one of them, everything they had that I lacked.

I told everyone who would listen that I didn't have an eating disorder. Of course I hated my body. I was five foot nine, too thin, and obsessed with obliterating myself (beginning with the pinch of fat below my belly button that only seemed to expand as I lost weight). I made myself throw up and took leftover Adderall so I wouldn't feel too hungry (though I denied both vigorously, because it seemed like cheating). But I'd known tons of kids who were fucked up with food; only the white and relatively well-off wound up in places like this. Like basically every other girl on the unit, I was white—and like most of them, I was blonde—but I felt our commonalities ended there. I bet that if I asked any of them, "What's your biggest weakness?" she'd reply, "I try too hard." They were too perfect for their own good; little darlings overwhelmed with the pressure to achieve their shiny destinies. From my vantage point, coming from a garbage house, their anorexia seemed like the physical manifestation of too much privilege.

"Why are you here if you don't have an eating disorder?" the institute's on-staff psychiatrist, Dr. Svenson, asked me. She smiled, bemused. She was pretty and youngish, with smooth skin and a round face like mine before I lost weight.

"I want to die," I said, explaining everything. I picked a blonde hair off my black XXL sweater and let it fall on her Oriental rug.

"Why do you want to die?" she inquired softly, as though this were a very delicate topic.

"The world sucks," I clarified. Dr. Svenson knew too much about me already from the intake. I knew better than to volunteer more—I'd learned that the more I complained, the worse I was treated. If one more person called me "histrionic"—the clinical term for "overly dramatic"— I was going to snap.

I swung my legs from the chair, tapping my taped-together Converse on the floor. When Dr. Svenson finished taking notes, she looked up at me. "Where do you want to go to college?" she asked.

"What?" I squinted at her, trying to assess if she was screening me for a personality disorder. My mom was always blathering about how smart I was, and nothing seemed to please certain people more than knocking us down a peg: the physician's assistant who'd met me once and decided my intelligence was "average," my academic performance "middling at best"; the uncle who had said I'd make a great secretary; Dr. Woods, who'd gone so far as to order an IQ test.

I bit my lip, willing myself not to step into Dr. Svenson's trap. But she sat perfectly still, purple pen poised, as if "dream school" were a standard psychiatric question.

"The University of Minnesota," I lied, looking away. "But I don't want to live that long."

Dr. Svenson replied that I was smart. Something in me melted. Then

I caught myself: shrinks buttered you up so that you'd do what they wanted. I wasn't going to trust anyone that easily.

"I'm not like the other girls here," I said. Just thinking about them—their skinny moms, the men they called "Daddy"—made me flush with shame. Compared with them, I was dirty, gross, trash.

"I know you're not," Dr. Svenson said. "I want to see you in college by the time you're sixteen."

Dr. Svenson's hair glowed as light shone in from the window overlooking the parking lot. For a second, she looked like an angel in her sweater and white coat with her name embroidered on the chest. I had no idea why she was saying this, besides the fact that I was at Methodist, with the rich bitches, but I was already doing the math in my head, figuring out how quickly I could qualify for Minnesota's state program to take university classes instead of going to high school.

"But if you want that, Emi, I'm going to need you to eat."

I sighed: adults made everything good conditional on my compliance.

"Can you do that for me, Emi?"

I picked at a cuticle, trying to act as if I didn't care. But I wanted what Dr. Svenson offered me.

FOR FOUR DAYS, I did everything I was supposed to do. I ate all three meals and all three snacks. In physical therapy, I lay on the ground and gently stretched. During Group, I tried not to roll my eyes when the girl beside me burst into tears and sobbed, "I can't believe I hurt my family!" The therapist told us that we were filled with goodness, that we just had to redirect our self-destructive energies to become great. I gritted my teeth, wanting to scream. I did not believe these platitudes applied to me. Rather, I saw the grace Methodist extended to its patients as evidence that they would excuse my mom's failings, as so many outpatient clinicians had before.

I was willing to do anything besides therapy with my mom. "It's not going to end well," I warned the doctors on rounds and the nurses. But like most clinics, Methodist treated adolescent anorexia as a family disease. They would train my mom to administer my medicine of food and, in doing so, heal me. I waited for our appointment, filled with dread. Fifteen minutes after our scheduled start time, my mom arrived with plastic shopping bags dangling from her arms. A dozen veiny necks craned to take her in. I refused to meet anyone's eye as I stood up, stars spinning around me, before I steadied myself and went to meet her.

"Hi, honey!" my mom said. "I have some things for you!" From beneath a layer of used paper towels, she extracted one of many journals.

"I don't want it."

"I got a great deal!" My mom was still talking about the sale when the therapist emerged. She wore an open-front cardigan and comfortable pants, topped off with a "fun" necklace: the uniform of eating disorder shrinks everywhere.

We sat in her office under Tibetan prayer flags. The therapist explained the protocol while my mom took eager notes. I seethed. My mom seemed to love this eating disorder stuff: it explained why I was miserable without putting any responsibility on her.

"You just want to let my mom control my life," I interjected. It seemed obvious that my mom should have less control over me, not more. No one seemed to agree.

The therapist turned to my mom. "What concerns you about your daughter's eating?"

"Well," my mom said, pushing her bifocals up her nose. "Emi is rotting her brain. Based on my SAT score, my IQ is 132. And Emi's even smarter than me!"

I elbowed her from my side of the sofa. When she said stuff like that, it made both of us look crazy.

"What else?" the therapist asked.

"Emi's really lost her breasts."

"Why does that matter?" I snapped.

"Emi had great breasts," she told the therapist. "She could have been a model."

I lunged out of my seat. "I'm in the hospital. I want to die. And all you care about are my tits?"

My mom was always pointing out old men who might be interested in me, as if my best hope was to marry better than she did. It only confirmed my nihilism; I would rather die young than grow up to suffer that fate. Now I stared at the therapist, willing her to call out my mom. Wasn't that a weird thing to say about a fourteen-year-old's body? Wasn't it inappropriate? What else did my mom have to say, what other evidence did they need, to see that she was part of the problem? How could this therapist, in her professional judgment, seriously believe that training my mom in force-feeding was the first step on my path to recovery?

But we were out of time. Of course the therapist said nothing.

THAT NIGHT, I GOT SICK. The nurses suggested that it was psychosomatic and recommended relaxation exercises, until my blood pressure fell and wouldn't go back up. I spent two days in the ICU. My mom couldn't make visiting hours when I got out and was returned to the eating disorder unit, so she scrounged up a substitute; the best person she could find was the father of the sixteen-year-old I'd dated when I was twelve. I begged my mom not to send him, but he showed up anyway. When I returned from our very awkward conversation, I walked back to the TV room. The other patients stared at me, knitting needles in midair.

"What?"

"Is that your dad?" a freckled blonde asked me.

"That's not my father!" I screamed.

"We just haven't seen him," another one chimed in.

"Why don't you stop making so many fucking assumptions?" I spun around, hating them. It wasn't even about Michelle; I couldn't imagine living in a world where it was inconceivable that a girl didn't have a dad.

Being among Methodist's well-off clientele benefited me when Dr. Svenson inquired about college instead of asking if I tortured animals. But now I felt naive to think that conversation meant anything. After treatment, my fellow patients would go back to their regularly scheduled bright futures. I'd return to my same shitty life with no end in sight.

I cried in a chair in the hallway. A nurse came to me and asked if I wanted to talk. I covered my face and refused. She asked if we could go somewhere private: my crying was triggering the other patients. "I hate this stupid place," I sobbed. "I want to die."

She put her hand on my shoulder and told me I was safe. I jerked away.

I said I'd kill myself as soon as I had the chance; next time I wouldn't delay. "If you make me live," I said, gasping for air between hiccups, "when I grow up I'm going to build a bomb to blow up the whole world, and I'll make sure Methodist Hospital goes first."

The nurse gripped my shoulder. I pushed her away. Another nurse appeared. Each took one arm and hoisted me out of my chair. They pulled me to my room, while I dragged my black Converse sneakers across the linoleum.

In my four times in the psych ward, I'd never gotten into trouble. But now I turned and saw the girls in the TV room, their mouths twisted into little Os. I believed they enjoyed the entertainment, savoring the spectacle of the outsider being hauled away.

When we got to my room, I broke free. I crashed into the bookshelf. My roommate's makeup clattered to the floor. I banged my head against the wall. Two nurses pushed me to the bed and held me down. My face smashed into the violet quilt. A nurse offered me pills, but I refused. I didn't want them to knock me out, to not even be conscious as my life derailed.

Bodies filled my room. Someone called security. Another nurse was on the phone, probably getting authorization to give me a tranquilizer shot.

When I heard her, fear sobered me. I wasn't actually nuts. I was just upset. Couldn't they see that? Obviously, they couldn't. Obviously, I hadn't acted that way. Tears streamed down my face as I begged them to just give me the pills.

They let one hand free so I could take the plastic cup. I swallowed them dry, like a prayer, as if they could erase what I had just done.

I WOKE UP in the darkness in another wing of the hospital with a phone pressed against my ear. "So you chose to be sick, huh?" It was Dr. Woods, my psychiatrist from the outside.

I was woozy from the drugs and dehydrated. My eyelids were swollen, my hair plastered to my forehead. Dr. Woods's voice made me feel warm: she'd woken up in the middle of the night and cared about me enough to call.

"I . . . I don't think," I tried to explain. Even if I had chosen to be sick—to act out and push away the nurses—how could I have chosen to be better?

Dr. Woods cut me off.

"Don't fuck this up," she said and hung up.

THE NEXT DAY, I watched TV in the ICU. A nursing assistant sat beside the door so that I wouldn't run. Every few hours, a nurse brought me Ativan to keep me calm. Trays of food came and went.

Dr. Svenson appeared in my doorway, silhouetted. I was surprised to see her. She let the assistant take a break and then dragged the chair close to my bed. The hallway lit her from behind as we sat in the darkness of my room.

"I heard you had a rough night," she said.

"You could say that." I wondered why she was being so kind. I worried that it meant she always expected that I'd end up here, banished.

Dr. Svenson explained that the doctors on rounds would monitor my vitals. Meanwhile, she'd manage my medication.

"Fine." I didn't want to let on that I was glad to see her. But each day after that, I waited for her. They transferred me to the children's wing, where I had no therapy, nowhere else to be. They held me down to put in a feeding tube. I didn't hear from Ingrid. Days passed as I watched freezing rain fall past a wall outside my window. But I was grateful not to be with the prissy girls. Their relative wealth and relatively functional families only confirmed what my mom replied when I complained: that most of our hardships were because we lacked means. I would rather sit alone all day than deal with the jealousy those girls stoked in me.

And, in the medical unit, I was allowed to have a laptop.

Dr. Svenson came and found me writing. It was the one thing that made me feel calm. Before getting sent to the hospital, I'd challenged myself to write fifty thousand words in November, for National Novel Writing Month. I didn't want to do any of the nonsense shrinks suggested, like meditate for three minutes, but I gladly spent ten hours typing, until my forearms cramped and ached.

Dr. Svenson asked what I was writing about.

"It's literary fiction. It doesn't have a plot."

"You should finish it," she said. She lingered next to my bed, her arms folded on the railing. "You know, Alexandra and I went to medical school together." It thrilled me to hear her call Dr. Woods by her first name, as if I were let in on a secret. "Before that, she studied French literature."

I looked into Dr. Svenson's blue eyes and implored her, *Ask me again about college.* I'd already decided that, if she did, I would tell her the truth: I wanted to go to Columbia University in the City of New York. The Ivy League. A friend's sister went there and bought me a T-shirt, which I'd worn until the decals started chipping off. For a year, I'd distracted myself, eschewing self-destruction, dizzy on the dream of hightailing it to Manhattan. Then an uncle had laughed at my plan. "People of your class don't go to Ivy League schools," he said. Why wouldn't I believe him? He repaired expensive French horns. Since then, I'd missed so much school that my bad odds had gotten worse. But if Dr. Svenson thought Columbia was possible, maybe I'd trust her word over my uncle's.

If she didn't treat my dream like a delusion, maybe I could find a way to talk about my situation besides "I hate it here," "I want to die," and "Everyone is stupid," though I didn't know what I'd say instead of those phrases. My mom infuriated me, but she didn't beat me or molest me. Sometimes she proposed that I could kill Michelle and solve all of our problems; we'd get the trust fund from Grandma Edna and not be broke anymore. She said it jokingly, but every time the plan was more detailed. But I wasn't going to tell Dr. Svenson about a divorcée's revenge fantasies. I could've told her about the house, but no one seemed to care. My mom had denied so many things that I wasn't sure if the mice screaming on mousetraps in our house were real, or if I was hearing voices.

Every time I talked about my ambition, and every time I complained, I risked proving someone right. How would it sound if, tube up my nose, I mentioned one of America's top universities? Dr. Svenson might write in her cursive, "delusions of grandeur." If I said something negative about the house or my circumstances, she might view me as spoiled and ungrateful, just as my mom argued.

Even though I liked Dr. Svenson, I couldn't risk the humiliation of bringing this stuff up. She had to be the one to ask. I stared into her face and willed her to pose another question.

She put her hand on my shoulder for a second before she left.


AFTER ALMOST FOUR WEEKS at Methodist, my team convened for a "care conference." My social worker, Ingrid, said I should go to a therapeutic foster home. Everyone, even my mom, agreed. I was fine with it—it meant getting out. But five days later, we met again. Dr. Svenson and Ingrid sat in plastic chairs at the foot of my bed and told my mom and me that I wasn't actually stable enough for foster care.

"That's fine," I said. "So I'll stay here until I'm stable and then I'll go home." I was almost done with my novel. I knew exactly how I'd kill myself.

Dr. Svenson mentioned residential treatment.

"No," I said. I knew about places like that: kids in the psych ward with bad or no insurance were put on Medicaid and sent there, sometimes after just one hospitalization.

"Just until you're stable," Dr. Svenson said.

"What about school?" I glared at her, willing her to remember how she'd said she thought I could go to college at sixteen. Then it occurred to me that she probably didn't even remember her offhand comment.

I felt so naive for liking Dr. Svenson. How was she supposed to save me? What options did she have that anyone before her had lacked? I didn't want to enter the child welfare system, and she couldn't make my mom change.

"You'll go to school while you're there," Ingrid said.

I stared at my mom, who had a journal balanced on her lap. "Are you going to let them do this to me?"

Her eyes were big and wet behind her bifocals. "I couldn't make you eat, but I can't just let you die."

"Oh my God, shut up!" I yelled at her. "Stop being so dramatic!"

Ingrid chimed in: Children's Residential Treatment Center in south Minneapolis had an open bed. They'd scheduled my intake for next Wednesday. No matter what happened, she never stopped smiling.

# Three

After a month at Children's Residential Treatment Center, they finally let me be alone with my mom. A social work graduate student shut the door of the wood-paneled visiting room. I listened to her steps get quiet and waited for the first locked door to click shut before I spoke.

"I hate it here. The Staff are a bunch of idiots."

"Of course they're not as smart as you," my mom replied. "That would be very difficult!" She offered me a can of Fresca from the cooler bag she'd brought.

My mom's flattery softened me slightly, but no matter how many times the Staff drilled into me that it was my fault I'd gotten locked up and no one else's, part of me still blamed her. Yet my mom was my only outlet: the Staff monitored my conversations with the other Residents, and my mom was the only person on the outside I could see or call besides Ingrid.

"All the Staff say is 'Accept this. Accept that,'" I told her, parroting the cure for suffering the Staff prescribed.

"Bastardized Buddhism," my mom affirmed, summing up the treatment of choice for young people like me with budding personality disorders.

The dogma was the same as in outpatient therapy, but it was more rigorously enforced: only you are responsible for your emotions. A poster on the cinder block wall declared a familiar slogan from cognitive be-havioral therapy: "Events don't cause feelings. Thoughts cause feelings." It didn't matter how you had been abused—not even the girls on Unit B who said they had "been prostituted" and were tattooed with pimps' names got a pass; the Staff told us we had complete control over our thoughts. Every night, Unit A gathered on dilapidated green-and-magenta sofas to listen to that night's designated teenager read a confession about an assigned aspect of their downfall.

When it was my turn, I had to take full responsibility for my sins: crying too much, refusing to eat, playing the victim, acting belligerent, dramatically declaring my intentions to die, engaging in "attention-seeking behaviors," lying to doctors. If I lacked sufficient candor or responded defensively in the interrogations that followed each presentation, I'd get punished with a Unit Restriction. I already was forbidden from going outside—I hadn't earned the Privilege—but on Restriction I'd have to stay in my room all afternoon, with no amusements allowed. If someone turned on a radio during our hour of free time, I'd have to leave the room.

My only consolation was that I was at CRTC, as we called our squat brick facility, and not somewhere worse, like jail. (I had threatened to blow up a hospital, they reminded me—I was lucky not to face criminal charges.) On my first day, the Staff had warned me twice that if I didn't comply, I'd be sent to a state hospital. I knew enough about those places to be terrified. Michelle had spent a year in one as a child, for reasons unclear to me, and told me about public masturbators, people peeing in the hallways, human waste smeared on the walls.

Sitting in the visiting room, my mom said, "Do you remember when your father was at Willmar?"

I sighed. "Of course I do."

It was one of my mom's favorite stories: One day Michelle recognized that no one cared if she felt better, only if she acted better. So she started saying she felt "fine," then "okay," then "better," then "good." My mom took a sip of her Fresca for dramatic effect. "And then they let him out!"

Usually, my mom used this as evidence of how manipulative her exspouse was. But this time, I heard admiration for Michelle's cunning.

"So what?" I said, sipping my pop.

"So you can pretend to get better, too. 'Play the game but don't believe it.' I think I heard about a book called that on KTIS."

"Fuck you," I hissed. "You let them lock me up and you don't even believe they're going to make me better?"

My mom looked at me over the top of her glasses with her most serious face. "Emi, you know how I feel about that language." She shuffled the deck of cards sitting on the table. "They say in Al-Anon, 'Only God can heal you. But even He has a hard time!'"

Something hardened in my chest. I never thought my mom wanted to hurt me, but it often seemed like she wanted me to be hurt. "I'm the mom!" she loved to say, staking a claim.

"Pretend to get better" was the nearest I'd gotten to confirmation that treatment was a power play, clearer even than her old threats to send me to Teen Challenge, an Evangelical rehab/boot camp. "I don't do drugs," I argued with her every time. "Pfft," my mom replied, and I knew what she meant: because I was a minor, she could have me locked up for any reason. I suspected Teen Challenge would welcome me with open arms.

"Why am I here then?" I asked again, unsure if I was seeking clarity or offering my mom an out.

"I couldn't make you eat, but I couldn't just let you die," she said, quoting herself. Before I could remind her that the Staff had already decided that an eating disorder wasn't my real problem—I'd have to gain thirty-five pounds on sugary junk food and institutional hot dish but would receive no targeted therapy—she interjected, "Now *that* would make a great title for a book!"

AFTER MY MOM left and the Staff searched me for contraband, I climbed up onto the desk bolted to the wall. I stared out the shatterproof window at the parking lot. Snow drifted down behind the metal bars. My mom sat in her car for a while, then finally turned on the headlights of her rusted '92 Toyota Corolla and drove off down the alley, probably on her way to the clearance section of Target or Rainbow Foods.

I pressed my hand against the chicken-wire glass, then my forehead and my cheek, trying to get as close as I could to the outside. I didn't want to go back to my mom's house, but I wanted to leave. I longed to feel cold again and then drink a hot coffee, to take an Adderall and feel the buzz of concentration, to go to a library and sit in front of a stack of books and read them one after another. I wanted to return to my favorite place in the world—New York—with the stores called "bodegas," a word that danced across the tongue, the entire island of Manhattan embodying the song "Diamonds on the Soles of Her Shoes" by Paul Simon. Then I'd fly off to the only conceivably better place, Paris. I'd say the words I'd practiced so many times in my mind, trying not to forget what I learned in middle school: Je m'appelle Emi. J'habite à Minneapolis. Tu t'appelles comment?

I couldn't understand why adults were so gung ho on life, but if they were forcing me to stay alive, there were things I wanted. Those glimmers of hope had felt far off, but maybe there was a way. Enduring eight to eighteen months of residential treatment seemed so impossible that it made going to college at sixteen look reasonable.

*I'll give it a year*, I told myself. If I wasn't any closer, I could kill myself then.

————

THE NEXT MORNING, I asked the math/science teacher, "What do I have to do to get into college?" I spoke softly so that the Staff sitting in the corner of the classroom wouldn't hear.

The teacher laughed. "That's so far away, young lady!" Most of the students loved our teachers, who could call us terms of endearment and give us Blow Pops, but I was annoyed.

"It's not, though," I whispered. "I want to go as soon as I get out of here."

"Just keep doing what you're doing," he advised.

It was a typical answer. Treatment presupposed that everything would be okay someday—regardless of how unlikely that was. Around me in the math classroom, the other high schoolers did multiplication and division worksheets. The next hour, in English, we read aloud from *Treasure Island*. Many of my peers struggled to sound out the words. It seemed as if we needed extra help, yet we only had three hours and twenty minutes a day of instruction, minus two hours a week for individual therapy and, theoretically, an hour for family therapy (which, to my relief, rarely happened). During the afternoons and evenings, when other kids were in school and doing homework, our graduate student counselors led us through various group therapy sessions.

The "keep doing what you're doing" strategy led to a specific future, one we prepared for after lunch in our weekly Life Skills training. We learned how to get GEDs and practiced job hunting in the *Star Tribune*. But the only jobs that paid more than minimum wage were night shifts at a rival treatment center. Even that required a college degree. The only way to balance our sample budgets was to allot thirty-two dollars a month to health care. My Abilify cost a thousand dollars a month; even if we *could* make ten dollars an hour, none of those jobs provided insurance.

When I mentioned the discrepancy, the counselor smiled at me, showing her small white teeth, and said, "It sounds like you're Catastrophizing."

I constantly got dinged for Catastrophizing. Part of "being a kid"—the edict given to us, which I was often scolded for failing to obey—was to leave the future up to adults. But how could I leave anything up to these adults, who seemed so clueless?

The relevance of education—and the options it bought—was so apparent that I couldn't understand why the Staff denied it. If my mom had had more money, she could have sent me to after-school programs or private school, leased storage units for all her junk, or let me live in the upstairs apartment instead of renting it out. Or maybe she wouldn't have compulsively clearance-shopped at all and instead embraced Pilates. Of course rich people had problems, but they seemed like easier problems. On the flip side, if we'd had less money, we could have been even more screwed. Kids were taken away from poorer families for stupid reasons, then sent to the county hospital psych ward and shipped to state hospitals right away. We never talked about racism, but you had to be blind not to see that skin color mattered, too: Unit A was all white, with the exception of one Latina girl, while all the other kids of color lived in Unit B. The Staff maintained that placement was random, but the upstairs counselors seemed meaner and more strict and the Residents often left for court dates.

In treatment, any factor not entirely within our control was not worth acknowledging. "Don't 'should' on yourself!" a poster on the TV room wall admonished. Simply wishing things were different was seen as a sign of delusion, a choice to stay sick. At CRTC, a narrow circle was drawn around our bodies. *This* is what you can control, they told us: your emotions, your actions, your attitude. For everything else, there's acceptance.

Maybe if I'd come straight from the psych ward, I would have heard it all, believed, and despaired. But at Methodist, among the rich girls, I had seen a completely different paradigm. No one was telling those girls to "keep doing what you're doing." No one pathologized their wishes for greatness.

Even though they were miles away, in suburbs far from our desolate block, I could imagine those skinny white girls at cross-country practice, taking final exams for their AP classes, packing for vacation with their parents in Cancún or whatever beach they visited to get sunburned. Their ghosts tormented me in the hours of Quiet Time. I would not let them get ahead, I decided. I would not let myself fall further behind while they seized everything I wanted for themselves.

ALL I KNEW about getting into college was that I needed a good SAT score, because my mom had gotten so much mileage out of hers. It was one thing to say "I'm smart"; it was another thing to explain your 1388 was in the ninety-seventh percentile. "It qualifies me for Mensa!" my mom exclaimed, letting cashiers and car mechanics know that she was a genius.

When the Unit went to the library on Activity, I asked one of the Staff to get me a prep guide. I waited all afternoon for them to return, terrified they'd deem the request "inappropriate." Just after sundown, once the fifteen-passenger van had pulled back in, a counselor came to my door. To prevent abuse, Staff weren't allowed in our rooms with us, so I popped up to meet her on the threshold to the hall.

"They didn't have any SAT books," she said.

My heart sank. It would be three weeks until the Unit went to the library again.

"I got you this instead. I hope it's okay." She held out *Barron's ACT 36: Aiming for the Perfect Score*. The words evaporated from my mouth. The Staff were so tied up in updating charts, enforcing rules, and doling out Consequences. This was the first real act of kindness a counselor had shown me.

"Thank you," I said, meaning it for once. I climbed up onto the desk with my new obsession. Hunched over, I started a practice test, writing the answers in the composition book I used to draft my confessions. The hours of Quiet Time that pooled around my days suddenly took shape.

I already loved standardized tests. They were democratic. It didn't matter that other kids went to real high schools. When we sat down with our Scantron forms and No. 2 pencils, we would all be judged the same, objectively. I believed, in fact, that I had the upper hand, because I had no homework, extracurriculars, or sports to distract me. Except for my twenty hours a week of treatment, I could focus on what mattered: standardized test preparation.

When I was finally allowed to go out on afternoon Activity, I got to check out three books at the library. I swapped one ACT guide for another and then picked up Annie Dillard's *Pilgrim at Tinker Creek*. I traced the silver sticker that said "Winner of the Pulitzer Prize." *Pew-litz-er, Pew-litz-er*, I chanted to myself, an incantation. I read it in between practice exams, as a reward, and wrote down all the big words to look up as soon as I had access to a dictionary.

Next to Dillard in the "D" nonfiction section, another book caught my eye: *The White Album*, by Joan Didion. My favorite essay, "In Bogotá," described a city nestled in the Andes, shimmering in the fog, filled with emeralds. The city seemed too magical to actually exist. I thought it must have been an elaborate metaphor.

Sitting on my desk, back against the wall, book propped against my legs, I felt happy. I wouldn't admit it to anyone, but I hadn't been so content in a long time. I could breathe without coughing. At night, I slept. No matter how low the windchill, it was always warm inside.

For years, I had been trying to minimize my expected suffering. Adults viewed suicidal ideation as a pathology, but for me, it was logic: weighing the bad against the good, projecting forward to decide if life was worth sticking around for. When shrinks heard that, they just claimed things were not that bad, which I refused to believe. But I could concede that some things were good: the sound of a fresh notebook cracking open, the smell of a sharpened pencil, four-syllable words, like "demonstrable," thick and luscious in my mouth as I mispronounced them.

THE NEXT TIME the psychiatrist came, I asked if I could get off Abilify. I was struggling with math practice problems (material I'd never learned and needed to teach myself) and wondered if my atypical antipsychotic was making me foggy.

"I was never psychotic," I explained to the gray-haired doctor in the empty classroom where he saw patients. He looked as if he were counting down the minutes until he could go back to ice fishing. "Really. I swear."

My list of diagnoses contradicted my statement: I'd been asked so many times if I heard voices that eventually, I said I did. The voice inside my head warned me to get out—that I was going to die living at home—and occasionally told me to cut my losses and kill myself. I was pretty sure this was just an internal monologue until adults labeled my thoughts "hallucinations."

But being psychotic wasn't really the point. Most other children I knew who were swept up in the psychiatric industrial complex took anticonvulsants or antipsychotics, but not because we had seizures or heard voices. These were blunt-force drugs that calmed people down, in many cases by masking the effects of abuse. The side effects could be serious— I knew kids who'd gained a hundred pounds in a year; others suffered permanent involuntary facial twitching—and Abilify wasn't yet approved for pediatric use, but that didn't stop antipsychotics from being the most profitable class of drugs of the mid-2000s. They were so widely prescribed to vulnerable populations that some states began requiring third-party approval before giving them to foster kids.

Almost as bad as the side effects was what having a medication listed in my chart communicated to doctors. I was only noted as psychotic once I was on my first heavy-duty drug. Unfortunately, the bad diagnoses stuck while the nuances slipped through the cracks. But going off of a medication raised its own set of red flags. Two weeks after Dr. Woods instructed me to stop taking Seroquel, my mom took me to an exorcist. The woman had forced me out of my mom's Corolla and screamed that she saw the devil in my soul. When I was upset afterward, a doctor assumed I was hallucinating. My mom failed to clarify that demonic possession wasn't my idea. Who would the doctor believe? A concerned mother who'd taken off work for an appointment or a thirteen-year-old who had recently been taken off her meds? The next day, I was on Abilify, my "psychosis" cemented.

The CRTC doctor folded his hands. "I want to keep you stable."

I bit my lip. He meant: "You're nuts."

As he gathered his papers, I cursed myself for my mistake. I couldn't just tell him *the truth* and expect him to believe me. My experience, and my chart, made me an unreliable narrator.

Back at school, I had plenty of time to seethe. I planted my elbows on my algebra book and dug my hands into my scalp, greasy as usual. Then I realized: I should wash my hair. Cleaning up nicely for my date with the psychiatrist, looking the part of someone who didn't need anti-psychotics, mattered more than the facts at hand.

Two weeks later, when the night-shift counselor woke me up in the 6:50 a.m. darkness for my shower slot, I was ready. The water ran just warm enough not to freeze the pipes, but I stepped in, yelping. Goose bumps broke over my skin. My feet numbed. I smeared shampoo from my ninety-nine-cent bottle of White Rain over my head. It wouldn't lather in the cold water, so I scrubbed as hard as I could with my chewed-off nails.

A counselor knocked on the door. It was 7:01 a.m. Shower time was over.

"I'm coming!" I hopped into the only jeans that still fit and my most dignified T-shirt. During school, I rehearsed.

When it was my turn in the empty classroom, I told the doctor, "I've been working through a lot of stuff in therapy." I stroked my fluffy dishwater-blonde hair. "But I feel really foggy. I think I could get more done in treatment if I felt clearer, you know?"

He asked what other drugs I'd taken. I tried to make it sound as if I'd never answered this question before: "Prozac, Zoloft, Wellbutrin, and Lexapro." I skipped the rest. I especially skipped the other antipsychotics.

He had access to all my medical records, of course, but I knew he wouldn't check. I doubted he even remembered our last conversation, two weeks prior, when he wanted to keep me "stable."

The doctor suggested Cymbalta, a new antidepressant.

I perked up. "I'd try that."

It almost made me sick, how easy he was to manipulate. Even if I had been hearing voices, it wouldn't have mattered, as long as I had washed my hair. And as long as my mom wasn't around to give her opinion.

## Four

Once I got off the heavy-duty drugs and was allowed to go outside, I made peace with living in a hermetically sealed box. They gave me a place to stay where I could read and study; I didn't cause trouble. It seemed like a fair bargain.

Then I started tripping over rules I didn't know existed. I talked too much to a boy who wore a necklace made of puka shells and rainbow beads. We got dinged for Exclusivity and couldn't so much as look at each other for a week. (After that, we were too skittish to resume our blossoming friendship.) Once, after I asked two different counselors if I'd gotten a pass approved to go out with my mom and see my brother's family, they slapped me with a Consequence for Manipulation.

Standing in front of the Staff table, fists balled, on the verge of tears, I asked, "Why?"

"You know why," the counselor who'd brought me the ACT book scolded. But I didn't know, not until she explained: asking two people for the same thing was the exact definition of Manipulation, even if the shift had changed and the first counselor was off for the weekend. They rescinded my pass, kept me indoors all weekend, and made me apologize to a jury of my peers.

Shortly after I got off Abilify, a counselor named Lori appeared at my door. She leaned against the frame nonchalantly, folding her arms. My heart raced as I waited to learn how I'd fucked up. "The Staff have been discussing your hair. It usually looks greasy."

My face felt hot. Someone must have noticed when I made myself pretty for the psychiatrist. "I have really fine hair. Normally, I highlight it, but there's nowhere to do it here."

"I think no one has taught you how to wash it," the counselor said. "So I will."

"What? I know how to wash my hair," I shot back, before I could stop myself from being defensive. It wasn't as if I *never* showered. But it was like eating: If I got used to doing it on a regular basis, how would I fare later, when circumstances made it impossible? I explained to Lori that the water was freezing during my early morning shower slot. She nodded with studied empathy; I would have preferred it if she had rolled her eyes. "Grab your towel."

In the bathroom, Lori gestured to the floor beside the tub. The cold tile stung my knees through my shredded Levi's.

"Put your head under," Lori instructed.

I stared at her, wondering if she was serious. I craned my neck to get under the faucet. Ocean Mist scent filled the air as Lori poured shampoo into her palm. I froze. I thought she was going to talk me through the process, not wash my hair herself.

My elbows dug into my sides and my legs squeezed together. I didn't want Lori to touch me. Revulsion made me feel vulnerable and small underneath her. But I knew there was no point in arguing, unless I wanted a Consequence. As the Staff reminded me, I'd gotten myself locked up. Everything that happened within those four walls would be the result of my previous choices.

"You can sit up," Lori said. She rubbed her hands together. "First you make a lather." She gestured at the bubbles. "Then you start at the roots." Lori dug her hands into my scalp. I seized up, frozen in space. Her long fingernails scratched as she massaged my head.

Warmth bloomed through my body. I wanted to puke into the tub.

"You can rinse now," Lori instructed. Then she repeated the process, explaining every step as if I were a street urchin from a Charles Dickens novel who had never heard of conditioner.

*I know how to wash my hair*, I wanted to scream, but my jaw was clenched so tightly shut that even if she'd asked me a question—for example, "Is it okay for me to touch you?"—I might not have been able to open my mouth.

If Lori sensed my distress, she showed no indication of it. She acted as if she were doing something sisterly and providing me with a luxury, like a blowout.

Lori was almost always nice. Her motivations seemed benevolent. I was supposed to see that and trust her, instead of fixating on the fact that the Staff had near-absolute control over our lives. There were certain safeguards in place, but the situation was rife with the potential for abuse. In the normal course of events, treatment was already so personal—the Staff policed what style of underwear I wore and the gender of my T-shirt designs—and the Residents had no way to set boundaries. It would be easy for a counselor to choose to step over a bright line, and easy to get away with it. If we had complaints, we had to trust our social workers enough to tell them; except for unsupervised in-person visits with our families—a Privilege—all other communication was monitored. The Staff alone would decide what was good for us, no matter how bad it made us feel. Lori told me to towel off. "Let me brush it." I stayed stone-still, listening to my heartbeat. She cocked her head to one side. "So pretty."

Back in my room, I sat down on my plastic mattress. My pulse throbbed inside my neck. I was upset with no words to say why. I would have said I felt "violated," if that word had any meaning, but it didn't. It was a sensation so ubiquitous as to be meaningless. "Violated" suggested I had rights in the first place, which felt untrue, especially after I arrived in an ambulance in restraints.

In treatment we were reminded again and again that the world owed us nothing. We could be hurt at any time, but good things would happen only if someone with power bestowed their benevolence upon us. But in this one place—when I climbed onto my desk and began to read—I could tip the scales in my favor. My hair dripped onto the library book's pages.

EVERYONE ELSE WAS gone on Activity when one of the Staff handed me a photocopied packet titled "Boundaries" in bubble letters. I sighed, irritated about the extra work, and set about completing it as quickly as possible.

"What are boundaries?" the first page read. I skimmed the inane list of examples designed for an elementary schooler.

"What are *your* boundaries?" it asked.

"People washing my hair," I wrote with my half-length golf pencil before crossing it out, not willing to risk a Consequence for snark.

The final page prompted, "Describe a time someone violated *your* boundaries." I wrote about the first thing that popped into my mind: the game of Truth or Dare in sixth grade when two of my friends held me down on my bed so that one of their brothers could rape me. Years later, I was haunted by the used ziplock bag he'd grabbed from a pile of detritus and wrapped around his dick as a makeshift condom. I'd begged my way out of it, instead agreeing to bow down and kiss the boy's penis, but I was still humiliated. I'd never told anyone, knowing my mom would be mad I'd let people inside our house and suspecting she'd blame me for what ensued. Despite everything coughed up in our confessions, in treatment we talked about what we had done, not what had been done to us. Besides, we weren't allowed to discuss anything "sexual." But this was only a packet, so it didn't seem to matter, even though just writing it down made me feel as if the room were contracting and soon I'd be crushed.

I turned the packet back in. The counselor leafed through it, squinting to read my bad handwriting. He got to the final page, then read it a second time.

He looked up at me. "You know this is assault, right?" I was stunned to hear that word. "It's not your fault," he added, and I felt even more startled: When, during my four months locked up, had anyone said *anything* wasn't my fault?

His sympathy felt good, like scratching an itch, but also uncomfortable. The man wearing the keys to the bathroom and the outside world on his lanyard stared at me, searching, as if he'd gone to social work graduate school specifically for a moment like this, to impact a young person's life.

I blushed. *No*, I wanted to reply, in the service of honesty, *I'm a slut*. I'd been told as much thousands of times. Then I'd been made to feel as if everything in my life were my doing, that I always played a role. When suddenly this man judged one situation to be assault and decided it wasn't my fault, why was I supposed to believe him?

The counselor asked me if I'd ever told anyone. When I said no, he said he'd have to report it to Hennepin County. I sat in the TV room and watched him through the big chicken-wire glass window into the office. He cradled his bald head in one hand, looking pained, while the other hand held the phone. A part of me relished being the subject of someone's distress, but another part of me was bitter: in immediate hindsight, the packet seemed like fishing, like CRTC wanted something concrete, something that would *explain*. A convenient traumatic event, even though often the subtle things were worse: the sense I had that if I told her, my mom would blame me for not fighting back harder; the way she'd told me to handle it myself when I was first assaulted by an older boy; the way she'd accused me of "emotionally raping" her after I spent a summer afternoon clearing out a place to stand in the kitchen. Of course the kids in treatment had been abused. But if the Staff assumed that, why did we sit in a circle every evening atoning for our sins? Why were we the ones locked up, when the people who hurt us and failed to protect us walked free?

It just seemed so opportune to make a big deal about this onetime event, with other minors, years in the past. After the report to Hennepin County, nothing would happen. I hadn't wanted to give them that simple explanation. I'd wanted to be like the protagonist of my favorite book, *The Stranger* by Albert Camus: rather than justify his actions, Meursault walked to his execution with his head held high.

But I was starting to understand that would never be my life. I couldn't simply choose to die; instead I'd be trapped inside the walls of CRTC until I surrendered my secrets.

Then I thought, *I'm going to get out of here.* They'd make me talk about what happened and then I'd get to leave. This realization made me hopeful and jaded and mad. For the first time, I understood that my past would be the price of my future, but only after it devastated me.

IN THE WEEKS THAT FOLLOWED, I emotionally excavated myself on demand, so much so that when I heard my name called during Quiet Time, I let myself hope I would be getting a release date. I stood in front of two counselors, a tiny blonde marathon runner and the nice twentysomething who'd brought me my first library book.

The blonde began, "We think it's really important for you to be a kid. It seems like you're using books to escape. They're not really age-appropriate."

I swallowed. "Is this about the ACT book?"

"That's part of it."

"I'm going to take the ACT later this year. I need to study for it."

"You're only fourteen. The ACT is years away."

"I want to take college classes next year. I have so much to catch up on."

"We need you not to worry about that now. Right now you have to think about being a kid and getting better."

I couldn't believe it. Had they forgotten the "Boundaries" worksheet? No one could tell me I wasn't opening up. If the past was the price of the future, I'd paid it. But my craving for upward mobility, to never again shake with fear, far outweighed any desire to "be a kid." Given the circumstances, what kind of childhood could I even have?

I looked from face to face. They remained motionless, silent. "Are you going to take away the ACT book?"

"From now on, you can only read appropriate teen fiction."

"What? Are you kidding?"

"You need to learn life's not about books and tests." What was life about then? Therapy? Board games? Washing my hair? "If you want to argue about it, you can take a Consequence."

The Andes receded into the fog.

I went back down the hall, everything in slow motion. My chest rose and fell. The little blonde counselor ran marathons—what was that besides a distraction? The Staff could all drive home, and drink, and date, and do whatever adults did to escape their shitty jobs working at this hellhole. I was just as stuck here as the furniture bolted to the floor. The counselor went into my room and gathered up *Pilgrim at Tinker Creek*, *The Best American Essays 2005*, Garrison Keillor's *Good Poems* anthology, and *Barron's ACT 36*.

When she left, I crawled into bed and tried to cry very quietly so the Staff wouldn't hear me. I didn't want to give them the satisfaction of knowing they'd crushed me.

*Five*

At the next family therapy session, my mom complained about them taking away my books. I sat close beside her on the sofa, us against the Unit supervisor.

"Emi loves to read," my mom told Tammy. "She was reading at a college level in fourth grade!" I nudged her. "She's not even in therapy." My last two shrinks had quit. Weeks had passed without them assigning me someone new, turning CRTC into a ten-thousand-dollars-a-month holding tank, although I wasn't exactly aching to talk more.

"Can't I just have the ACT book back? Just during school hours."

"You don't need to be worrying about this now."

"I do." I reminded her of all the school I'd missed—that I was missing. "At Methodist Hospital, even my psychiatrist was talking about college."

"Well, that's there, and you're here."

"Here, everyone is just trying to graduate high school, get a GED, *maybe* go to community college." The odds weren't good: Ingrid said that in her thirty years as a social worker, she'd never had a client attend college.

"You sound a little judgmental," she said, making a face, as if she'd just realized I was a reprehensible elitist. "Maybe you need to change your expectations."

I sighed.

"Emi is *really* smart," my mom added. "She is a genius." I elbowed her to shut up.

"Of course Emi is smart, but let's not get carried away here. College is a long way off."

"I want to take college classes next year."

"Do you really think that's realistic?"

"If I get out of here, yes," I said. I could knock out my Gen Eds at a community college and transfer later. I could still be in college by sixteen, like Dr. Svenson said she wanted.

"Definitely, if you gave my daughter some kind of an education," my mom said. "I can't understand why you don't let her have the ACT book. Emi's bored to death here."

"I think you're using college as a distraction from your problems." Tammy smiled at me. "You can't avoid them anymore. You're going to have to deal with them here."

I sighed, exasperated. What problems did she mean? My mom's hoarding? The assault I'd discussed again and again? My unnatural ambition and delusions of a better life?

Tammy was right: I *was* using college as a distraction. I had a dream. In the pursuit of it, I felt calm. When I studied, I could return for a few hours to the old feeling that God had a plan for my life; I didn't have to worry about the obstacles or the odds, as long as I gave my all. Even though I no longer believed in a higher power, work was a form of faith. And I wasn't sure what more the Staff could want than a young person hell-bent on self-improvement. Sitting on the sofa, the anger in my chest hardened into something cold and solid, a diamond I promised myself I'd never drop.

At the end of our session, I hugged my mom goodbye tightly, that familiar smell of hair grease and mouse pee suddenly comforting.

———

I DID EVERYTHING I could do to stay busy. I read appropriate teen fiction, books on meditation from my therapist, Black History Month books from my teacher at school. (Toni Morrison's *Beloved*, to my delight, was even darker than Joan Didion.) In tiny script, I wrote poems in the composition book assigned to me for my confessions, but they weren't very good.

When Ingrid came on her mandatory monthly visit, I was prepared for her final rhetorical question: "Is there anything I can do to help you?"

"Actually," I said, as she slung her cracked pleather purse over her shoulder. "Do you think you could find someone to help me with my poetry?"

She paused, keys in hand. "To help with poetry?"

"Yeah. Like a mentor?"

She pursed her lips, like she did when she had bad news. "I'll see what I can do."

I assumed Ingrid meant she would do nothing, as usual. I felt dumb for asking, even though I knew I had to. From then on out, I'd have to beg for any little thing that could possibly make a difference.

THE NEXT MONTH when Ingrid came, she was in a good mood. I was surprised. Before, Ingrid seemed to have only one affect: constipated yet pleasant. She clapped her hands together. "Prepare yourself. I found you a mentor, and she looks *just like you*."

"You actually found me a mentor?" Dreams of the Pulitzer Prize fluttered through my head. I just had to write something as good as *Beloved* or *Pilgrim at Tinker Creek* and then I would definitely get into college, ACT math be damned.

Ingrid opened the door to the visiting room. "Emi, this is Annette."

Annette stood in front of me, a few inches shorter, with dark hair and a thin nose.

"Don't you look so much alike? I can't believe it. She looks more like you than your mom." Ingrid looked from Annette to me and back again. "I'll leave you two alone."

When the door clicked shut, Annette said, "I don't think we look that much alike. It's just because we're both German."

"Are you from Germany?" I asked her. Although my mom told me my ancestry was 55 percent German, 12.5 percent Swedish, and 5 percent Welsh, I didn't know anyone who had actually been born in Europe and was, therefore, cultured and sophisticated.

"I grew up in Germany and then moved to Bogotá," Annette said. I recognized the name from Joan Didion's essay, though I hadn't realized other people knew about Bogotá.

"Where is Bogotá?" It sounded flat coming out of my mouth.

"It's in Colombia."

I nodded and took a mental note. "Do you speak French?"

"Poorly. But I do speak German and Spanish." I tried hard not to seem too impressed.

"Are you a writer?"

"I'm actually a physician," she said. She was an MD *and* had a PhD. I couldn't believe my luck. Annette had signed up for a program through Hennepin County to be a mentor and now she was here, to mentor *me*.

She folded her hands on her frumpy capri pants. "Let me be frank. Ingrid told me you were looking for someone to help with your poetry. I'm not that person. I don't like art."

I looked Annette up and down. How could someone not like art? Art was the antidote to mediocrity, to conformity. "Do you want to see if we can get along anyway?" she asked. "Maybe we can go for a walk?"

"Wait, you can take me out of here?" I reined in my shock. If she wasn't allowed to take me out, I hoped she wouldn't find out until we'd already left. "Walking is great."

But the next time Annette came, she couldn't take me out. Instead, we sat in a visiting room where we were allowed to talk for exactly one hour. She didn't mention the possibility of our outing, which made me think she'd decided she didn't want to be alone with me unsupervised. But she did ask if she could bring me anything. I had no idea what she meant. "Do you like apples?" she asked. "What's your favorite kind of apple?"

I didn't want to sound entitled. Eventually I offered, "Honeycrisp?"

I wasn't allowed to call Annette or even know when I'd next see her, but six weeks after our first meeting, the Staff called me during Quiet Time and brought me outside. Annette waited in her clean silver Hyundai. She made me wear a wide-brimmed hat and apply sunscreen twice before our three-mile walk around Lake of the Isles. Afterward, she took me to a Thai restaurant with servers and everything. I had no idea what to order.

I worried that, just as she didn't like art, Annette wouldn't like me. When we pulled back up at CRTC, she turned to me and said, "Look, I'm sorry."

I stared out the window so I wouldn't have to watch her say it.

"They didn't have Honeycrisp apples at Whole Foods. So, I got you Pink Lady instead. They're my favorite."

I exhaled. "Oh my God. Thank you." I took the bag.

"Don't be silly. It's nothing." She hugged me so just our shoulders touched.

While I walked back up to the Unit, I cradled the apples. I studied the sticker that said ORGANIC. I calculated that they must have cost at least two dollars each. She'd spent at least eight dollars on apples, for me. The next four nights at Fruit Snack, while the other Residents ate the woody Red Delicious that never went bad, I savored a giant gourmet

Pink Lady. I couldn't help but feel that the fruit—like Annette—had been sent from the future. A future where I'd eat two-dollar apples all the time like no big deal.

In June, while I was on a pass to leave CRTC with my mom, she stopped by the house to grab a coupon she'd forgotten.

"Can you get my journals?" I asked. For months, I'd been asking her for the notebooks I'd filled up in the hospital, eager to search for any sign of improvement in my writing.

"You know I can't find them." She pulled the Corolla into park on the gravel spot in the alley behind her duplex and shut the door behind her. Sulking, I took a sip of my lukewarm Diet Dr Pepper. I wasn't supposed to go inside, per my treatment plan, but now I wanted those journals.

I unbuckled my seat belt and followed my mom, who knew the rules but didn't care. On the back stoop, cardboard boxes slouched beside a broken barbecue grill. My mom pushed open the door to her apartment as far as it would go—halfway—and I slipped into the darkness. The stench crashed into my face. A mélange of piss, mold, and rotting fruit hung in the humid heat. I sucked in air through my mouth.

In the kitchen, teetering stacks of boxes and receipts and paper grocery bags covered the washer/dryer and the oven and the counters. A narrow strip of almost-bare floor connected the back door to the bathroom and my mom's room. I could easily imagine it all bursting into flames. In my recurring nightmare, I was trapped in a fire among the piles of detritus, unable to escape. (I swore to my therapist it was not a metaphor.)

"Do you want some ice cream?" my mom asked. "I have seventeen flavors!" I ignored her as she rattled off the options. She was probably living on energy bars, yogurt, Wendy's dollar chili, Moose Tracks ice cream, and reduced-fat chocolate chip cookie dough.

I waded through the dining room, where waist-high piles rose beside a foot-wide path, carpeted in papers and littered with mouse poop. Plastic storage bins towered in the center of my bedroom.

"What's in my room?" I yelled.

"Feather boas!" she called from the kitchen. "I got a great deal. Ninety percent off!"

"What are you going to do with them?"

"I'm going to throw a party! Someday!"

I balled my fists. It felt like she'd sold the life we could have had for all of those somedays.

I squeezed in beside the tubs, searching for my journals, but my room wasn't what I remembered at all. The bookshelves contained mildewed, never-read castoffs. On the desk under my loft bed, there was a line of small vases full of pills. I'd thought it was cool and trendy to arrange the capsules like summer camp sand art, but now it seemed grim, especially with one tipped over, Adderall pillaged. I didn't dare touch them. I fingered a too-small dress and noticed holes gnawed into the polyester. I couldn't find the journals anywhere.

I stumbled out and into the backyard. The brightness hurt my eyes. A patch of overgrown grass glowed almost fluorescent green, flanked by hostas and orange-flowered trumpet vines—lower maintenance than grass. I dug my hands into the pockets of the khaki shorts a counselor had selected at Target before throwing away all my old clothes.

Eventually my mom emerged, humming. "Don't you want me to come home?" I yelled at her. "You said you're working on the house. You lied."

She finished locking the door.

"I've been talking to my therapist about it. I think we've made a lot of progress."

"Yeah, but you haven't *done* anything, and that's what matters. I'm in treatment, busting my ass to get out. You're not doing your part!"

"I'm not the one who weighed next to nothing."

"Do you really think that's the point? Don't you think your house has something to do with me being locked up? The mice? The junk? The smell?" Of course, it wasn't just the house, but everything that the house meant: that she couldn't take care of me, that she hadn't changed, that I lived in an unnecessarily bleak world.

"Oh, Emi." She pursed her lips, her face, when she was done talking. "Don't you think? Don't you think?"

We drove back listening to the car's fan blow futilely. It was too humid to even sweat.

When I got back upstairs, I presented myself at the Staff table. "I went home," I confessed, as much to get it off my chest as anything. "It was bad. Worse than when I left."

I went back to my room and didn't even care about what Consequence they'd give me, heavy with the knowledge of what I'd seen. I felt like a fool—what had I expected? I hadn't exactly thought the house would get better. But I guessed I'd forgotten it was ever that bad. Or I'd never understood, because it was all I'd known for years, except for a few weeks of respite in a hospital.

All through Quiet Time, I expected a counselor to pop into my door-frame and issue me a Unit Restriction, or worse, but no one came. Maybe it was because I'd owned up to breaking the rules. Or maybe reality was punishment enough.

AT OUR NEXT family therapy appointment, Tammy began the conversation I'd fantasized about for the previous seven months: discharge.

"Emi has two options," Tammy said. "She can go to a foster home and start the school year at a new high school. Or, if we want to discharge her home, she's looking at at least another year here—assuming we work out the issues there."

"I think it's obvious," I said. "I should go to foster care." I knew my mom wouldn't change. Ingrid said I was too young for independent living programs. Group homes were holding pens for teenagers families wouldn't take. There were no other conceivable options.

My mom looked at me. "I let them take you away so that you could come home. We haven't tried to work it out at all."

"I've tried to work it out! I work it out all day, every day. You're the one who's not working it out. You're the one who hasn't done anything to the house."

My mom looked at Tammy. "You can't take her away from me."

I doubted that. If my mom didn't comply, I suspected they would call Child Protective Services. I suspected she knew that, too.

"It'll be voluntary," Tammy said. "You'll sign off."

My mom turned back to me. "If you think foster care is going to be better than living with your mother, you're wrong."

"I really don't want to go to foster care. Believe me, I don't." Guilt rattled me. I hated that this was being presented as *my* decision. "What choice do I have? I've dealt with my issues. I can't sit around waiting for another year so you can deal with yours."

My mother started crying. "Fourteen is too young. It's too young for you to take my daughter away."

"Don't be so dramatic. I'm the one who has to go to foster care."

"I'm the one who's losing my daughter."

"Oh, come on."

"You're not really *losing* her," Tammy countered. "Just think about it as a year. A year to improve your relationship. If everything goes well, she can come back home."

"That's not the first time I've heard that one," my mom quipped, her voice thick with disdain.

After that session, my mom was seriously mad at me, for the first time in my life. There was a theater of villains in her mind: my father, her first husband, her parents, Tammy, Ingrid, the psychiatrist who referred my case to the county. Now I was one of them.

My mom sat coldly during our remaining visits. "I'm just going so I can go to a good school," I pleaded: a place with AP classes in a district where we couldn't afford to live. I'd get my books back and get closer to college. I'd study all day, every day, in the quiet calm. I'd be so busy I'd hardly even notice my surroundings, let alone the people who took me in. I would definitely never love them.

My mom softened, but only slightly. She protested even as she signed the papers, letting me go into foster care but maintaining the right to take me out at any time. I hated siding with the shrinks who took every possible opportunity to remind me my emotions were my problem. My mom seemed to be the one person who believed in me, even when her faith wasn't rooted in reality. But I couldn't wait, locked up, forever.

# Six

There's no better family than the Parkers. Great family," Ingrid told me in the CRTC visiting room. "You're not going to find a family better than them."

"Who else is there?" I asked, trying to consider my options.

"There's no other families," Ingrid said.

"None?"

"You can start tenth grade at Lakeville South—it's a great school, by the way—or you can wait. But it will take a while. Like I said, you're not going to find anything better."

All I knew about Dave and Jan Parker was that they lived in a far-flung suburb, newly carved out of the cornfields forty minutes south of Minneapolis. "What are the odds you'll find something else before the new school year?"

"Zero," Ingrid said, upbeat. I studied her positivity, the way she could present the only option as a great choice, as if that weren't an oxymoron.

I knew it was nearly impossible to find foster families for teenagers. Most Residents who didn't go back to their parents went to group homes to wait out the time until they turned eighteen and were released. For all the trouble the Staff gave me for studying, it probably had helped me get a placement. That and being white.

When I met Dave and Jan, they seemed nice: she worked with special needs children and he used to build furniture. Jan had a master's degree, which impressed me. They were fostering Dave's relative—kids were supposed to live with family whenever possible—and besides her I'd be their first foster kid. "Can I be vegetarian?" I asked. I'd stopped eating meat when I was nine, after getting a mailer from PETA, but Methodist and CRTC didn't allow vegetarianism. Jan said it was okay; she tried to stay gluten-free. I was sold.

When my "D-Day" (discharge day) arrived, after eight and a half months at CRTC, I packed my stuff into paper grocery bags. The doors clicked shut behind me as I descended the stairs a final time. I stood in the parking lot and stared up at the cloudless sky. The other Residents who could go outside sent me off. To my surprise, I cried as we hugged, touching for the first and last time. We knew each other's secrets, but we weren't allowed to know anyone's last name, so I prepared to never see them again.

I got into Jan's car and watched Minneapolis recede into the rearview mirror. Edina and Bloomington blazed past. We crossed the Minnesota River valley, the southern edge of my known universe.

Then it gripped me: I was going to live with a family I had met once, about whom I knew almost nothing. Outside my window, the roadside turned into prairie and big-box stores. I swatted away a tear with the back of my wrist and told myself to toughen up.


DAVE AND JAN LIVED in a cul-de-sac in a development filled with Mc-Mansions. I toured the three stories and then brought my stuff into the converted guest room where I'd sleep. I had a queen-size bed covered in a flower-printed bedspread. A little needlepoint above the bed read WELCOME HOME. I cringed every time I saw it.

The best part of my new room was the ACT book my mom had bought me—my very own, that I could annotate, with no one else's pencil marks. I displayed it on the center of my desk.

Sandy, Dave's seventeen-year-old relative, showed me her room filled with pictures of horses and her medals from the Special Olympics. That night at the dinner table, Dave asked me if I wanted to say grace. I remembered a prayer from CRTC: "He's the cheese on my Cheeto: God is really, really neat-o."

Sandy laughed until she snorted and leaned back in her chair, almost falling over backward before she caught herself.

"Well, that's one I haven't heard before," Dave said. He unfolded his paper napkin on his lap.

Still laughing, Sandy slapped her leg. Jan snapped her fingers and yelled at Sandy, "Get yourself together." Jan took an exaggerated deep breath and motioned to exhale. Sandy followed suit, only to burst into giggles again.

"Sandy can't really help it," Dave said. "She has some developmental issues."

"Her mom is a hoarder, too, just like your mom." Jan took a bite of salad. "It got so bad, Sandy ate cat food."

Sandy stopped laughing. "Just once. I ate it myself. Nobody made me. It actually tasted really good." She sighed, closed her eyes, and smiled, as if savoring the memory.

Jan motioned for her to cut it out. Sandy shrugged.

I decided I liked Sandy. I was used to passive-aggressive midwesterners. She was straightforward.

Over dinner Sandy talked about her day doing a work program. "But I really want to be a veterinary assistant someday." I felt an instant connection to her.

"That's a great goal! You'd be a great veterinary assistant."

Sandy beamed.

"Don't get your hopes up," Jan said. Jan explained to me that the goal for Sandy was to have a job, any job, and to live on her own. Given her intellectual disability, it would be hard, but that would be success. Having high expectations set you up for failure, Jan said. "Believe me, I've been working with special needs kids for a long time."

I didn't believe Jan. I couldn't believe her. When Jan had to force Sandy to brush her teeth after dinner, I silently took Sandy's side: Why brush your teeth if you don't have your hopes up? Why get up in the morning? Why not die eating cat food in a house full of garbage?

Of course I knew that putting that much importance on my goals meant the possibility of failure clawed at me. But that was the price.

After dinner, I dove into my ACT book until Jan called me down for "family time." Looking at her and Dave in their matching brown leather recliners, I knew they wanted to do good by taking me in. They wanted me to be a part of their family. But I felt repulsed by the idea of them getting close to me. I already had a mom. *I don't need Dave and Jan*, I thought. *I don't need anyone.* "I'm studying," I told Jan, afraid this would be the first of many conflicts.

When I clarified that I was preparing for standardized tests, Jan sighed. "Why do you need to worry about the future so much?" She spoke as if she were reciting from a therapy handbook or reading off an inspirational needlepoint. "Just enjoy the present." I stared at the television so she wouldn't see me roll my eyes. Maybe Jan imagined I'd complete her family, but I couldn't imagine how *I* was supposed to enjoy the present moment: my very first day in foster care.

*The Biggest Loser* contestants were weighing in. I could not care. Even if I'd enjoyed reality TV, the idea of simple pleasures completely evaded me. By the time I counted to ten, anxiety buzzed in my limbs. I didn't want to be in the beige-carpeted den in this too-big house that smelled like potpourri.

"Can I grab my ACT book?"

"Fine," Jan said.


DAVE DROVE ME to school to sign up for classes. Lakeville South High School rose out of the newly razed fields, a metal-and-glass box ringed by an ample parking lot. In the guidance office, my counselor handed me a schedule, but I was shocked to see no AP classes. I had understood that "suburban school" meant AP classes. Ideally, only AP classes.

I eyed the man sitting behind the computer. He wore a blue shirt tucked into shiny dress pants. His name placard announced DEAN BOCHE.

"Dean Boche, I'm so excited to be joining Lakeville South." I gave him my biggest, fakest smile, the same one I used with the psychiatrist at CRTC. "I've heard all about how great your AP classes are. Can I take some?"

"Well, unfortunately, registration was in February. Everything is full now. You can take them next year."

"Okay." I bit my lip, blaming myself for not signing up for classes earlier, even though in February I'd been locked up with no clue when I'd get out. Being in foster care meant taking whatever was left over. But it also meant that Dean Boche knew nothing about me or what classes I'd taken before. I went through my schedule hour by hour, bargaining, until I'd managed to get him to switch me into almost all AP or honors classes.

"Maybe I shouldn't be in choir. I can't sing. What other AP classes do you have?" I asked when we got to the last slot.

"You have to take an art class," he said, exasperated. "If you don't take an art class, you won't graduate. You can take woodshop."

I tried not to reveal my true opinion about woodshop, which was "You've got to be fucking kidding me."

After a pause, he looked at the computer. "We also have a spot in photography."

Lakeville South had a full darkroom, with chemicals and everything, Dean Boche explained. I was realizing that this high school was in a different league from the one I'd attended in Minneapolis before Methodist, where each table of students shared a graphing calculator. I took the spot in photography.

Outside the office, Dave asked to see my schedule. He squinted. "Don't you think it's a little . . . intense?"

"Good. I like intense."

"Are you going to have time to hang out with friends? To just be a teenager?"

Fear flickered through me. Would he make me go back in and drop the classes? I didn't want to hang out with friends or "be a teenager"— what would I have in common with my peers? After having my books confiscated, I wanted to fill every minute of the day with new facts. My sparkling future all started with tenth grade at Lakeville South.

I shrugged. "I'm sure I'll have time."


BEFORE SCHOOL STARTED, Dave took me to see my psychiatrist, Dr. Woods. She'd only been my shrink for two months before Methodist, but I'd thought about her prophecy that they'd throw away the key if I stayed sick every day while I was locked up. I wanted to admit that she was right—even though I wasn't sure, really, how I could have chosen to be well.

When she came out, her bobbed hair was gray. Shadows ringed her eyes. She looked a decade older than I remembered. I hoped she'd worried about me so much that it aged her.

Dr. Woods shut her door. "Look, I'm not playing those games anymore," she announced, preemptively warning me not to lose weight. "I tried to give you a lot of leeway. But if you want to mess around, you can do it at Methodist."

I sat down. The standard-size chair felt child-size across from her desk. Nervous, I sat on my hands. I was at my "goal weight" from the Eating Disorder Institute, and I wasn't plotting any funny business. "I'm sorry."

"Don't apologize. You were sick. That's what sick people do." It sounded as if she were trying to convince herself.

I didn't really believe that I was sick in any way that excused my behavior. But it was generous, better than the alternative: that I was an asshole.

"How do you like Burnsville?" she asked.

"I'm actually in Lakeville," I told her. We'd driven through Burnsville on the way to Dave and Jan's.

"Oh. I'm sorry. Way out in the sticks."

"It's not that bad. I get my own room and the school has a lot of AP classes."

Dr. Woods leaned back in her chair and smiled. "Just admit it, you're in the middle of nowhere."

I shrugged.

"How are you going to cope?"

I sighed. I didn't know if this was a mean "I told you so"–type comment or a real question about "coping skills." Either way, it didn't matter. "I'm only going to be there for a year. And then I'm going to go to college."

"I don't think that's what you should be worried about right now."

I didn't bother asking what Dr. Woods thought I should be worrying about instead. I figured it would be something stupid, like that I needed to address my "trauma," a term devoid of meaning in the context of my life.

Anyway, I knew I couldn't bear to look backward, not while I was living in Dave and Jan's guest room. I longed for Dr. Svenson from Methodist, for her to lean over my bed and ask about my literary fiction. But she'd just given me pills and sent me to residential. She was gone.

Now my hope resided in Dr. Woods, Dave and Jan, Lakeville—and my mom, in a roundabout way.

When Dr. Woods led me to the door at the end of our session, she handed me her business card. "Call me before you do anything stupid."

Dr. Woods's pessimism faded from my mind within the first fifteen minutes at Lakeville South High School, when a teacher handed me a twelve-hundred-page, almost-two-hundred-dollar textbook. I held *Gardner's Art through the Ages* to my face and breathed in the new-book smell. I refused to put it in the "cute" pink-and-purple tie-dyed backpack Jan had bought me with county money. Instead, I held it up to my chest as I walked through the halls, part shield, part AP Art History badge of honor.

The French teacher announced, in French, that we'd only speak French. "This isn't French One, tout le monde!" She explained she was just like us. Once upon a time, as a young monolingual Wisconsinite, she'd dreamed of the glamour of La France. "Remember, those who speak ze most will speak ze best!" Then Madame asked the new students to stand up and introduce themselves. "En français, bien sûr!" My eyes darted around the room. Only one other girl stood. "Je m'appelle Lena," she said. Lena was seventeen and an exchange student from Poland who stood out as impossibly cool in her white Converse sneakers and tight jeans. She probably even smoked.

Then the eyes turned to me. I folded my arms over my Diet Coke T-shirt. It was the coolest item of clothing I'd acquired at CRTC, before the Staff threw away almost everything I'd owned. I looked, accurately, like I had been dressed by a social worker.

"Je m'appelle Emi. J'habite à Minneapolis." *I'm Emi. I live in Minneapolis.* But I had to correct myself: I *lived* in Minneapolis, past tense. I noticed the other students were already sorted into cliques, girls with high ponytails, boys in swim team shirts. Coming from the city, I felt more out of place than Lena, with none of the cachet. In the hallway, I kept seeing students extract glass rectangles from their back pockets. They hunched over them and poked. I had no idea what they were doing—did a new iPod come out, one with no buttons?—but I had no one to ask. Only when the English teacher announced a zero-tolerance policy for iPhones did I realize what they were.

I was still feeling like an outsider when I finally found the photography classroom. The teacher stood in front of her desk, cleaning her glasses on her dowdy sweater. As soon as the second hand swung past twelve, indicating class had begun, she killed the lights.

"My students call me Miss J.," she said. Then she changed the slide. I recognized the image, which she explained was Ansel Adams's *Half Dome*. He had hiked for hours, carrying forty pounds of equipment and film, which back then consisted of large sheets of glass. I liked that he'd had to suffer. I wanted to do something like that.

Miss J. flipped to the next slide. She asked, "What is photography about?"

My hand shot up.

"It's about light," I said. Heads turned to look at me, the new girl. I repeated one of my mom's favorite mantras: "Photography means writing with light."

For the rest of the hour, I hung on Miss J.'s every word, until the course fee came up. It was forty-eight dollars for film and twenty-five pieces of photo paper. I had five dollars to my name, handed to me in an envelope when I left CRTC. Dread filled me all the way until dinner, when I asked Dave and Jan for the money. I showed Jan the info sheet.

"Why don't you just do the free option?"

"You only get six rolls of film and then they shred it at the end." I couldn't handle the idea of my work being destroyed.

"You can use your allowance." I was going to get ten dollars a week for cooking weekly dinners, doing dishes every night, and cleaning the bathrooms—more money than I'd ever had, but I didn't want to be in debt already.

That night, when I called my mom for our ten minutes, I asked her for the cash. "It could be an advance birthday gift?" My mom launched into how much Dave and Jan were getting paid for taking me in, the maximum amount possible because I had so many diagnoses. "Fine," I said, annoyed and ashamed. "Forget I said anything."

Almost as soon as I hung up, Jan called me downstairs and muted *Deal or No Deal.* "You can't do that," she said, exasperated. "You can't ask us for one thing and then go behind our backs and ask your mom."

"It's manipulative," Dave said, but I already knew that from CRTC: asking two people for the same thing was the definition of manipulation. Now Dave and Jan might consider me conniving forever.

I considered switching to woodshop, but I liked Miss J. I braced myself all day for her class, knowing what I had to do. The sound of my heart filled the room as I waited for the other students to leave. When I went up to Miss J.'s desk I checked, again, that we were alone. Even in the silence, her face had a mild look of shock, as if she were a turtle awkward outside of her shell. "I'm in foster care," I whispered. I had never told anyone this fact and didn't plan to tell anyone ever again. "Is there any way I can get a waiver for the fee?"

I prayed she wouldn't tell anyone I'd asked, worried about my consequence for manipulative triple-asking. Miss J.'s expression didn't change at all. She looked as uncomfortable as I felt.

"Sure. It shouldn't be a problem. I mean, for most kids forty-eight dollars isn't a problem, but I'll see if there's a form or something. But you're good."

"Thanks," I said. I felt indebted to her with this secret, which terrified me.

As I left, I realized she knew more about me than anyone else at Lakeville South.


My mom was supposed to arrive at 8:00 a.m. on Sunday before Dave, Jan, and Sandy left for church.

"Where is she?" Jan asked, pointing at her watch.

I called my mom, who said, "I'm five minutes away!"

Ten minutes later, Dave and Sandy climbed into the car. I stood on the stoop with Jan, folding my arms tighter and tighter.

Fifteen minutes after that, my mom pulled up. "Hello!"

Jan said, "I thought you were coming at eight."

"It's right around eight." My mother smiled, completely oblivious.

"It's eight thirty. Our church is starting now."

"Oh. How nice of you to wait with Emi!"

"We can't leave Emi alone," Jan said.

"Why not?"

"It's the rules."

"I don't think that makes a lot of sense—" my mom started.

I grabbed her arm and tugged. "Bye." I waved to Dave and Jan.

My mom dropped me off at 7:15 p.m., fifteen minutes late. She followed me to the door, wanting to catch up. Jan told my mom that, from then on, they'd leave for church promptly at 8:00 a.m. If my mom was late, she could pick me up after the service had finished.

The next week, after the service ended, I paced in the parking lot while Dave and Jan and Sandy leaned against the car.

Finally, my mom pulled up. I hopped in and slammed the door shut.

"Hi, sweetie!" my mom said. Once we were in the car, she added, "I can't believe they made me come here. It's totally out of the way."

"You can't believe it? I just had to sit through an hour-long sermon about how God will give you a big-screen TV if you tithe. How do you think I feel?"

"Why can't you just wait for me at their house?"

I felt my blood rush into my arms. I was ready to rip open the car door, jump onto the shoulder of the freeway, and run. I could hide in the trees beside the exit ramp, and when the coast was clear, I could sell my body for a bus ticket. I'd make it to Chicago, at least.

Or I could have strangled my mom. That would've worked, too.

I compromised by screaming, "I would love to wait for you at their house, but I can't! They aren't allowed to leave me alone! I don't have a key!"

She shook her head. "Why can't they be more flexible?"

"Why can't you come on time? There are a million rules. I have no control over them. I get to leave once a week and you can't show up fifteen minutes earlier? For *once*?"

I just wanted her to take some responsibility for my situation. Just 25 percent, even 10 percent; I'd accept the rest. But she didn't. Whenever she mentioned foster care, always in passing, she emphasized the "therapeutic" part: I had been too sick to be safe at home. I suspected that was the story my brother and sister-in-law had heard, if they even knew where I was living.

"I'm sorry," my mom eventually said. She spoke softly, meekly, in a voice that reminded me of a slapped child's.

I stared straight ahead as the skyline came into view.

"Do you want a pop?" I offered. I took out a peach Fresca from the soft-shell cooler she'd packed for us, novelty sodas, all bought on sale, chilled, then selected for our visits. I popped open a diet cream soda and sipped, trying to feel how much she loved me in the aspartame.

As soon as I gave up on her sharing the blame, she got brighter, just a mother and a daughter on an adventure. "What do you want to do today, sweetie?"

———

NORMALLY, Dave and Jan had to heckle Sandy to do her homework, but one night she came upstairs with her school folder. I was standing at the kitchen island, cutting out photocopied pictures of mummies and labeling them. Over the course of the year, we'd have to memorize more than five hundred significant works of art. I was thrilled out of my mind.

"Can I have some note cards?" Sandy asked.

"Sure." I handed her a pack. My mom got them on sale, cheap.

Jan came upstairs to get a Diet Dr Pepper. "Sandy, I can't believe you're doing your assignment!" She beamed. "Emi, looks like you're a good influence." I couldn't help but smile, too.

Sandy and I stood back to back. I paged through *Gardner's*, labeling each piece with its title, date, and location. Sandy copied her vocabulary words.

After fifteen minutes, she asked me, "Doesn't it make you sad not to watch TV?"

"No. I like to learn." I thought about it for a moment. "If I work hard, maybe I'll achieve my dreams and then I'll be happy."

Sandy nodded. We worked silently for a while. Then she went down to watch *Deal or No Deal*.

A few weeks later, just before the unit on antiquity, Jan called me downstairs. She and Dave held court in their brown leather side-by-side recliners.

"We need to talk," she said. "Why have you been printing out pornography?"

"What? What do you mean?"

She held up the batch of pictures I was about to cut up. The incriminating evidence was Michelangelo's *David* in grainy black-and-white. In the same voice she used to tell Sandy to brush her teeth, she told me, "This is not acceptable."

"That?" I laughed. "That's my art history homework."

"How do they call that 'art'?"

"Why can't they just put some clothes on?" Dave added.

"I don't know, I don't get it either." I shrugged. "But it's for school."

"Do you really have to print these out?" Jan asked.

I explained that my teacher would check the next day that I'd affixed each to a card and labeled it with the appropriate facts.

Jan sighed. "Fine. Just make sure Sandy doesn't see." She held out the stack of papers. As I took them, she added, "I really don't like those pictures of naked people in my house. They make me so uncomfortable."

I felt a twist of guilt seeing the look on Jan's face—even though it was ridiculous, the nudes made her feel bad. Shouldn't she get to be comfortable in her home? It made me uncomfortable to think of myself as an imposition. I preferred the version of the story where she and Dave boarded me for cash.


SHORTLY AFTER THE "pornography" incident, I asked my mom if she would take me figure drawing, something she'd done in college. At a grain warehouse converted into a studio, she showed me how to clip newsprint paper to a board. We sat on drawing horses, facing a podium.

I was a little nervous: I'd never seen a naked adult before who wasn't my parent, let alone stared at one for three hours. As an Evangelical Christian, my mom didn't even like it when women wore short shorts or bikinis in public, but this was art and thus different. I wondered if the model would be more Kate Moss or Venus of Willendorf when a mostly bald man in a bathrobe strode onto the stage. I held back a nervous giggle. *A butt is a butt*, I told myself. *Be mature.*

When it was over and I got in the car, I said, "Don't tell Dave and Jan. They'd flip." I opened a Diet Mountain Dew, now lukewarm, and told her the story about *David*. We both laughed, my mom extra hard.

Outside my window, houses thinned out beside the freeway. For a minute, I wished I were going home. I wished I were going to sit down with my textbooks and study without Dave and Jan bugging me about family time. But I knew my mom would have me back on heavy-duty drugs before throwing anything away.

My mom pulled up in the cul-de-sac. In one breath, I said, "Bye, Mom, I love you," then threw the door open before the car was fully stopped. I ran up to the house and turned the dead bolt before my mom could try to come in to chat.

When I finally saw her car pull out, I sighed, once again able to focus.

ONE OF MY PHOTO CLASSMATES, Jessica, invited me to her house to model. With Miss J.'s advice, she had rigged a lighting system from Home Depot parts in her bedroom. Dave and Jan found it weird that two teenagers didn't want to go to the mall or see a movie, but they seemed relieved I was doing *something* and agreed to let me go.

Jessica drove me to her house after school. She wrapped me in Christmas lights and stuck a flashlight under my neck, taking long exposures with a tripod while I undulated, creating white streaks in the exposure. I held her cat and made existential faces. After we finished shooting, we drank Diet Cokes in her giant kitchen with no adults around. Looking at the tile floor, Jessica said, "This is just my dad's house." Her parents were divorced. I felt my ears fall from my shoulders: I wasn't the only sad one. I promised to come back soon.

A week later, a girl from AP English invited me to write with her at a coffee shop. Rachel wanted to do National Novel Writing Month. She was impressed I'd already written a novel, the one at Methodist, even if I'd never dared reread the mush I'd produced. We planned a date to make outlines. Dave and Jan thought this was an even odder pastime than taking pictures, but they gave their blessing.

Rachel picked me up on a Saturday afternoon in her beat-up car.

Minnesota Public Radio's alternative station—89.3 The Current—played on her radio. She drove us a few suburbs north, to the nearest non-Starbucks coffee shop. We outlined side by side for hours and then chatted about our ideas. When I held Rachel's attention and her hazel eyes locked with mine, I felt myself melt. Before she'd even dropped me off, I was thinking of excuses to see her again.

I felt elated to be making such cool friends. If nothing else, they were a good way to get out of Dave and Jan's house. When Ingrid came for her monthly visit, I bragged about them.

"Why, that's wonderful!" Ingrid said, folding her hands on the kitchen table. "Where did you go? How did you get there?"

I gushed, proud of the fact two different people trusted me enough to let me ride in their cars.

"Well, I'm very proud of how well you're seeming to adapt."

That night, Dave and Jan called me downstairs during a commercial break. "Emi," Dave said. "We spoke with Ingrid."

"Yeah?"

"She says you can't be riding in cars with other teenagers. It's policy."

"What? Why?"

"I know, I don't agree with it," Jan said. "But it's a liability."

"But how am I supposed to make friends? I made a date to take pictures again this Wednesday. Do you think you can drive me?"

"Well, that's the other thing," Dave said. "Ingrid doesn't think you should be going over to other people's houses either."

I cursed myself for telling Ingrid anything. My mom was right: social workers only caused problems. I had dropped my guard just a little bit, blabbed, and now I couldn't have friends. "This is insane."

Jan shook her head and sighed. "Rules are rules. If you want, you can invite people over here when we're home."

"Thanks," I said, but I knew I never would. What would I tell people about the Parkers? Would I call them "Mom" and "Dad"? My "foster parents"? I knew I would die friendless before I said any of those words.

I had no other choice but to cancel the photo date I'd made. I tried to make it sound as if I'd done something very bad and very cool to result in this terrible punishment. Later that week, Rachel invited me to a poetry reading. I had to say no. After that, the invitations stopped coming.

THE BRIGHT SIDE of the ban on friends was that I got to spend extra time in the darkroom. Dave agreed to pick me up after school. I paid attention to Miss J.'s schedule until I knew exactly what days she stayed late, listening to oldies on the radio and singing under her breath whenever Paul Simon's "Kodachrome" came on. I savored the ritual of processing film: starting the timer, filling my canister with developer, waiting, agitating, flipping the can upside down, tapping it on the counter. The vinegar stench of stop bath grounded me.

Usually it was just us, but the night before a homework deadline, my classmates frantically worked around us. In front of the sinks, a girl punched a boy's arm and he tried to steal her film canisters. Miss J. looked up from her computer, set down the ziplock bag containing her afternoon sandwich, and glared at them.

I'd finished two days after receiving the assignment, so I was processing film for my own projects: pictures around the Lakeville subdevelopments, shots of Minneapolis's Stone Arch Bridge from Sunday visits, a few I took of a baby in a stroller before its mom noticed and threatened to call the police. I loved the weight of my mom's old Canon A-1 around my neck. It let me pretend this wasn't my real life: I was just an observer, passing through.

When everyone else was gone, Miss J. came over.

"Hey, I have something for you," she said. She held out an envelope of photo paper, ILFORD in bold caps printed across the top. The course fee included unlimited film, which we rolled ourselves, but only one pack of paper. It was expensive, nearly a dollar per page, so I'd started a campaign to get my mom to buy me a box for Christmas.

"I found it in a closet," she said. "It's extra." She set it down on the counter next to me. I smiled at her, my eyes squeezing shut at the edges. "Don't tell anyone."

JUST BEFORE I turned fifteen, my mom turned fifty-five. To celebrate, she invited all of her friends for happy-hour half-price appetizers at Green Mill. She and I wore our matching sweaters from Old Navy and pretended for her guests that I wasn't in foster care. As my curfew got closer, I stared at my watch, growing more and more nauseous with anxiety.

I put my mouth next to my mom's ear. "We have to go." I didn't want to do it. Her friends were all there. But I had to go. I had to go back. I grabbed her arm and tugged. She swatted me away. Finally, she said all of her goodbyes. I sunk down in the passenger seat, stray potato chips crunching under my butt. I fought not to yell, not to say anything mean, to let my mom have as good of a birthday as possible, even if it included driving her daughter back to her foster home.

When we got to Dave and Jan's, even later than usual, she managed to sneak inside to chat with them as I picked my cuticles and said "bye" at every pause in the conversation.

As soon as the door closed, I said, "I'm sorry." I slouched in the foyer, exhausted from my mom, exhausted from the party. "I'll be on time next time."

Jan folded her arms and shook her head. "I'm going downstairs." Dave followed her.

On autopilot, I went to the kitchen and gathered up my note cards and tape and blue-handled scissors. I threw it all on my bed, shut the door, and pulled down my black Levi's.

I opened the scissors and I pressed the blade against my thigh. I drew it along the skin. The flesh split open, a red mouth. For a moment, I could only see the open flesh and the layer of fat I'd cut into. Then the blood came in droplets to the surface until it ran down my leg.

I grabbed a washcloth and held it to my thigh. I lay back on the bed and passed out as calm washed over me.

THE NEXT MORNING, Jan apologized for getting huffy. "It's not you; it's your mom."

I shrugged. I didn't know what she meant, what difference there was.

She explained, "We can't let her push our boundaries." People rarely suggested that my mom pushed my boundaries, too—instead, because I preferred my mom's company to my foster parents', I constantly felt like part of the problem.

Dave and Jan seemed to expect me to confide in them. But in the same way that I despised their lack of ambition, their kitschy plaques, and their Butter Lovers popcorn, I figured they thought I was a pretentious snob. For my fifteenth birthday, my mom got me a subscription to *The New Yorker*. Every time Dave handed it to me, a look of revulsion twisted his face, as if it were the screenplay of *Brokeback Mountain*. (I didn't even read the magazine; I didn't have time after studying. I just stacked it next to my pillow, beside my camera, and tried to pick up sophistication through osmosis. Every once in a while I opened the cover and traced my finger over the big words, trying to spot "élitist"—so fancy with the little accent.)

I already needed to read people constantly—to know where I stood, in the passive-aggressive Minnesota culture, where "sorry" masked vicious-ness; to appease the adults who had so much power over me—and I didn't want the direct criticism I feared would come from getting closer to Dave and Jan. Jan yelled at Sandy at least once a day, usually about brushing her teeth or doing her homework or crossing the street at the wrong place. Sandy never flinched; often she screamed back. Once Sandy did what she was supposed to do, she'd cuddle her head against Jan's chest and Jan would pat her hair. But Sandy was family. I was a stranger with a mom.

One night at dinner I asked Dave, "Can you pass me a fork?"

"What are you missing?" Jan asked.

"A fork. I have a knife and a spoon."

"What else are you missing?" I cocked my head, confused. Jan con-tinued: "You're missing 'please.'"

"Sorry. But it's just a fork."

"No, it's not 'just a fork.' You never say 'please' and 'thank you.'"

"Yes, I do. I just forgot to say 'please pass me a fork' this one time."

"You sometimes say 'please,'" Dave said.

"No," Jan corrected. "You never say 'please,' not for anything we do for you."

"Look. I'm sorry. I just thought it was a normal thing to pass me the fork and I didn't have to say it."

"You think this is normal?" Jan gestured around her at the plaques on the walls, at the pasta on the table. "This dinner, tonight, here with my family?"

"Yes. I think this is the definition of normal."

"You're naive." She smiled and handed me a fork. "What do you say?"

"Please?"

"No, damn it, you say 'thank you'! I gave you the fork. You say 'thank you.'"

"Thank you," I said. "Thank you so much." I only barely tried to hide my true meaning: *Fuck you. Fuck you so much.*

"You're welcome." I read into it: *Fuck you, too, you ungrateful bitch.*

I puked in the shower after dinner.

All that week, I said "please" for every fork, knife, and spoon, "please" for every plate and open door and cup. I said "thank you, thank you, thank you" all the time, in addition to my chronic "sorry." I hoped Dave or Jan would get fed up, but they seemed to smile every time I said it.

"How are things?" Annette asked at the beginning of our visit in October.

Normally, I never complained to Annette: her time seemed too valuable to waste with my grievances, especially now that she had to drive south to pick me up. But that afternoon, I couldn't help it. Tension with Dave and Jan had spilled into every aspect of my life. Even at school, I wasn't calm unless I made myself throw up or ate so little that the world compressed into calm focus.

I didn't tell her about that. Instead, I tore into my foster parents' backward views—that they thought it was "weird" I wanted to write fifty thousand words in the month of November, that they enforced the ban on friends, that they found Michelangelo's *David* pornographic.

"Come on, Emi. They're just Minnesotans. Don't expect them to be cosmopolitan. Bohemian artists do not take in foster kids."

I sighed and scratched the scabs on my legs through my pants. "We got into a fight over how often I should say 'please' and 'thank you.' They think I need to say it every time they give me anything."

"They're trying to do a good thing by taking you in. Most people can't take in foster kids. You should be grateful for them." She glanced at me before looking at the road. Every word from her weighed on me, chastened me. I wanted to apologize for complaining, despite the toll the situation was taking on me. "Even if you're not," she told me, "you should try to pretend."

When she pulled up at a stoplight, Annette looked at me. "You look thin," she said. "Have you lost weight?"

I rubbed at my ribs through my jacket, my sweater, my shirt. I looked back out the window. "No."

WHEN NOVEMBER CAME, I started writing my new novel, a heavily autobiographical work starring a thinner protagonist in a coastal city, whose teachers happened to all have the same names as mine. Emotions tore through me. My tears landed on the keyboard. Snot dripped down my nose. All I noticed of the outside world was the sky above the cul-de-sac turning from pink to periwinkle to black.

Hunched over the counter, my spine screamed from my tailbone to my neck, but no pain could stop me. It seemed clear no one cared about my experience when I just said it. But if I could write well enough, I could trick a reader into caring. Even if I couldn't change my mom or make Dave and Jan palatable, it seemed completely possible that a teacher could read my manuscript and then decide to keep me. Then, not only would I get rich and garner critical acclaim, I'd have the home and family I always wanted.

Jan did not seem to understand that the stakes could not have been higher. She kept inviting me to watch television. I always had the same reason to decline: "I have to work on my novel."

After one too many nights of this excuse, Jan grew frustrated.

"Why do you *have* to do it?" She turned down the volume, suddenly attentive. "This sounds like your writing compulsion again."

Was it a compulsion? Once I was done studying, I had to write. If I didn't write, bad things would happen. Like never becoming a famous author.

"If I don't work on it, I won't finish it."

"What makes you think it's worth finishing?" Jan asked. She looked at Dave for backup. "I think you're trying to avoid your problems."

I thought about residential treatment, how the Staff confiscated my books after I told them about the assault. It made me feel impotent, like a little girl again, cowering in underwear. I lobbed back at Jan, "I think I want to make something of my life."

She turned off the TV. "You aren't special. You're normal, just like everyone else."

I clenched my fists so hard my thumbs popped. This seemed like the cruelest possible insult.

Jan went on, "If your expectations weren't so high, you wouldn't be disappointed all the time and you wouldn't be so depressed."

My molars locked together. Here it was again, this hated idea that I was choosing my misery. This time, it was the good thing about me—my ambition—that supposedly architected my defeat. It was no-win logic; either I'd be resigned to Lakeville, depressed by my circumstances, or I'd be hoping for better things, depressed by my failure to achieve them.

It hurt so much because I worried they were right: that I was normal, average, unremarkable, forgettable. I could die with nothing but my diagnoses on my tombstone. I had no way to prove them wrong. In fact, they were probably right.

But I couldn't show any vulnerability. I feared they'd twist my doubt against me. "Maybe you're right. But I'm going to go work on the book." I turned around and went upstairs as the pressure built behind my eyes. I passed the kitchen counter and headed up to my room. Voices in my head bickered: whether I would ever succeed, what that meant, why I felt unhappy. I picked up the kiddie scissors and didn't put them down until the noise shut up. I pulled my jeans back up, right over the fresh cuts, and went back down to write.

I STARTED HAVING TROUBLE SLEEPING. Dr. Woods suggested I try Benadryl before bed. It didn't help. I jolted up, the moon shining on the bare trees in the yard.

One of my cuts got infected. As it grew hot and red, I started to panic, wondering how I would explain. When I accidentally sliced my hand on a film spool, I laughed with relief as the blood dripped on the classroom floor: I had an excuse to go to the doctor and get antibiotics.

Shortly after that, I said I was going to take pictures in the woods behind the backyard. When I got to the county road, I turned in the other direction and walked under the freeway to the shopping center. I bought NoDoz with my allowance at Walgreens. At the hardware store, I got a box of razor blades: one hundred, each wrapped in cardboard. At least that would be sterile, the cuts clean.

I hated the therapist I saw every week, at a clinic in the basement of a subdivision that called itself a "healing center." There were stockpiles of herbal tea and a burbling portable waterfall. It was supposed to be an eating disorder clinic, but my shrink stopped weighing me after our first session. I was glad, but it also made me lose any respect I'd had for her. Each Tuesday night, she questioned me about my "behaviors"—purging? restriction? self-harm? I said no to every question. I never felt bad about lying, because I didn't think the therapist cared about me, just the be-haviors. If I did open up, I figured she'd just suggest deep breathing—as if being in the present moment, in Lakeville, Minnesota, was a solution instead of the problem.

Only Dr. Woods saw through my bullshit. As soon as I walked into her office she asked, "How's the whole eating thing going?"

My heart rattled. "My first inclination is to tell you everything's fine."

"So you've still got an eating disorder. Congratulations." Anger bolted through me: I'd come the closest I ever had to admitting I had a problem, and she was glib about it. Dr. Woods cleared away a pile of plastic dinosaur figurines and extracted a scale. She made me take off all my sweaters until I was in my jeans, leggings, and T-shirt. "You have to gain six pounds by the time I see you next."

I protested—that was more than I could possibly gain in a month healthfully, even if I'd lost more than that—but she was sick of excuses.

"And stopping hacking on yourself while you're at it."

I stopped tying my shoelaces and stared at her. "How do you know?"

She gestured to her computer. "I saw the prescription for antibiotics."

I preferred Dr. Woods to almost anybody. At least she paid attention. She seemed to see treatment for the game that it was. She didn't make the rules, but she was the referee. Her straightforwardness made me feel less alone. "You're lucky," she added. "Next time you're going to get staph and they'll have to amputate." I couldn't help but smile at the dark humor, even though I left feeling down about her ultimatum.

Every day, I woke up in the darkness and trudged down to the bus stop. As the sun rose, I stared at the identical streets of indistinguishable houses. iPhones lit my peers' faces, making them like ghosts. When we arrived at school, it wasn't fully light yet. During lunch, I ate the skin off my Granny Smith apple but then felt sick and threw my tray away. I cut myself in the bathroom with a razor blade I carried in my bag. By the final bell, dusk hung over the cornfields. I couldn't imagine going through another winter, snow on the ground until May, maybe June. It was even harder to imagine summer, the ground cracking open in green.

I lay in the converted guest room after homework and dinner and fishing bits of food out of the shower drain. Headlights projected onto my wall from the county road. I missed God. Once I'd picked up my mom's copy of *The Purpose Driven Life* by Pastor Rick Warren; just the introduction overwhelmed me with the idea that the Lord had a plan for my life. It was predestined, fate. All I had to do was find it.

When I woke up at night, I prayed to nothing. I didn't ask for perfect scores or the Pulitzer Prize; I just wanted to know that my life would turn out okay. I needed some certainty, something I could rest on, and then I could make it through.

Eyes squeezed shut, I begged the heavens, "Please let me believe."

But I couldn't.

DAVE AND JAN tried to cheer me up. They treated Sandy and me to an a cappella concert. They offered to take me to the chiropractor, but I refused. One Saturday afternoon, Jan's adult daughter came over. "Come tanning with me and Sandy. It's good for your vitamin D. That's a natural antidepressant."

"It gives you wrinkles and cancer."

"Oh, come on. Don't be a spoilsport. Come with us. We can have girl time." Sandy did a happy dance.

I grimaced. "No, thank you."

With each well-intentioned suggestion, I felt worse about myself. Was I obligated to roast myself or let a quack crack my spine in order to feel better?

On Ingrid's visit, she told me about a book I had to read, her eyes lit up with excitement. "The parents are exactly like your mom. It's astonishing." She made me get a scrap of paper to write down the title. "It's called *The Glass Castle*."

When Annette came to visit, she brought me a paperback of the book. She stood in the foyer with Jan, arms folded, and told her, "The mom in this book is so similar to Emi's, I couldn't believe it."

It was possible that Jeannette Walls's bestselling memoir was going to offer me the insight I needed, but I no longer had a lot of time for pleasure reading. Besides, I didn't really want to read an entire book about a woman who was just like my mom; it was enough to deal with her every Sunday.

The book recommendations kept coming in. The next time I saw Jan's daughter—toasty skin, highlights aflame—she suggested the title that was really going to help me. "It's a number-one bestseller." I perked up. "It's called *The Secret*."

She summarized "The Law of Attraction": We "attracted" reality to us with our thoughts. Our mindset would determine if we were rich or poor, healthy or sick. A quick Google search turned up that, yes, some adherents claimed negative energies had created the Holocaust. She offered to buy a copy—I could read it first and then give it back to her—but I declined.

"Suit yourself. But don't say I didn't try to help you!"

## Seven

Over winter break, my mom and I drove to Washington, DC. I worried about spending ten days with her, but the alternative was spending the holidays in respite care at a facility or another foster home, because my bad mood was dragging down the house. Dave and Jan needed family time without me. My mom was elated—Ansel Adams and another photographer, Annie Leibovitz, both had exhibitions at the Corcoran. In the weeks before we left, we collected film spools, chemicals, and empty two-liter soda bottles so that we could take photos along the way and process film in hotel rooms. With each acquisition, my hesitation about the trip fell away. Then we loaded up the back seat of her new (used) Buick, boatlike and merely cluttered. (She'd kept the Corolla as a portable storage unit. At every opportunity, she reminded me, "I'm saving it for you!")

With traffic and snow, the one-way trip took twenty-four hours. My mom thought it was important to show me the country, even if that mostly meant our nation's freeways. At rest stops, I shook out my legs and tried to unroll my shoulders from my ears, but I never complained—each mile away from Lakeville was freedom.

Every time we saw an object from Simon & Garfunkel's "America," I played the song on my iPod rigged to a cassette adapter, and we belted out the words. We weren't good singers, but we harmonized perfectly. My mom said it was something about genetics.

On the road, we were free. My mom's shortcomings no longer bothered me. There was a cooler full of pop and Light & Fit yogurts to sustain us in the back seat. We stopped at Burger King every night and split king-size fries for dinner. We begged the cashiers for extra ketchup packets, then squeezed it directly into our mouths with every bite for the perfect hit of salt and sweet, washed down with pop from home that made it easier for me to vomit. We only went to a sit-down joint once, for Thai food on Christmas Day. My mom said spicy food helped people with depression. I added sriracha until tears cooled my cheeks.

MY MOM TOOK FOREVER at the Ansel Adams exhibit, pulling up her glasses to study the prints and standing so close she triggered alarms. I preferred Annie Leibovitz. The show included her celebrity portraits—several of whom I recognized, like the very pregnant, very naked Demi Moore—but also a lot of candid shots with Susan Sontag, her life partner. It was subtle enough that my mom didn't say anything derisive about homosexuality (or, as she sometimes did, inform me that lesbians were smart not to bother with men). I was mesmerized by the couple's life: Sontag sprawled on a sofa in their house; their travels, including to a war I'd never heard about in a place called the Balkans; most of all, Sontag's manuscripts. An itinerant existence, which I could relate to: two artists, together. It was a fantasy of domestic bliss that I could wrap my head around, unlike the girls at Lakeville South blabbering about boys with whispers of mustaches.

Everywhere we went, my mom made friends. Whenever she saw a group posing for a photo, she offered to take it. At the National Cathedral, she approached a family who handed her their camera.

"Okay, you're taller so you should go behind her. Good, now bring him into the center." They shuffled around in front of an altar. "Great. Perfect. Now get close and pretend you like each other."

My mom took one shot, fiddled with the exposure, then snapped a dozen more. She didn't reveal her disdain for the digital camera, even though analog was better.

When the mother took her camera back, she exclaimed, "These are wonderful!" She invited us to dinner at their house. They cooked us many vegetarian courses—fried patties, korma, paneer tikka masala—and sent us off with gallon-size ziplock bags full of leftovers. My mom tucked them into her fanny pack and we ate straight from the bags on the National Mall.

It would have been rude to throw it up, so I didn't.

AT NIGHT IN THE MOTEL, when I felt my mom's weight sag her side of the mattress, I realized how much I missed physical contact. Most weeks I touched no one at all, except for hugs from her on our Sundays. My mom had told me the story of baby monkeys taken from their mothers who clung to terry cloth substitutes. That was how I felt, I realized, but I didn't even have a stuffed animal. I couldn't get used to that soft, mushy feeling that left me weak and vulnerable, pathetic. I loved my mom, but I knew my attachment to her was a liability.

On the day I was supposed to return to Lakeville at 7:00 p.m., a major snowstorm hit while we were still hundreds of miles away. We'd have to drive straight through at full speed to make it.

I called Dave and Jan at 6:00 p.m. from somewhere in Wisconsin. I turned my mom's purple flip phone over in my hand. I knew what they'd say; it was always the same thing. We were always late and I was always sorry.

After nine, my mom drove into the cul-de-sac. The porch lights were off. The inside was dark, too. I could tell they were sending a message.

When we pulled into the driveway, the motion-sensor lights flicked on, illuminating the hood of the car, the snow all around us, the drive-way scattered with salt.

"Don't come in," I said. "Just let me go."

"I want to chat."

"No." I grabbed my tie-dyed JanSport and slammed the car door. I pulled my paper grocery bags out of the spot we'd cleared for them in the trunk. I ran up to the doorstep and rang the doorbell. By the time Dave and Jan came—slowly, to make a point—my mom was standing behind me. "Just let me go," I hissed.

My mom invited herself in. We all stood in the foyer.

"It's late," Jan said. "We're going to bed."

My mom kept talking. Jan opened the door. An icy breeze blew in but, for several excruciating minutes, my mom didn't budge.

After she finally left, Jan shut the door. "Why can't you ever be on time?"

"I'm sorry. I can't control my mom. If I could, I wouldn't be here. But I can't."

"This house is not a hotel," Jan told me. "Stop treating it like one."

I wanted to call my mom and have her pick me up. We could drive away, fugitives on the run. But I was stuck.


BEING BACK IN Lakeville felt even harder after being gone. I cut myself in the bathroom stalls at school. Another wound bloomed pink and hot. I stroked it through my jeans, trying not to scratch. I couldn't deal with another infection, so I just hoped it would go away on its own. I started avoiding the darkroom. I didn't want to embarrass myself by looking crazy. At night, in the shower, I found solace in putting my fingers down my throat, emptying myself until I was weak enough to feel calm. The whole time, I dreaded my appointment with Dr. Woods.

When the day arrived, I ducked out of precalculus with a used Dasani bottle. I stood in front of the drinking fountain, ready to drink approximately ten bottles of water to gain six pounds and replace the extra weight I'd lost, but then I thought, *Fuck it.* I hadn't washed my hair either, which always drove Dr. Woods bonkers.

In her office, I pulled my feet up onto the chair, my legs against my chest. I plucked lint off my sweater. I expected the scale to come out, followed by a lecture about personal hygiene.

Instead, Dr. Woods asked me, "Are you thinking about killing yourself?"

I looked out her window at the parking lot. "Kind of."

"Do you have a plan?"

The sides of my eyes twitched. "Not really."

"Good." She sounded sincere. "You can kill yourself when you're eighteen. For now, you've got to stay alive." I glared at her. I knew it was supposed to be a dark joke, but I resented the reminder that I was a minor and, therefore, powerless.

"Do you have anything you're looking forward to?"

"I submitted some photos and poems to the Scholastic awards. I want to see if I win. I want to get a thirty on the ACT in February."

"That's good. Do you have any other reasons that you should stay alive?"

"I don't know." I bit my lip, too exhausted to play ball. "I just don't know what the point is. Is my life ever going to be worth living?"

"Look, you don't have to worry about figuring out the meaning of life. You don't need to worry about becoming some great genius. All you have to do is not kill yourself."

I sighed. Why did she, like everyone else, treat my dreams as a secondary concern? I felt that if I knew I would achieve my goals, I could keep going. But week by week, they seemed more and more far-fetched.

"Am I ever going to feel better? Am I going to go through my whole life like this, where I just keep getting more and more depressed?"

Dr. Woods paused and pushed her hair behind her ears. "It's probably like cancer. You'll go into remission for a while and then it will flare up. We'll adjust your meds and then you'll feel better again."

All of the evidence seemed to point toward that conclusion, that whatever was wrong was a problem with me that wasn't going to go away. I appreciated her honesty, but it felt like a pop can crushed behind my sternum.

Dr. Woods turned to her computer and clicked around, offering, "I can try increasing your Cymbalta."

I sighed. "Okay." I agreed to a Safety Plan: before I attempted to end my life, I'd tell an adult or call 911. I wrote it down on a form and then signed, probably releasing my providers from any liability if I offed myself.

At the end of our appointment, Dr. Woods stood at the door. "Look, it would really bum me out if you killed yourself. Maybe that's a good enough reason not to." Tenderness jolted through me. I wondered if she thought about me between appointments. Then that sweet idea grew heavy, into obligation. Dr. Woods smiled and added, "Although I doubt you care."

A FEW DAYS LATER, on the Wednesday before finals, I stood in front of Miss J.'s door, just out of her line of sight. Two more cuts, swollen and oozing under my jeans, had gotten infected. If I wanted to live, I'd have to talk to someone, get antibiotics, risk punishment. It seemed like a good time to kill myself so that I wouldn't have to bother.

I peered into Miss J.'s classroom, where she sat behind her computer eating her sandwich. I wanted to tell her how much she'd meant to me and how much I'd loved photography. Then I decided that if I did I'd almost certainly break down crying, so I walked away, back to the cafeteria.

The next day, I did the same thing, but Miss J. followed me. I walked quickly and she kept pace, right behind me. "What's wrong?" she asked.

"Nothing." Even as the word came out of my mouth, I hated myself for lying.

She paused. "You seem sad."

"I know, I mean, I just kind of am."

Miss J. raised her eyebrows behind her glasses and kept walking behind me for a while. "See ya, I guess."

"Au revoir," I replied.

That was it, I decided, as I sat alone in the cafeteria. I'd gotten my last chance to connect with someone and I'd thrown it away. I could write novels and take dozens of rolls of pictures, but I feared I'd never be able to let anyone really know me.

THAT NIGHT, I wrote a note, articulating the two outcomes I saw: "Maybe, somehow, I'll stay alive and achieve greatness. Or maybe I'm going to cut my losses and die now." I wasn't sure if it was a suicide note or not.

Then, on a sheet of notebook paper, I wrote a second letter to Miss J., saying all the things I couldn't say in person about how much she meant to me. How even if she didn't know it, she had been who I needed. That way, if I never saw her again, she'd know I loved her. In the morning, when her classroom was empty, I went in and dropped it on her desk.

In AP Biology, I zoned out during the lecture and went through my mental checklist: I'd written letters. I had a bottle of caffeine pills, enough to give me a heart attack. Straight out the doors, into the woods across the street from the school, swallow them all and bury my body in the snow. I had my completed homework in my backpack, to prove I was a good student until the very end.

Then I remembered my binder of negatives and contact sheets—it was still in my tray in the photo lab. If I died, Miss J. would have to deal with it. She'd have to take everything out and give it to my mom or to Dave and Jan. When I'd cut my hand on the film spool and laughed, her face turned white and she'd run out of the room. How would she feel when I was dead? Especially after she'd tried to talk to me.

I stood up. "I feel sick," I announced to the class in the middle of the lecture and walked out.

I stood in the doorway of the nurse's office. "I think I have an infection," I said. She gave me a set of shorts from the lost and found. In the bathroom, I peeled off my black jeans, ripping off scabs as I went along. Then I stood in front of the nurse, a hundred-plus wounds crisscrossing my legs.

She wheeled herself over on a stool, leaning in to look at the cluster that had turned pink and swollen. "Do your parents know?"

"No."

"Are you thinking about killing yourself?"

"Yes."

"Do you have a plan?"

"Yeah." I crumpled on the cot. I knew those were the magic words. I knew what would happen: phone calls, ER, psych ward. I believed that saying those words would throw away my shot at leaving for college early and instead move me backward. But I had to say them. If I could have dreams, I wanted to live. And if I wanted to live, I had to do something, because I was afraid of myself.

The nurse sat with her arm on my back. When I finally blinked my eyes into the real world, she told me, "You did the right thing. Now you're going to get over this. It's going to be better from here."

Somehow, she sounded so certain.

JAN LEFT WORK EARLY to drive me to the emergency room. She seemed flustered. "Why didn't you talk to us? Why did you go straight to the school nurse?"

I shrugged. I knew Jan was upset I hadn't come to them first. In her vision of a successful family, I shared my struggles and they helped me work them out. She took me to McDonald's and bought us fries. We sat at a small table under the fluorescent light in our parkas, eating in silence.

"Do you still want to do it?" she asked after a while.

"Do what?"

"Go to the hospital," Jan said, irritated.

"Yeah," I said, tucking my hands inside my sleeves.

After the long standard evaluation, a checklist of tragedies, I curled onto the exam table in the room where I waited, not even studying.

The psychiatrist on call came in last. They'd let me leave the ER and go back to Dave and Jan's, right then, if I agreed not to hurt myself. "Can you contract to safety?"

I sat up, bleary-eyed and exhausted. "No," I said. It felt strange not to lie.

WHEN I GOT to the psych ward, Jan was alone in the intake room. She wore her jacket, as if she were ready to leave. "Your mom's not coming," she told me.

"What?" I was confused: Was my mom supposed to come? Why would she? I was just getting admitted.

"She has a church thing, so she's not going to come tonight."

I shrugged. I didn't know what my mom had to do with anything. Jan stared at me and spoke slowly. "Her daughter is in the hospital and your mom is going to church instead." I felt personally attacked, even though she was criticizing my mom. Of course my mom was going to church. What was I supposed to do about it? Love my mom less? It was as if Jan wanted me to switch my allegiance, love her family more because of my mom's failings—but love didn't work like that.

When I didn't respond, Jan continued, "Do you think I want to spend my Friday night like this? The Friday before the long weekend?" I clenched my jaw until pain bloomed through my cheeks. Jan detailed her plans: antiquing, watching a movie, baking some gluten-free muffins. None of that was going to happen now, because instead there would be paperwork and counseling sessions and guilt. "And your mom's not coming," she repeated.

I could tell that Jan was upset, as if my confession to the school nurse were a display of disrespect, a rebuke of her competence as a foster parent, and an attack on her character. Her insecurity spilled into frustration. I sensed that Jan wanted someone to pat her on the back and tell her that she was a Good Person doing a Good Thing, or for me to confirm that she took better care of me than my "birth mom" (a term I hated).

Instead, I wanted to tell Jan that she could just leave. She and Dave had known my diagnoses and gotten extra money for them, yet now they were making me feel like such a fuckup, like I really had failed by winding up hospitalized again. Even if all I did was follow my stupid Safety Plan.

The world always seemed to urge me to ask for support, as if the problem were that I chose to stew in my despair instead of reaching out to the community who would break my fall. Yet when I admitted to an authority figure how bad I felt, this was what I got: Jan implying that my mom didn't love me, that she and Dave were better than I deserved. There were so few acceptable ways to need help.


As the doors locked behind Jan, I felt my body soften. A twenty-something counselor gave me a pair of scrubs to sleep in and a quilt, probably one some lady had made for sick children, as if I were actually ill and not just choosing the wrong path. It pressed me tight against my plastic mattress, containing me. Ativan filled my legs with sand.

In the morning, I ate Frosted Flakes from a little box with a pink carton of skim milk. The other kids shuffled cards, fanning them into bridges every time. It was the closest to summer camp most of us would ever get. We did Group and said our feelings, but no one tried to fix us. We all felt sad and it was okay. I was not an imposition. It was other people's job to take care of me, and they did. I didn't have to pretend to belong to someone else's family.

On Saturday, my mom came for visiting hours. "Hi, honey!" She hugged me and brought me cans of pop and some paper for drawing, and we didn't even talk about what happened. It was just another day, the visiting room just another place to conduct our relationship, like McDonald's or Rodeway Inn or the library. I didn't have to think about her house because it was so far away. She left at the end when they told her to and I went back to the TV room.

The psych ward felt like the one place I could be a kid. I understood why I came back again and again. If I was honest, Dave and Jan were right that my goals stressed me out. I imagined either success or death. In the hospital, there was neither, although I wished I had my books. Unlike any hospitalization before, I had a life outside I ached for: I'd have finals the next week and was losing time to study.

At dinner, I ran into a girl I'd known at CRTC. She'd been quiet, never caused trouble, prayed before each meal. She fiddled with her cross necklace and told me that next she was heading to a state hospital.

My heart caught in my throat. I wondered how it possibly made sense to lock up a depressed bulimic and expect her to improve. We had only a handful of acceptable ways to suffer, but the shrinks had even fewer options for how to help.

ON SUNDAY AFTERNOON, Dave and Jan came to visit with Jan's adult daughter in tow. After a few minutes of chitchat, Dave and Jan left.

Jan's daughter and I sat across the table from each other. In the visiting room, it was clear how blonde she was, how tan. Surely, she had excellent vitamin D levels. "Do you see what this selfishness is doing to us? You can hurt yourself, you can hurt your mom, but I won't let you hurt my family."

At that moment, with no pretext that I belonged to Dave and Jan's clan, I admired them. Jan's feelings were hurt and—as baseless as I found those hurt feelings—her daughter was defending her mom by attacking the outsider. They were a real family.

"I didn't mean to hurt anyone," I said.

"Stop. On Friday night, your mom didn't even come to see you. So you can see how much she cares about you. Next time, we're not going to come either." Jan's daughter picked up her purse and left. I sat in the visiting room alone. Her words didn't hurt; my disdain for her shielded me from their impact. But what she said sunk in. I believed her: I had no more wiggle room. I could never come back to the psych ward and leave with a future intact; people would give up on me. It didn't matter how much I was suffering or how suicidal I felt. Getting locked up, for any reason, was no longer an option. That meant killing myself wasn't an option either. Any attempt was too likely to fail, putting me back in the psych ward, or worse.

When I woke up the next morning, the most beautiful light filtered through the air shaft. I rolled over in bed, reaching for my camera. But of course it wasn't there.

LATE MONDAY MORNING, I sat across from a therapist on staff. My mom sat on one side of me. Dave and Jan sat on the other.

"Do you regret doing this?" Jan asked me.

"What's *this*?" I asked.

"Getting sent to the psych ward."

I felt like Dave and Jan wanted me to apologize. I did feel like a horrible person for doing bad things, like cutting, lying, and puking, but I didn't regret going to the psych ward. That felt like too fine of a distinction to explain, so I stayed defensive.

"No. I'm happy I followed my Safety Plan when I felt unsafe." I hated the term "Safety Plan," but the therapist nodded in approval.

"Emi should not have gone to the hospital," my mom said. She looked at Dave and Jan. "There's no reason she should be here."

"I really was suicidal," I told her.

"Emi came back from this trip with her mom and everything went downhill from there," Jan told the therapist. "Emi's mom is a big trigger for her."

Dave twiddled his thumbs.

"*They* do not support Emi's intellectual development," my mom said.

"Emi's mom has an inflated view of her daughter's IQ. She's giving her expectations she can't live up to. That's why Emi's so stressed," countered Jan.

"Look, I'm not going to kill myself," I said. "I made a decision." The adults fell silent.

The therapist nodded, but Jan glared at me. "How are we supposed to believe you? How do we know you're not going to keep hurting yourself in our home?"

"I'm going to stop cutting myself for Lent. And I'm going to stop listening to pop music unless it's in French."

"I'm glad you plan to stop cutting," Jan said. "But your plan is incredibly disrespectful. You're not even Christian."

"I'm culturally Christian. And you're not Catholic. Do you even do Lent?"

"This sounds like a great conversation for outpatient therapy," the therapist cut in. "If Emi contracts to safety, then we can go ahead and discharge her."

"I don't believe Emi," Jan said. "I think she should stay here awhile longer so she can think about the consequences of her actions."

"What actions? Saying I had a plan to kill myself when I did? Following my Safety Plan? What do you want from me?"

"If Emi contracts to safety, we have no reason to keep her here. Can you agree with that?" The therapist looked at Jan. I wondered what would happen if Jan said no. Would I be sent to another home? Part of me wanted that. But if I left, I would have to change schools. How would I get into college without even a single full year anywhere? And I suspected Dave and Jan were as good as it got.

"Fine." Jan picked up her purse.

I filled out the safety contract. If I felt like hurting myself, I would listen to Carla Bruni or MC Solaar, or write. I signed it first and handed it around the room to collect adult signatures. Dave scribbled down his with his face twisted into disapproval.

"Bye, honey!" my mom said, hugging me, fishing out her keys to go shopping.

The therapist led me back to my room, where I put my clothes into a garbage bag. She handed me my purple tie-dyed backpack, filled with my homework, razors, and NoDoz still at the bottom. The doors locked shut behind us. I followed Dave and Jan to the car in silence.

*Eight*

As soon as we got back from the hospital, things changed. Whatever minor trust Dave and Jan had in me vanished. From now on, I'd no longer be allowed in my room except to sleep. My time staying after school would be limited. Dave would administer my Cymbalta, Zyrtec, and stool softener from a locked case, aka a flimsy plastic box I could have pried open with a butter knife.

As soon as we got back to their house, Jan said, "I'm going to do a baseline inspection of your legs." I chuckled at the term "baseline inspection," how Jan was trying to sound so official, but she was not amused.

She waited outside my door while I changed. I hesitated putting on my shorts. As much as I refused to show vulnerability, I didn't really want Jan to evaluate my body. I looked at the window, wondering if I could climb down three stories into the backyard and escape.

I stepped out.

Jan put her hand over her mouth and ran toward the stairs.

I felt satisfied that the evidence of my suffering had made her sick. I hated it when people called self-harm a "cry for attention" and hoped the damage I'd done silently proved it had nothing to do with attention. Maybe Dave and Jan would realize that I hadn't said I was suicidal just to make their lives harder.

That night, they told me I had to drop AP Art History. "The stress is making you sick." I tried to argue that my "stress" did not come from flash cards of naked marble men with tiny genitals, but Dave took me to speak to the guidance counselor. I made big overachiever eyes at Dean Boche, pleading. I wound up in two more advanced classes. When we left the office, Dave seemed humiliated. I wanted to tell him I wasn't trying to hurt him, but I also wasn't above savoring the feeling that I had won.

LATER THAT DAY AT SCHOOL, I was called to the office. Miss J. was there, holding the letter I'd written to her. My chest twisted with guilt as I sat down.

"You're so eloquent," Miss J. started. I felt a flicker of pride, but then she reached a finger below her glasses and drew a tear away. I squirmed. "When I read it, it just crushed me. It was like all the pain you feel, I felt." She put a hand to her heart. "And I had no idea."

"I'm so sorry," I said. I'd wanted Miss J. to worry, but I didn't want to make her sad. She was supposed to be rolling her eyes at the other students or circling my best shots with her black Sharpie, not dealing with my problems. "I feel better now. Things are going to get better from here." I nodded in order to convince myself.

She gave me an A-frame hug. The next week, alone in the photo classroom, she asked me, "Do you miss living with your mom?"

"Sometimes," I said, though I often fantasized about Miss J. or another teacher wanting to adopt me. If she'd offered, I would have moved in that night. "I miss living in the city."

"Maybe you can go to camp this summer," Miss J. said. "Like a photo camp or something?"

"I don't know if they'd let me." I thought about Dave and Jan in their recliners. They did not seem amenable to the idea of camp, especially not after my trip to the psych ward.

"I'll write you a recommendation letter. Just tell me what you need."

"Thanks," I said, trying to sound nonchalant, but afterward I couldn't stop thinking about it. My fifth-grade band teacher had told me about Interlochen Center for the Arts in Michigan; I'd applied to their programs two years earlier, shortly before I attempted suicide and wound up spending that summer in the psych ward. Sure enough, they had a photo camp.

Miss J. helped me pick out my best photos. I didn't tell Dave and Jan about my plans. My mom signed the forms: she was eager to help me pursue art, especially because Dave and Jan disapproved.

Just a few weeks earlier, my life had felt bleak, hopeless, the winter eternal, every night the same TV shows, the same stupid power struggles. Filling out the application was a thrill—I could compile a packet and get to trade my old life for a new one, a life that I wanted to live.

As soon as I walked in the door to Dave and Jan's, I could tell something was wrong. Dave came into the kitchen and opened the fridge. He extracted a Diet Dr Pepper but said nothing. A few minutes later, Jan came through the front door early. She plopped her purse down. "Sandy's in the hospital." She looked at me. "How do you feel about that?"

"What happened? Is she okay?" I imagined her struck by a car, lying in the gray ice that lined the roads.

"She tried to eat blue snow." I winced. Every so often, a kid mistook a patch of leaked antifreeze for a sweet winter treat. Jan folded her arms and clarified: "She tried to kill herself." Apparently Sandy had seen Dr. Woods—"who you adore"—who had changed Sandy's meds. "Then she saw you go to the hospital. You know Sandy looks up to you. You let her down."

"I don't exactly adore Dr. Woods," I said. The muscles in Jan's jaw clenched. I knew I'd said the wrong thing. "I'm sorry. I'd never want something bad to happen to Sandy."

"Well, you're going to tell her that when she gets out. You're going to apologize for making her do this."

I still wasn't exactly sure how I'd made Sandy eat blue snow, but I could see the logic: I had gone to the hospital, then Sandy had. I had come into their life, then something bad happened.

A few days later, Sandy returned. She slid across the floor in her socks and sang under her breath, seeming back to normal. Jan led her into the kitchen and stood in the doorway, hands on her hips. I swallowed hard. "Sandy, I'm sorry."

"Sorry for what?" Jan asked.

"I'm sorry I went to the hospital and was a bad influence on you."

"I think it was the pills they gave me." Sandy made the crazy sign next to her head and stuck out her tongue.

I smiled, relieved, but Jan stayed stony. I had upset the balance of their home. I hoped that if we just ignored it—and if I ate and followed the rules and didn't hurt myself—that things would just go back to normal.

But not long after, Dean Boche came and pulled me out of class. Dave was waiting for me in the office. "Is it Sandy?" I asked, scared.

"No," he said. "We're going to go see Dr. Woods."

I had no idea what was going on. At the office, Jan and my mom were waiting.

Before I could sit down, Jan asked, "What is this?" She held up a gallon-size ziplock bag containing pills, razor blades wrapped in cardboard, Dr. Woods's business card, a paintbrush, a jar of India ink, contact sheets, and several 8 × 10 photos. "Dave searched your backpack. You've been taking weapons to school. You could have gone to jail." The word "jail" made me seize up, though I tried not to show it, not wanting Jan to have a point.

Dr. Woods had her arms folded. My mom looked at me.

"Look, I haven't cut myself since the hospital. You knew I cut myself; I had to be using something. Are you really surprised?"

"Yes!" Jan said. "That you're dumb enough not to get rid of this stuff!"

I paused. "That's a good point."

"Yeah, Emi, why didn't you get rid of this?" my mom asked. Her voice was soft, almost insulted.

"No, that was dumb of me. I'm sorry," I said. I looked at the faces in the room. "I'm sorry. I'm sorry. Okay?"

"Okay." Dr. Woods folded her hands. "Let's come up with a consequence and then move on. Emi, I trust that you're not going to keep more contraband around."

"No, I want to talk about this," Jan said. "What are the pills?"

"Caffeine."

"That's cute."

"I was really tired."

"Where did you get this paint?" Jan held out the ink.

"My mom."

"It doesn't even matter that you had it! I'd let you paint a wall in your room if it meant you didn't cut." Jan looked at my mom. "I can't believe you got it for her to sneak into my house."

My mom took off her glasses and cleaned them on the bottom of her shirt.

Dave pulled out the contact sheets and prints. "Explain these." He handed them to me. The contact sheet contained the photos my classmate had taken on our autumn photo date. In one of the prints, I was wrapped up in Christmas lights like a human shrub. Another zoomed in on my torso, the thin lines of scars visible on my left arm while I petted a cat sitting on my lap. "These are satanic. What are they supposed to mean? I don't want the occult in my home."

"I didn't even take them! If I took them, they'd be in my binder at school, not in my room."

"They're glorifying cutting," Jan said.

"Come on," my mom said. "Emi is an *artist*."

Before they could fight too much, Dr. Woods cut the session short. She warned Dave and Jan it was unproductive to try to figure me out. To my foster parents' credit, they wanted to understand me. They seemed to think that if they could crack my code, and if I decided to trust them, I could join their family, confront my past, and have a few years of a normal childhood before embarking into adulthood. This, to me, seemed like the dumbest idea in the world. Not only was my past far from being past, Dave and Jan were totally random people. I couldn't suddenly belong to them when I still belonged to my mom.

Every night when the phone rang, Dave and Jan winced: they had to let me talk to my mom, although it seemed like Jan would have preferred to shake her and scream about the choices she was making. The goal of foster care was supposed to be family reunification, but I could tell Dave and Jan believed that my mom was fundamentally bad for me. Arguably, they weren't wrong, but because they were the alternative, she seemed like the better option.

In the midst of the conflict, Interlochen accepted me to camp, with a modest scholarship. It was still expensive, but my mom promised to find the money. She'd tap into her George W. Bush stimulus check and dig into funds she'd saved for my college. I was over the moon, elated to spend six weeks in the woods wearing knee-high socks, surrounded by thousands of my fellow young artists.

When Dave and Jan found out, they were incensed. I wondered why they thought I should have asked them: I knew they would have said no. Jan wrote to Ingrid, asking who to contact at Interlochen to tell them I wasn't stable. Ingrid said she'd take care of it. One of them must have called, because the camp rescinded my admission.

THE NEXT TIME I SAW DR. WOODS, she shut the door and said, "You need to get out of Lakeville."

I looked down at my sneakers. "I was hoping to go to camp for the summer." I was ashamed to admit my wish, now that it wouldn't happen.

Dr. Woods picked up a figurine and played with it. "What about next year? You need a different place to live."

I'd walked into her office expecting her to chew me out for the razor blades and caffeine pills. But, unlike Jan, Dr. Woods didn't seem to view me as a terror. She looked at me as if I were a sad girl who hurt herself but was otherwise harmless. If anything, Dr. Woods trusted me more because I'd shown my ability to follow through on my Safety Plan. I could never tell who would be happy and who would be upset about any given action.

I explained there was nowhere I could go and keep attending Lakeville South. "Should I move back in with my mom?"

"No." Dr. Woods glared at me. "She'll drive you crazy again and then you're going to be a hundred pounds and die of a heroin overdose. Can you go away to school? Like, live in a dorm?"

"Like boarding school?" I imagined a rolling field in the English countryside.

"You're always talking about college. Go to college next year like you said. But live in a dorm."

"Don't you think I'll go crazy there?"

"You're going to go crazy if you stay here."

"Do you think I can actually go? You've always told me not to worry about college."

"That's because I'm worried about you sleeping under a bridge."

"Really?" It never occurred to me that my life could get worse.

"Yes. Come on, Emi," she chided.

We brainstormed college. It was too late to apply for admission to the main campus of the University of Minnesota, but my mom had gone to a satellite campus in the rural town of Morris. She'd been sixteen, only a little older than me. The state's Post Secondary Enrollment Options program would pay for my tuition, fees, and books. I'd only need to cover room and board, which was probably cheap because Morris was in the middle of nowhere.

It seemed like the perfect plan, the one way to make everyone happy. My mom would get me out of foster care. Dave and Jan would get my pornography and chaos out of their occult-free home. I'd replace my family problems with 24/7 knowledge acquisition.

The next day during lunch, I asked the guidance office to send Morris my transcript. I had no idea what grades I'd gotten at CRTC, let alone what schools it might have listed before that; I was too afraid to look and it was too late to change anything. I printed my application at the school library so that Dave and Jan wouldn't see it. I filled out the single-page form, attached an AP English essay, and gave my ACT score. I'd taken it in February, just as a trial run, and got a thirty-one out of thirty-six. Placing in the ninety-seventh percentile wasn't enough for somewhere fancy—but Morris wasn't fancy. It felt so satisfying to fill out all the boxes—each one a little wish for my future—that I understood how someone could get addicted to applying for things.

DAVE AND JAN heard that my mom was petitioning Interlochen to take me back. They said that if I was hoping to leave for the summer, they'd have to give up my bed "to another child in need." They phrased it as a moral obligation, but the cynical part of me thought about money. I knew they got more than one thousand dollars a month for my care, because my mom complained it was more than half of what she made working full time.

"I understand," I told Dave and Jan, trying to sound solemn, even though I was elated about the possibility of ditching Lakeville forever.

"Where are you going to go after?" Jan asked. "To your mom? What's your plan?"

When I said I didn't know, she seemed disgusted, but I wasn't going to tell them about my application to Morris, in case Jan called them, too. That Sunday, when my mom came to pick me up, she wouldn't stop smiling. "I have something for you."

She reached beside her seat and extracted from the debris an 8 × 11.5-inch envelope, printed with UNIVERSITY OF MINNESOTA MORRIS in maroon and gold. It was thick. I was in.

"Yes!" I said. "Yes!" I reached across the center console and hugged my mom, the joy almost too much. I'd have my wish and live in a dorm, with no adults telling me my ambition was wrong. My mom would be 155 miles away—a safe distance.

We filled out the forms at McDonald's. Room and board cost $6,710, but Grandma Edna had set aside enough money to pay for a few years of in-state tuition, and we hoped she'd cover the room and board instead. Because Child Protective Services had never gotten involved and my mom had signed me into care voluntarily, she could take me out.

Later that week, I came home from school and found Dave holding my maroon-and-gold envelope.

"When were you planning on telling us? Were you planning on just having your mom pick you up and leaving?" The side of his face twitched. The anger in his voice baffled me. They'd already told me they'd give away my bed, even without a confirmation from camp; no matter what, I'd have to live somewhere else in the fall. I felt like he should have been happy I was going to college—Ingrid's first client to do so. But to him the surprise envelope was another reminder that I'd failed to become part of the family.

Dave shook his head. He took a Diet Dr Pepper out of the fridge and slammed the door.

———————

WHEN ANNETTE PICKED ME UP, I gushed about Morris. I'd studied the course catalog and devised a plan to graduate in three years. As we drove to the local ski slope, I explained how I'd major in either French or English, and then become a doctor.

Sitting on the opposite end of the chairlift from me, Annette said, "I didn't realize you were so unhappy in Lakeville. Is it really that bad?"

Normally, she seemed detached. Her question surprised me.

"We just don't get along," I said. A few weeks before, I'd forgotten a bobby pin in a pocket and broken Dave and Jan's washing machine. They charged me three hundred dollars for the repair, turning down the money from the county's fund for accidents, telling Ingrid I had to learn to face the consequences of my actions.

"Can you really not fix things? Do you think it's your attitude? Is it your mom?"

"It doesn't matter now. I'm going to leave. I'm going to college."

We hopped off at the top of the hill. I'd only skied once before, so I pointed my skis straight down. She chased after me, yelling at me to turn.

Once we were on the next chair, she asked, "What are you going to do on breaks?"

I shrugged.

"Is going to college at fifteen really going to solve your family problems?" She told me about a school near her house. "You can take any AP class you want. If they don't offer it, they'll find a teacher. Everyone has to learn foreign languages." I looked out over the hill, covered in ice in the Minnesota spring. "Do you think you'd be happy at a school like that?"

"Of course." I looked farther out, as far as I could look, at the frozen prairie beyond the parking lot. Of course I would have liked to live with Annette and go to a school like that and eat only organic fruits, but I couldn't. That was the whole point.

"Be honest with yourself, Emi. If you weren't trying to get out of Lakeville, would you really be happy with Morris?"

I clenched my jaw, hard. The question seemed cruel. Cruel and futile, especially because I wasn't sure of the answer.

MY MOM TOOK ME to go see Morris. We drove a hundred miles until the freeway ended, then fifty miles more down one-lane roads. Wind turbines rose out of cornfields. The stench of manure filled the car, even with the windows rolled up. My mom showed me her old dorm, and I hoped they'd place me in the same one.

After I spent a day observing classes, my mom's favorite professor took us to dinner at the fanciest place on Main Street.

"What do you think about Morris?" he asked.

I felt embarrassed even speaking to him: he'd graduated from Harvard. "I like it." It was college, after all. I'd even placed into third-year French, my all-time proudest academic achievement.

I expected a flattered smile, but instead I saw a look of concern. He said he wondered if I'd be happier somewhere else.

"Why? Like where?"

"Like my alma mater, Harvard. I think students there are a little more intellectually curious than they are here. More like you."

I sat, stunned. Why would he say that about me, that I'd fit in better at a place like *Harvard*? How could he know? We'd talked for twenty minutes.

My face flushed with pride while frustration rattled me: Why couldn't everyone just be happy for me? A year earlier, I'd been locked up, book-less, hopeless, worried about going to a state hospital. Now I could get my bachelor's degree at nineteen. I could escape.

"Well, can she transfer?" my mom asked.

"Harvard hasn't been taking transfers for a few years."

"What about Yale?" They started discussing how difficult it would be for me to graduate from a renowned institution. Looking at my mom, lit by the votive candles on the table, I wondered who she would have been if she had gone somewhere other than this rural campus. Maybe she would have a fancy job and know how to pronounce the names of different pastas. Maybe she'd be happier, not even hoarding.

This vision filled me with fear. I thought of all the fights where I'd yelled at her, "If Stanford rejected you because you were too young, why didn't you wait to reapply?" going for the spot that hurt, and she'd told me she had to get away from her family. Watching her talk to her professor, it seemed completely possible that her life would have been different if she'd just had another year, one more chance.

Tears stung my eyes. Maybe Annette was right. But I couldn't imagine two more years of foster care just for the *chance*, the tiny chance, to go somewhere prestigious. For years, adults had told me to stop thinking so far ahead. Finally, they seemed right.

EVEN THOUGH DAVE and Jan were upset with me a few weeks later, I still ventured downstairs to ask for a favor. During a commercial break, I asked Dave, "Do you think you could pick me up tomorrow after school?"

Jan turned down the volume. "For what?" she asked.

"For a club meeting."

"What club?"

I bit my lip. "One of my teachers leads it." It was the Gay-Straight Alliance, run by my art history teacher. I'd been going for months, claiming it was French Club. (To my credit, the membership was essentially the same.) We were unveiling our campaign against the ubiquitous insult "that's so gay" with a pizza party, then covering Lakeville South in rainbow-colored flyers.

"What's it called?" Jan asked again.

"The GSA." She waited. "The Gay-Straight Alliance."

*Deal or No Deal* came back on. We all looked to the television for a moment, where women in tight dresses clutched numbered briefcases. Jan didn't take her eyes off the screen. "Well, you don't need to go because you're not gay."

"So what if I'm gay?" The sharpness in my voice startled me. I didn't know what I was, if I liked boys or if bisexuality was real. In my family growing up, homosexuality was a sin, but bisexuality was worse, because it seemed like more of a deliberate choice. It also implied having multiple partners in one lifetime, which made someone a slut. Even after Michelle transitioned (and converted to Unitarianism), she remained critical of any sexual orientation besides her own.

Jan looked at me in shock. "I can't believe you've lived here all this time, putting Sandy in danger."

"No offense," I yelled, "but I have no interest in Sandy!"

I stormed back upstairs to my room and shut the door, even though I wasn't supposed to. No one came after me. As soon as my pulse slowed down, I felt relieved. The tension between us had finally cracked. I'd never been able to articulate my discomfort or justify not making myself vulnerable to these two well-meaning adults, and I suspected they were relieved, too. Finally, they had proof that I had terrorized their home and a good reason to explain why, despite their best efforts, things didn't work out. Later that night, they told me I had to move out after my last AP test. I'd still have two weeks left in the school year, but that wouldn't be their problem.

Afterward, we became more cordial. They took in a new girl—a diabetic Wiccan with bipolar disorder—and I delighted in how ill-equipped they seemed to be to handle her, hopeful they would miss my relative simplicity. In my last week at Dave and Jan's, Interlochen reaccepted me to camp. When they'd called Dr. Woods, she'd affirmed that I was stable. "I said a change of scenery would do you good," she explained at our appointment. I wanted to throw my arms around her, even though I knew that was against the rules. The evening following the AP Biology exam, I promised Sandy I'd come back to visit, although I knew I wouldn't. When my mom arrived, I ran out to her car. I spent the next half hour waiting in the driveway while she "played Tetris" to make room for my four bags.

The upstairs apartment my mom rented out was temporarily vacant, so I lived there, sleeping on a green foam aerobics mat. The fridge was stocked with expired Light & Fit yogurts and Diet Coke.

For the final two weeks of school, my mom had to drive me, even though it made her commute ninety minutes each way. Her efforts reminded me of just after the divorce—her proving how well she could parent me—and I hoped it would stay like this forever.

Every night after the school shut down, I waited for her in the entrance. I did all my homework sitting on the floor, then rested against my backpack. After getting up early to get on the road, I was exhausted. But my mom had to stay late at work to make up for her long drives. By the final day of class, each hour was a tired blur of goodbyes, mostly to my teachers, the majority of whom I knew I'd never see again.

I clutched my binder to my chest as I stood in front of Miss J. "Bye," I blurted. I threw myself into her for a hug and darted out.

From my spot on the floor in the entrance, I watched students skip out in twos and threes, excited for summer jobs scooping ice cream and attending volleyball intensives. I fell asleep on my backpack and woke up to a mom shaking my arm. "Are you okay?"

"Yeah. I'm just waiting for my mom to come get me."

"It's late." The sun was setting, so I figured it was around 8:30. The woman let me use her cell phone to call my mom, who said it would be awhile.

"It's fine," I told the stranger. "We do this every day."

After she left, no one else passed through. I eyed the janitor through the window, mopping the last marks of the year from the cafeteria floor.

Finally, the headlights of the Buick cut through the twilight. I grabbed my stuff and hopped into the car. I was so eager to leave that as Lakeville got small behind us, I felt nothing.

# Nine

The drive to Interlochen took eleven hours, the pines beside the high-way stretching taller as we got into the woods. When we said good-bye, my mom swiped tears from behind her glasses. I was elated to watch her car disappear.

For six weeks, no one from Minnesota could even call me—they'd have to mail a letter or relay emergency messages through the office staff. My peers grumbled about the no cell phones policy, but because I didn't have one, the rule made me feel normal. I loved the uniform: cornflower-blue polo every day except Sundays (when we wore white), navy shorts, color-coded knee-high socks. At the opening ceremony, two thousand musicians and painters and filmmakers gathered in the amphitheater, all wearing matching outfits. For once, I fit in.

A breeze blew in from Green Lake as the sun set. An administrator told us, "Shakespeare wrote, 'The purpose of art is to give meaning to life.'" I sighed with relief: finally, here was an adult taking the meaning of life seriously, even if the Shakespeare attribution seemed like a stretch. When the ceremony drew to a close, an orchestra onstage played a sim-ple, melancholy tune: *Les Préludes* by Franz Liszt, the Interlochen theme song.

As I followed a crowd back to the high school girls' section of the woods, the smell of sap filled my nose and the music echoed in my head. As I got back to Cabin Nineteen, I looked up and gasped at the tangle of stars.

WHEN CLASS STARTED, I gathered with three other photographers, while our teacher, Kurt, sat just outside the door to the lab. Kurt explained that during the school year, he taught at a community college. Camp was his favorite time of year, because we cared so much.

"If you wanna keep it that way, you've got to take lots of pictures. At *least* a roll a day. You can use all the photo paper you want." Kurt got up and went to the closet where we'd process film. He came out with a stack of Ilford envelopes. "If y'all use up all the paper, I'll make them buy more."

Kurt reminded me of the dads visiting their daughters at Methodist. He doted on us. I couldn't help but like it. He'd sit outside, watching wildlife, and I'd bring him contact sheets. He circled the good photos in red grease pencil. "Not enough," he said, shaking his head. "Take more." It felt strange to have someone push me, instead of criticizing my drive.

I had never felt younger.

The four photographers grew close. We spent a lot of time trying to cheer up Anthony, who'd gone to private schools before his mom lost her job during the financial crisis. He seemed as depressed as the city he was from, hard-hit by the recession. "I'm never going to get out," Anthony said, looking stricken under the red light of the darkroom as he moved his prints from the fixer tray to the stop bath.

"Just go away to college, Anthony," one of the girls from the Chicago suburbs told him. We all chimed in, saying he could do it, that he was so smart, that high school was almost over. Even when Anthony told us about the hopelessness of his school and his hometown crumbling around him, I thought he was just being negative: no matter what problems were going on in his life and in his world, higher education was the answer.

"You guys don't understand. You have no idea what it's like."

Kurt kept urging us to apply to Interlochen's boarding school, assuring us there was financial aid. We sat through mandatory info sessions/ sales pitches. Whenever the Academy came up, Anthony hardened, as if he couldn't stand this thing he couldn't have being dangled in front of him. We all saw how badly he wanted it.

I wondered if I was just as transparent when I folded my arms and said I wasn't going to apply, tilting my head up and declaring, "I'm on my way to college in the fall."

WHENEVER I WASN'T with the other photographers, I hung out with my cabinmates. We were all fifteen-year-old rising high school juniors, all young for our grade, overseen by a prudish tubaphone player who wore her hair in two long braids.

Our days started at 6:30 a.m., when reveille blasted into the slats between our wood plank walls. We lined up on the tennis court to do calisthenics while a counselor announced that evening's performance schedule. We went to one another's shows and readings and gallery openings.

When girls asked about the red scars under the hem of my shorts, I tried out stories: "I fell through a glass coffee table," "I got run over by a lawnmower," "A tiger broke into my family's car during a drive-through safari in Wisconsin, then it mauled me." But for the most part, we didn't talk about the past, only the future.

After lights out, we whispered in our bunks, asking ourselves what mark we would leave on the future. Every surface of the cabin, from toilet stalls to ceiling beams, was covered in Sharpie: quotes, poems, song lyrics, bars of sheet music, riddles, each signed with a name, a year, and a discipline. We combed through, searching for celebrities. But the cabin floor in the center of the room was sacred: each year's residents wrote one shared slogan for posterity.

When giggling woke me up in the middle of the night, I knew what it was about. Five girls huddled in the center of the room, between our bunks.

I crawled out of my bed, climbed down the ladder, and joined them. "We have to make a decision," Taylor, a musical theater actress, stage-whispered. "Tonight is the night."

As the discussion heated up, only a few girls remained in their beds.

"Look, I have it," Taylor announced. "Cabin Nineteen"—she paused for dramatic effect—"we turn gay guys straight."

A gasp escaped from the circle.

"Sorry, but that doesn't make any sense," I chimed in. "Who here has ever turned a gay guy straight?" None of us had even kissed a boy during that summer: they lived almost a mile away, barricaded by the woods. "Who here has *ever* kissed a boy?"

Three hands went up.

Taylor asked me, "Have you, Emi?"

"Yeah, of course." Tallying up my experience in middle school, I said, "Lots."

An oboist looked distraught. "Even if I had the chance, I wouldn't know how."

"You have to practice," Taylor told her. She turned to me and looped her long blonde hair on her finger. "Emi, will you kiss me?"

I hesitated. I'd only kissed girls in Truth or Dare. The eyes of the circle looked at me, and I reached forward and took Taylor's face in my hands. My lips touched hers.

I expected she'd pull away, but instead she kissed me back. She felt so soft against me. I felt like a pilot light flicking on next to a match.

Eventually, Taylor pulled away. "Emi's really good," she announced. "Kiss me again."

So I did. Then the oboist said she needed help. Her face trembled in front of mine and then it melted. She agreed with Taylor: "Emi *is* good."

The group giggled. Another cabinmate came beside me. I kissed her, too. They lined up and our faces reached for one another. I dug my hands into their hair—red, black, blonde. Seven, I counted, when around me laughter exploded and I let go of the embrace. Our counselor stood in the doorway between our bunks and her room.

"We're coming up with the slogan for our cabin," Taylor explained. "What do you think about 'We turn gay guys straight'?"

We all laughed and went to bed. The ladders creaked. The holdouts lay mummy-still in their sheets. Despite my best attempts to sway popular opinion, we wrote in bubble letters on the floor, "CABIN NINE-TEEN: We turn gay guys straight."

I WAS WITH the Cabin Nineteen crew at a Saturday night mixer when the song of the summer came on: Katy Perry's "I Kissed a Girl."

Taylor abandoned her doomed mission of dancing with a boy and pushed back to us through the throng. "Emi!" She put her hand to my ear, as if telling me a secret, and yelled, "This is your song!"

Everyone laughed. My cheeks flared. I was ready for them to call me a slut or say something cruel about how I *liked* kissing them, that it wasn't just practicing. Instead, Taylor started screaming out the chorus, scaring away any potentially straight males.

AFTER A BARBECUE DINNER, I wandered off to the woods behind the cabins. When the voices turned into faint murmurs, I bent beside a tree and reached into my throat.

I gagged and then a question gripped me: Why?

I'd always had a reason to hurt myself: the low-grade nausea I called "existence"; the wrapper of my skin, stretched too tight; unhappiness that seemed prehistoric, as vast as Lake Superior. I had been told that I was so sick that I would most likely be sick forever. But in these normal circumstances, I was suddenly normal. That night, I realized, I had no reason to make myself throw up besides habit. I wiped the spit off my hands with leaves and went to rejoin my friends.

WHEN I GOT sick of photographing trees, I started taking pictures of my cabinmates. I hung a sheet in the woods and made my models wear the same black tank top that looked good on everyone.

Kurt loved the shots: the complicated, contradictory faces. He shook his head. "I'm too old to shoot pretty girls. Now it makes me a creepy old man. But you can. You ever taken pictures with a big negative?" I'd heard about the 8 × 10-inch plates of glass Ansel Adams hauled up mountains to shoot Yosemite, but I only had my mom's 35mm camera. Kurt dug around the film-development closet. He emerged holding what looked like a black brick with two lenses.

"Be careful. It's heavy." He placed the camera in my arms. I cradled it. That Sunday, an opera singer and I trudged out to the practice huts. They were scattered among the forest that separated the genders like a DMZ of heterosexual tension.

It was almost sunset. Gold light spilled onto the plank floors. I found that my tripod was broken, so I had to hold the camera very still. I drew a deep breath and held it, pausing before each shot. I had twelve chances to get it right. Each click of the shutter felt vital. If I couldn't capture the light on the singer's shoulders, how would I remember those moments? I needed proof. No matter what had happened before, no matter what came to pass, for that evening I was filled with joy.

During photo class later that week, Kurt dug up 16 × 20-inch photo paper and found some extra-large development trays. When I'd made the prints—one of the singer's collarbone and one of her back, with the focus just on one point of skin, everything else blurred—he pinned them to the wall of the front room and told me, "You should apply to the Academy."

"I'm going to college. I already have a roommate and everything. I got into third-year French." My chest tightened. I'd been able to relax at camp because my future seemed set. If I didn't go to Morris, I'd want to go to Columbia, like I had when I'd worn my old T-shirt constantly. The odds of getting in were so low that I'd be looking at two years of uncertainty shredding me.

"Maybe they'll give you a scholarship." Kurt folded his glasses and put them in the front pocket of his denim shirt. "Just apply."

IN THE FINAL DAYS OF CAMP, I followed his advice. As soon as my application was in and I went home to Minneapolis, I felt sick. My mom forwarded me the two-page email she'd sent Interlochen, explaining our finances. After putting aside money for medical expenses, she grossed $28,250 each year. She received $150 a month in child support. Some years, she made a few thousand bucks on her rental apartment; in 2007 she'd lost $2,400. She owed $3,300 in car repairs. She had no savings besides her retirement accounts, which would only cover her health insurance premiums. Her department at work was closing, and she might be forced to retire the month I graduated from high school. She'd spent all of her spare cash—and more—on camp for me that summer. I felt loved and slightly guilty, but mostly scared to see the facts laid out frankly; even if my mom's shopping hadn't been an issue, our situation was tenuous.

Anthony had applied, too, and we emailed almost every day, sharing our anxieties and hopes. As we waited to hear back from Interlochen, I went back to sleeping on the aerobics mat in the upstairs apartment. I showered three times a day and read naked in front of a fan, but the August humidity clawed at me. Luckily, McDonald's had a special for ninety-nine-cent Happy Meals, so my mom and I went there every night. I luxuriated in the air-conditioning as the Beijing Olympics commenced on a muted television.

One evening soon after I returned from camp, my mom declared, "It's time for you to do driver's ed."

"I don't have time." I had two weeks and one day before move-in day at Morris, although I didn't like to think about that.

"You have exactly the right amount of time." My mom dunked an Apple Dipper in caramel. She reminded me that she'd saved her Corolla for me, a rust bucket that shared my birth year.

For years, I'd begged my mom to teach me to drive in a church parking lot. Now I shot back, "I don't want to learn." I blamed it on safety: my mom got into a lot of fender benders, even when she wasn't falling asleep at the wheel. "Micro-dozing," she called it.

"Pfft!" my mom replied to my worries. "What's wrong with my teenage daughter that she doesn't want to drive? Cars mean freedom, independence, adulthood!" She was right. That was the whole reason I was scared: whether I left for Interlochen or Morris, I was entering adulthood. Dr. Woods even suggested I become emancipated, but I was almost offended at the suggestion—I wanted to be my mom's daughter, which finally seemed possible, now that I didn't need her.

Despite my complaints, every afternoon I biked two miles to a strip mall storefront and joined the other fifteen-year-olds on plastic chairs. Sunburns peeled under spaghetti strap tank tops. The boys' farmer's tans made their arms look like corn dogs. I couldn't absorb the acronyms for stop signs and parallel parking. All I could think about was Interlochen Arts Academy. I realized why I had resisted applying, why I had shoved the dream of Columbia out of my mind and settled for college, any college, now: the uncertainty was agony.

The driving instructor popped in a VHS tape. On the TV mounted to the corner of the room, a mom in a tracksuit sobbed for her slain honors student, dead behind the wheel.

I dashed out of the classroom, leaned over a planter, and chucked Diet Mountain Dew and bananas.

THE WEEK BEFORE move-in at Morris, we still hadn't heard back from Interlochen. For the first time, Annette took me to her house, a bright split-level by a nature reserve.

She offered me Sanpellegrino from a glass bottle, taken out of a whole case in her pantry. I tried not to gawk.

Once I sat down on her sofa, she asked me, "What are you going to study in college?"

"Maybe English literature? Or French. And I'll do premed."

"Emi, listen." She sighed. She said she knew how I loved French, loved books and writing. "But that's not responsible." The people who studied those things had families who supported them. I needed to be able to get a job when I graduated.

"Maybe I could become a doctor? Go to medical school after?"

"Do you know how expensive that is?"

I shook my head.

"Promise me you won't major in anything with 'French' in the name. Or 'Literature.'"

I exhaled, angry and sad. But I also understood, thinking of how many times I wished my mom had studied something other than art. I swirled the water in my glass, bubbles tastefully dancing to the surface, and agreed.

That night, we met my mom at the mall for dinner. We sat on Big Bowl's patio, overlooking the parking lot. Everything felt bittersweet: the cooling air, the crickets chirping, the fact that I was finally leaving.

My mom talked all about her summer while Annette listened. I kept eyeing my mentor. I hadn't kept in touch with anyone from Lakeville or CRTC—just one girl from the psych ward—so I felt sure that after I went away to school I'd never see Annette again.

When my mom left to go to the bathroom, Annette flagged down the waiter and handed him her credit card. Then she reached into her purse and pulled out a greeting card envelope. "Open it later, when you're at home."

When my mom came back out, I hugged Annette. I made myself stiff so that I wouldn't care about saying goodbye.

I went into my mom's apartment so that I could pack. But first I needed to open the card and get it over with. Breathing through my mouth, I shoved my way past the teetering piles into the bathroom. It had the only door in the apartment, besides my mom's room, and the only place to sit other than her bed. Next to me, empty peanut butter jars and dirty laundry spilled out of the clawfoot tub. On the floor, I spotted the shoebox full of inhalers I'd used when I lived there.

I tore the envelope and slid the card out, expecting something about goodbyes and nice-to-know-yas. Instead, there was a cap and gown that said "Congratulations," as if I had graduated. I opened to a poem about new beginnings and then a check fell out.

I plucked it off the floor, which was carpeted with receipts and discarded instruction manuals, and then flipped it over: two thousand dollars.

I gasped. It was more money than I'd ever held in my life. Tears stung my eyes. "Gratitude" wasn't a strong enough word. Suddenly, I grasped the questions I'd shut out because I had no answers: How would I pay for laundry? Where would I go during breaks? Would school really solve my problems?

Annette had thought about this stuff. My mentor had considered me and what I needed. I knew that she wasn't saying goodbye.

———————

THREE DAYS BEFORE I was due at Morris, Interlochen called. I was in, but tuition would cost more than ten thousand dollars, money we didn't have. My mom had scraped together everything she had to send me to camp, and there was nothing left. She wrote an email appealing, and we waited. On the Sunday I was supposed to move in at Morris, I didn't want to ask my mom what we were going to do. In silence, we watched the hours pass: the dorms opening, key pickup starting, key pickup ending.

The next night, still no word, I couldn't sleep. I flipped from left to right. I heard the door open. My mom came and lay down next to me on the matted carpet. "Do you want some aerobics mat?" I offered her. Her face was wet. It shocked me to see her so somber.

"We need to pack up and go to Morris tomorrow," she said.

I nodded. I knew that was the only thing that made sense, even though I ached for the smell of sap. I wrapped an arm around my mom, wanting her to know that I recognized she had tried.

I DIDN'T HAVE a lot to pack. I stuffed my twin-size sheets from camp into my tie-dyed backpack and shoved in the clothes Hennepin County had paid for.

I went down into my room, looking around one more time. I dug through my old clothes, everything musty. Then I saw a flash of sky blue and gasped: it was the Columbia University T-shirt. I held my breath as I unfolded it, inspecting for holes or mouse pee. But somehow, it was intact. I ran my fingers over the white letters of the faded name.

The phone rang, and I ran to it, just missing a call from Interlochen. I dialed my mom at work; she was on the other line with Interlochen's financial aid office. When my mom called me back, she was sobbing.

Interlochen had given me eight thousand extra dollars. I heard relief in her voice, but also shame, as if the waiting had revealed that without luck like this, her best intentions might come to nothing.

Anthony got in, too, but Interlochen asked him to come up with twenty grand, even though his mom was unemployed, staring down the worst job market since the Great Depression. When I heard the news, I struggled to understand how I'd gotten more than a kid whose immediate situation—when I stopped to listen—seemed more dire. I was afraid for Anthony, afraid of the specific dangers of being a teenage boy who would not get the benefit of the doubt adults extended to me as a reasonably attractive, if disheveled, white girl. I believed that boarding school would save us, that especially horrible things would happen to him if he couldn't be safely ensconced in the wooded campus. And in my estimation, if you missed one chance, there would never be another.

Interlochen granted me a "merit" scholarship, but what did that mean? Art was so subjective. I just took pictures of teenage girls; it wasn't hard to make them beautiful. *Why me?* I wondered, the knowledge setting in that when I got good things, it meant someone else would be deprived. I'd hoped I'd beat out faceless spoiled morons, but instead I was getting an opportunity denied to my friend. Every time this came to mind, I had to shut my eyes and shove the thoughts away. They would drive me crazy.

When my mom got home from work, I ran out to the alley and hugged her, all sweaty, beside the fence covered in trumpet vines. "We did it!" she said. I was so grateful for her. Dave and Jan never would have let me go. At CRTC, this outcome would have been inconceivable. I felt like I had been right all along to stick with her.

"Well, should we celebrate?" my mom said. "Happy Meals?"

## Ten

I sat in the guidance office at Interlochen, tapping my leg and clutching a Post-it note with the first part of my plan to get into a top college. It could actually happen now, and if it did I wouldn't risk my life turning out like my mom's. I was ready to dedicate every moment to the cause. All I needed was some help, and I was about to meet the woman who could provide it.

"Emi?" a woman asked from the doorway. I popped out of my seat and sized her up. "I'm Kelly," she said. *My savior*, I thought. A bob fell around Kelly's face, making her look serious despite her loose green sweater and mom jeans.

As soon as she shut her office door, I started, "I really want to get into a great school. Maybe Columbia University—the Ivy League one."

"We don't talk about college until the spring," Kelly told me matter-of-factly and sat down at her computer.

"Well, I was *going* to be at college right now but I came here," I said.

"We need to pick your classes."

I bit my lip and read off the list from my Post-it.

Kelly clicked around. "These are all full." She printed me off a schedule of what was open, including two hours a day of drawing and two hours a day of sculpture.

"Can I take photography instead? That's why I got in. Plus I don't really draw."

"All visual art majors have to take drawing until they're proficient. The director of the department insists." I could tell that whatever patience she'd had toward me had worn off.

"Okay," I said, settling for any crumb of advice. "What else do I need to do to get into a top school?"

"Like I said, I don't have time for junior-year anxiety." Kelly smiled and took a sip from her Bowling Green coffee mug. I felt that if Kelly knew anything about my circumstances, she'd understand that I needed to think about getting in *yesterday*. If Dr. Svenson hadn't asked me where I wanted to go to college when she did, I would have been screwed. Why was it that an inpatient psychiatrist had taken my potential more seriously than the guidance counselor at my fancy boarding school? I suddenly felt fat.

Back in the waiting room, a line of students queued to finalize their schedules. Kelly had no more time for them than for me, but it still disappointed me to find my ambitions an inconvenience, my fears branded as irrational without any chance to explain the situation. I crumpled my Post-it note and threw it in the trash.

AT ORIENTATION, the president announced, "The mission of the Academy is to prepare students for a career in the arts." I folded my arms and wished I'd read the fine print. He rattled off the number of students who'd gone on to Juilliard, the Eastman School of Music, and other conservatories. At the mandatory info sessions for campers, they'd rhapsodized about these statistics—17 percent of America's orchestras were alumni of either the camp or the school!—and I'd assumed Interlochen's success in producing first violinists would also transfer into Ivy League admissions. After my chat with Kelly, I knew I had assumed incorrectly.

On Thursday, the visual artists congregated for our first mandatory presentation from an art school. I was eagerly waiting for Rhode Island School of Design, the best school, which had cross-registration with Brown. "No one gets into RISD from here," a senior with pink hair and an industrial ear piercing told me with an eye roll. "We're too *conceptual*."

"What does that mean?" I asked, fearing it meant no one was very good.

The head of the department, a mustached man named Kaz, prone to wearing kilts, skulked in the back row, waiting for someone's attention to fade so he could pounce on them. Kaz had been nice, even effusive, while courting me to come to the Academy. But he'd never mentioned the requirement to take drawing, or that I wouldn't take photography, or that my four hours of daily art classes would weigh more heavily on my GPA than all my academics.

A woman dressed like an edgy therapist flipped through a PowerPoint of her school: photos of alternative-looking students making colorful things, topped with some crisp graphics. When she got to the slide about tuition, I gasped and smacked my hand over my mouth: it cost fifty thousand dollars a year to earn a degree like the one my mom had. "Any questions?" she asked us.

I waved my hand in the air. "Do you offer financial aid?"

Kaz glared at me.

The admissions officer babbled about Pell Grants, merit-based awards, and loans. She meant that I'd graduate from her school with two hundred thousand dollars in debt. That was more than my mom's house was worth, an unfathomable sum. I didn't know how student loans worked, but I doubted anyone would even lend me that much cash.

I was starting to understand that getting into college was only one hurdle; I also had to think about funding. It was easy to assume that the best schools were the most expensive, but that wasn't true. Since taking the ACT and handing over my email address, I got spam from colleges every day. The local schools emphasized the simplicity of their applications, but when I clicked through I was appalled by the prices of places I'd never heard of. When Dartmouth and Yale sent notes, they advertised their financial aid initiative: families who made under sixty thousand dollars paid nothing. Ivy League–caliber schools competed with one another to offer the most money, while even the very good schools one tier down simply didn't have the funds. The pressure to get a full ride felt even more urgent because I was spending my college money, which would have covered a few years at the University of Minnesota, on arts boarding school.

I was grateful to be out of Dave and Jan's and away from my mom, but sometimes I worried I'd made a mistake. For many of the richer students, boarding school was a mental health intervention, their post-breakdown retreat and escape from tensions at home. The Academy had the same institutional feel as CRTC. I lived with 150 girls in a cinder block dorm with alarmed doors and hospital furniture. We even ate the same meals as in treatment at Stone Dining Hall, "where all the food tastes like rocks." (Wise students hoarded bananas.) It didn't help with the feeling I'd had ever since being in residential—on edge, convinced that the powers that be were indifferent at best, and out to get me at worst.

That suspicion of doom intensified two weeks into the school year, when a bank called Lehman Brothers collapsed. I stood in front of the TV in my dorm's lobby, rubbing my forearms as carpal tunnel set in from all the drawing. I'd heard about a recession, somehow connected to how some relatives had lost their house in the summer of 2006, but suddenly things seemed serious. My mom called later that day, frantic that she'd lose her job or her pension, which, like my college fund, was invested in the stock market.

"Do you think they're going to kick out the kids on scholarship?" an oboist asked me during our mandatory "community service" shift work-ing in the cafeteria.

"Can they do that?"

"Why not?" He shrugged, taking a sip from a glass of chocolate milk. I clenched my eyelids shut and tried not to think about it.

My coworker squeezed out a rag to wipe down another table. "This," he said, gesturing to the bucket of dirty water, "is our real preparation for a career in the arts."

BEFORE CLASSES EVEN STARTED, I decided to treat art as an inconve-nience. I'd do the minimum to get A's but focus on my academics. It didn't matter that Interlochen sent few students to the Ivy League; I'd will my way there.

Then my physics teacher announced that instead of problem sets, we'd make art projects, inspired by the *ideas* of reflection and optics. After class, I walked up to him and introduced myself. "Will this prepare me for the AP Physics B exam or Physics C?"

He rubbed his beard thoughtfully. "A test isn't really the point."

I stormed down the hall, fighting back tears. In my English classroom, I found the teacher perched on his desk, a Harvard sweatshirt straining against his belly. I exhaled. Maybe his Harvard affiliation meant I had a better shot at getting in there.

"I'm Professor Wescott," he announced, then took a sip from a Harvard-branded mug. "There are many ways of knowing. Spatial, kinesthetic, visual, musical. Verbal intelligence isn't the only kind." This pronounce-ment felt like a barb directed at me, as if Wescott could tell that the only way of knowing I cared about was knowing how to get into college.

He launched into a story about a two-week class on education he'd taken at Harvard, hence his branded lanyard. I figured he must have spent most of his two weeks at the gift shop. When I got to AP Calculus, I sighed in relief. Not only did the class have "AP" in the name, it seemed normal. The teacher, Mrs. Z., stood in front of a chalkboard. "They tried to replace it with a whiteboard!" she said, shaking her head. Chalk ghosts danced on her navy pants.

She started class on time, telling us a story to lead us to understanding derivatives. "Most of you will drop out," she announced at the end of the hour, seeming pleased with herself. That declaration pleased me, too.

THE STUDENTS WHO remained in AP Calculus gathered in the classroom after dinner to do homework. One of the regulars, a pianist named Charlotte, spoke fluent French, so we huddled beside each other at the seminar table, guessing at math translations: dérivitif, intégral, le chain rule. Unlike most students, Charlotte never skirted the uniform rules and always wore a cornflower-blue oxford tucked into navy trousers. She looked like the Little Prince with glasses.

One evening, she invited me to do homework on Saturday night. I was thrilled: I couldn't remember *ever* having Saturday night plans. I waited for her in the basement of my dorm. Underneath the fluorescent strip lights, the vending machines buzzed. Laundry spun and tumbled, making the air warm and linen fresh.

Charlotte arrived. "Je suis désolée," she apologized, for being three minutes late. From her L.L.Bean backpack, she extracted a Tupperware full of cookies. Sensing my confusion, she explained that she'd made them that evening. I knew Charlotte lived off campus, but did people with families just bake cookies on a Saturday night? The idea was novel to me. I set it aside and took one, still warm. Sea salt sparkled on top.

"Très bien!" I told her. "Merci, merci." We ate for a while as violas and pianos echoed from the practice rooms. Laughter and bass sifted in through the windows at the top of the cinder block wall, the sounds of a student dance. For once, sitting beside Charlotte, I felt content to be an outsider.

When we wrapped up our homework for the week, Charlotte went back to the beginning and checked her work. Normally, I never verified my answers. But there was nowhere I'd rather be, and I wanted Charlotte to like me, to want to do homework again.

AT THE BEGINNING OF OCTOBER, I found a card in my mail slot. I thought it might be from Grandma Edna, but it didn't have the usual return address, where she always called herself "Mrs.," followed by her late husband's name.

The card had a little-girl fairy on it and proclaimed "Happy Birthday" in glitter. Inside, beneath the Hallmark poem, were two lines: "Hope you're well. Love," followed by Michelle's signature.

My chest ached. Five years had passed without any contact. Grandma Edna or my cousin who wrote the checks from my college account must have given her my school address. I knew I was supposed to be grateful: this was something. How many times had adults told me to be patient toward my parents, understanding, willing to forgive, right up until their final breaths?

I wanted to crumple the card and throw it in the recycling bin. Living at school had let me pretend that I was away from my family for noble, normal reasons. Any actual reminder of my parents challenged that illusion. Yet I couldn't throw the card away, which would feel like a symbolic end to our relationship. Worse, *I* would be the person ending it.

In my room, I slipped the envelope into my bottom desk drawer and tried to forget about it. As I struggled to do homework, the fairy card taunted me, reminding me that I was still my parents' child. They had a claim to me, even if I had no claim to them.

A FEW WEEKS into the semester, my mom announced she was coming for Family Weekend.

"It's my birthday," I begged her. "Please don't come. As a birthday gift to me." I had my first "reflection journal" for English class due just after. Worse, the week after was the PSAT/National Merit Scholarship Qualifying Test. It had "scholarship" in the name, so I *had* to qualify. Plus my mom's gas would cost money—money she claimed she didn't have. (Annette's check covered my rubber cement and laundry quarters.) Most of all, Interlochen was *my* space, free from my mom. I couldn't articulate why I didn't want to see her, but I didn't.

She asserted it was her right to come, and she'd show up whether I liked it or not. The fact that she was correct made me even angrier.

The Friday before my birthday, my mom drove all night. We had class on Saturday, so at 8:00 a.m. I glared at my mom across the studio. Her clothes were wrinkled, hair lopsided from grease. Because we didn't look alike, I hoped no one would recognize us.

"The assignment today is to draw your parents," the teacher announced.

My mom beamed. "Hi, honey!" she said, sidling up to my drawing horse. I would have to stare at her for the next two hours.

As revenge, I decided to make contour drawings, where I traced her face without looking at the paper, resulting in a tangle of lines that—I hoped—would render her hideous. My mom relaxed her expression, although she could not hide the pleasure in being studied so closely. I seethed, clenching my jaw, and paid special attention to her wrinkles, the sun spots on her cheeks, the hairs sprouting from her chin and lip.

When the teacher called time, I'd drawn her twice. I looked down at my board and saw two pictures: in one, my mom looked dignified, loving, like when I called her "Maman," French for "Mommy." In the second, she looked like "Mother," lip sliding off her face, grotesque.

To my horror, they were the best drawings I had ever made.

I TOLD MY MOM I was too busy to see her and that I already had dinner plans. The parents of a girl down the hall took two cars full of her friends to Traverse City's fanciest restaurant to celebrate their daughter's birthday. I ate butternut squash ravioli for the first time; they melted on my tongue as we dined in candlelight. A pang of guilt racked me when I thought of my mom, who was probably eating a protein bar for dinner in her car. Then, when the waiter brought out dessert, there was a candle in a cake for me, too—my friend had told her parents it was my birthday, and they'd passed it along to the restaurant. I wiped at the side of my eye.

When we got back, just before curfew, I thought of my mom again. I opened the curtains and stared into the pine trees. It was too dark to see anything, but I imagined my mom out there, journaling in her Buick before sleeping in the reclined driver's seat. The image seemed so lonely that I went to the bathroom, ran the shower, and threw up dinner as penance. Then I hated myself for puking such nice food.

The next day, I relented and called her. At the mall, I led my mom to Borders. "If I'd known we were coming here, I would have looked for coupons," she said, sadly.

"I need an SAT book, okay?" I snapped. Even after two years of study, my math scores weren't where I needed them to be. I'd already gone through all the books at the library. I picked up a tome called *1000 New SAT Math Problems*. "Let's get this one."

To my mom's credit, she'd get me things I needed—and many things I didn't—if she could find them on clearance. But in her mind, if she couldn't find a deal, it wasn't a necessity. Reluctantly, she pulled out her Visa for the SAT prep guide.

I clutched my new book to my chest. My face hurt from gritting my teeth. I felt like a bad daughter, but I wasn't done. Before she could protest, I led my mom to a shoe store. "I need running shoes," I told an employee. I showed her my feet, pronated inward from wearing the same cheap sneakers for too long.

My mom asked if they had anything on sale. The cashier said no. My mom's face pinched, as if someone had screamed at her. But she still offered her credit card.

As soon as the cashier handed me the bag, I wanted to apologize to my mom. She'd proven she loved me; now we could return the stuff. I knew about money: Once you'd spent it, it was gone forever. You might miss it for the rest of your life.

But I also had needs. If I didn't get the shoes and the book now, I didn't know when I would. I hardened my face and gripped the bags as if I deserved what they carried.

I followed my mom out to the car. She started driving back to campus.

"I thought we were going to get dinner, for my birthday."

"Where do you want to go?" my mom asked, not looking at me.

"I don't know. Somewhere." I remembered the birthday candle the night before, the ravioli. I hated myself for thinking about something so expensive, for calling that love.

My mom pulled over onto the shoulder. "You have to tell me what you want."

"I don't know!"

"We can get fries at Burger King."

"I don't know where a Burger King is around here."

"McDonald's? Emi?" There were places in the mall, all sit-down, but I knew my mom didn't want to spend that kind of money and I wouldn't ask her to.

"I don't know." It was all I could do to keep the tears from streaming down my face, embarrassing me. I could tell my mom was mad at me, but I felt I needed a boundary. I couldn't give her the chance to tell me I didn't deserve the scraps I could extract. "Just take me back to campus."

We rode in silence. My mom would have to drive all night back. She'd go straight to work in the morning. I felt so bad for being mean to her. I wanted to throw up, even though I was hungry.

"Thanks for the stuff." I watched her pull away, wanting to break down, wanting her to no longer be mad at me. Dinner was over, the dining hall closed. I went into my room and grabbed the X-Acto knife I used to sharpen my pencils. I pulled down my pants and sliced the flesh over my hip bones, eight times on each side. As the cuts opened, I felt ashamed of myself, as if I'd regressed. But at least I could exhale and focus enough to read.

AFTER THE NEXT weekly arts school sales pitch, Kaz called me into his office. "What's going on?" I asked, sitting on my hands. Like Wescott, he'd dinged me for failing to incorporate enough ways of knowing in my work, but I hoped that he wouldn't accuse me of cheating; my drawings weren't good enough to be copied from photographs.

"Your mom said you weren't happy with art."

"What?"

Kaz leaned back in his chair. "If you have a problem, I'd like to hear it from you first."

I knew there were a lot of things he could say. About my B's. That I'd gotten a very large scholarship and now produced mediocre work. Every week, my sketchbook contained a Post-it note listing that week's failure: "too many colors," "excessive erasing," "not enough sources."

"I don't know what she's talking about," I told Kaz and tried to smile.

But the final straw came when I sat down in the cafeteria for the PSAT. Heat rose in my throat as I bubbled in the letters of my name. When the proctor called time, I headed straight to Kelly's office.

"I need an intervention," I told her. "With the way things are going, I'm never going to get into the kind of college that can give me a scholarship. I did not do well on the PSAT. I know it."

"Look, I'm packed solid with seniors who have real crises, who won't get into college *anywhere* unless I help them right now."

"But you don't understand." Kelly didn't know my family situation. She didn't understand how "college" was a metonym for safety, security, for my entire future. But I didn't know what to say about my mom, or how much it mattered—all I could talk about were numbers and my not-good-enough grades.

"I don't have time for juniors worried about their test scores." Kelly stood by the door of her office, looking exhausted, newly drained by everything I needed. "Please don't come back without an appointment."

CHARLOTTE AND I finished our homework early one Saturday, so we went for a walk. A line snaked out of the Melody Freeze ice cream shop, the scent of Bosco Sticks and the sound of Top 40 jams filling the plaza. But it felt like we were in our own universe, dizzy from calculus, walking alone.

Charlotte kicked a rock down the street. She dug her hands in her navy trousers—she hadn't bothered to change out of uniform. I liked that about her. She shunned fashion, trends, and current events, which made me feel as if my ignorance of all three were an admirable choice.

Leaves crunched under my feet and dangled from the trees, catching gold in the streetlights. In the piano building, a few lights were on in the practice rooms.

*I used to love piano*, Charlotte admitted in French, in the past tense. She explained how she practiced almost forty hours a week.

"Quarante? Vraiment?" I asked, unsure I understood the number. She said she practiced four hours each weekday and eight hours each Saturday and Sunday. She shook her head, biting her lip, and said she was the worst pianist at Interlochen.

Interlochen wasn't what either of us expected. Art had felt very different as a private passion—a rebellion—than it did as a discipline to be studied, trained, graded.

Charlotte and I passed the Opera Field where teenagers acted out great tragedies and dramas. Shadows rustled under a tree, either squirrels scurrying or a couple making out. We turned around. In the center of campus, in front of the wood-beamed Writing House, Charlotte said in French, *I wish I were a writer.* Her dream was to move to Paris and work at a bookstore called Shakespeare and Company. She'd dedicate herself to poetry and live in artistic poverty.

Charlotte's innocence charmed me, even though I knew enough to want money. I wasn't going to tell her that my dream was to own a separate refrigerator just for beverages.

"Transfère?" I suggested. Students occasionally switched majors—I'd seen the form in the guidance office. If she hated piano and loved writing, how hard could it be?

Charlotte shook her head. "Non." Charlotte explained she had signed up for piano. Switching out would be giving up.

Her persistence seemed noble, if fatal. She had a pride I lacked. In her position, I'd drop piano in a heartbeat. I couldn't go out of my way to prove my virtue; I was too desperate trying to achieve my goals. But no one could tell me what achieving them would take.

MY ENGLISH CLASS was discussing our Thanksgiving reading, Truman Capote's *In Cold Blood*, when the classroom phone rang. Professor Wescott nodded, listening. "Okay, I'll do that right away." He strode over to the door, Harvard lanyard bobbing, and cut the lights. "I need everyone to remain calm, but there's a shooter on campus."

Students gasped. We hid under the seminar tables. Wescott barricaded the doors and then returned to his desk, where he watched us with his hands in his trouser pockets. The girl beside me rocked back and forth, putting the back of her hand in her mouth to muffle her sobs.

For all my thoughts about suicide, which seemed like the ultimate act of self-determination, I feared dying at the hands of someone else, powerless. But now that it was happening, I felt calmer than I had in weeks. It all made sense: *Of course* I'd get out of residential treatment and foster care just to die in a rampage. *Of course* I wouldn't actually go to an Ivy. I'd wanted too much, and this was my consequence.

I lay on my back and waited, reading the graffiti on the underside of the table.

Twenty minutes later, Professor Wescott flipped on the lights. "You can get up now." Dazed, we stood, straightening our uniforms. "There's no shooter. This was just to illustrate the themes of *In Cold Blood*."

Someone stormed out of the classroom. Sniffles filled the room. I exhaled.

I knew what I had to do: I had to transfer to writing. As long as I was alive, I could change my life. Drawing was not going to help me; a good college essay would. In a burst of energy, I sucked up to my teachers for the final weeks of class. "I learned so much about the ways of knowing," I told Wescott, showing him how I'd splattered my B− drawings with red paint, allegedly inspired by Truman Capote.

One afternoon, I snuck across the street after an art school presentation and met with Mika, the head of the Writing Department. She was thirty at most, terribly skinny, and almost buzzing with shyness. I'd sent her one of my typo-ridden novels, along with several poems.

"Why do you want to transfer?" she asked me.

"I love reading and writing," I decided to say. I said it as if I were still capable of loving purely, free from strategic concerns. Mika signed my transfer form.

# Eleven

After finals, I found a ride to Chicago and then took the Megabus back to Minneapolis, where my mom picked me up. My mom said I could stay with a friend of hers over the holidays, but she backed out at the last minute, if she had ever agreed. Instead, I shivered on the back porch as my mom searched her pockets for the keys.

As the door opened, the stench hit me. I hesitated.

"Come in! You're letting out all the heat."

I pushed my way inside, which wasn't much warmer than outside. The kitchen looked like the alien landscape in *WALL-E* with debris stacked to eye level: cans of Campbell's Chunky vegetable soup, bags of Chex Mix, brown bananas, unopened cardboard boxes, empty peanut butter jars, plastic shopping bags. The piles seemed to have grown two feet since the summer.

I waded to my bedroom. The lump of covers in my bed moved. I shrieked.

"Who is that?" I asked, mad and also a little curious if my mom had a new lover.

"Well, you moved out." My mom explained her roommate had been sleeping on the sofa at Love Lines, the prayer hotline where they both volunteered (and showered). The woman had nowhere else to go, so my mom let her move into my room.

"Can you make her move out now?"

"If you give me a couple of hours, I can clear off the couch." I stood in the doorway of the living room, where the path from one room to another abruptly ended. Just reaching the sofa would take hours. Once we'd cleared that path, we'd have nowhere to move the mounds of photo albums, construction paper, and toys that covered the cushions.

At the start of December, my mom had agreed to give me two hundred dollars a month—the child support she received, plus fifty dollars—to cover all of my expenses. Her parents had done something similar when she was young, and though she still resented them for it, it seemed like the best solution for us both. But I hadn't realized the money was meant to include housing, too. At least at college I could have found a boyfriend to take me home during breaks, as my mom had when she was young.

I didn't know where else I could go. My mom had rented out the upstairs apartment. I couldn't remember the last time I spoke to my brother one-on-one; my mom suggested that he thought I was a bad influence on his kids. "I want to stay with Grandma Edna," I announced. Normally, I just called her for ten minutes on holidays, before she thanked me for calling and hung up. I'd never spent the night. When Grandma picked up, her voice was shaky on the other end of the line. "Hello?"

"Hi, Grandma. How are you?"

"I'm fine." She was ninety-one. "Fine" was the best I'd heard since I was little. "Who is this?"

"This is Emi. I'm in Minnesota. Can I come stay with you?"

She paused. "When would you like to come?"

"Right now if that's okay." I glared at my mom.

"Well, my house is too messy. And I don't have anything to feed you for dinner." I knew this was her polite way of saying no.

"That's fine. Thank you, Grandma. We'll be there in about two hours. Love you." Two hours later, I rang Grandma Edna's doorbell. My mom waited in the car, in case my grandma turned me away.

My aunt Colleen, whom I'd met once before, greeted me. Nearing seventy herself, she'd moved in to take care of her mom.

"Emi!" my aunt said, hugging me. "It's been so long!"

She led me into the kitchen. It was spotless, as always, although a whiff of urine hung in the air. Grandma Edna sat in front of the television in a pink sweatshirt with an appliqué poodle on it and matching pink pants.

"Hi, Grandma." I leaned down to hug her.

She replied with her standard greeting: "Go comb your hair."

I SLEPT IN Michelle's old room, wood paneled and smelling like cedar. In the morning, I dutifully combed my hair before I came down with the test prep books I'd checked out of the school library. Over cereal, I explained that I'd just taken the SAT and now had to prepare for three more subject-specific tests. Grandma seemed pleased.

All morning, I studied at the plastic-sheathed kitchen table. A corkboard of family photos looked down on me. During breaks, I peeked up to look at the unfamiliar faces of my relatives. Before I was born, for unclear reasons, Michelle had burned bridges with her siblings, which meant I hardly knew anyone. The most recent photo of me was as a first grader with a bowl cut that Grandma made me get, wearing a fancy dress that she gave me.

Colleen and Grandma silently played rummy 500. After lunch, Grandma took a nap and I did a practice test. In the late afternoon, we washed down spritz cookies with caffeine-free Diet Cokes and played a game of cards together. When the phone rang, Grandma took the receiver to her bedroom.

I figured my studying pleased Grandma, because for once she didn't criticize me. When I saw her as a kid, she made me cry almost every time: my ragged haircut, my bad posture, my midriff exposed in outgrown shirts. This time she just asked me how long I planned to stay. "Maybe a few days?" I offered, though the dorms didn't open for two weeks. I hoped that if I gave this answer every day, she'd let me stay indefinitely. On Christmas Day my aunt went to visit friends and left us alone. Grandma Edna watched D-list celebrities sing Christmas carols on TV while I followed my usual test prep regimen. The phone rang early.

When Grandma came back, she lowered herself into her chair and said, "That was Michelle. He calls me every day. He's unhappy, as usual. She misses you." Every time Grandma misgendered Michelle, I flinched, remembering Michelle crying as her mother messed up the pronouns. Grandma confused them, even when trying to apologize. "I asked if he wanted to talk to you but she says it's too painful," she told me.

"It's okay, Grandma," I tried to reassure her. "I'm used to it."

A gasp snuck out of Grandma's lips. I'd never seen her cry before. I looked up from my test, wanting to comfort her, but it seemed rude, so I stared back down.

"I wish Michelle were dead. She'd be happier that way." Tears slipped from her eyes. "I wish I could just die. I don't want to go on living anymore." She went through each of my cousins, bemoaning the fate of her family: the forty-year-old who'd never married, the one with cancer who wed a good-for-nothing, the pretty one who was cohabiting and would never get engaged, the student with a dead dad who couldn't finish college.

I felt relieved she'd skipped me.

"I'm sorry your parents are so useless," she told me. "You were a good kid. It breaks my heart."

"It's going to be okay, Grandma." I put my hand on top of hers. The skin was thin and cold, stretched taut over veins and ligaments. "I'm going to be okay," I said, to myself as much as her.

Grandma Edna pushed her chair away. "I'm going to take another nap." She hobbled toward her bedroom.

I looked at my practice test open on the table. I felt like such a burden. I knew my grandma loved me and that's why this was so hard, like it hurt her to see me. When Grandma Edna said it so plainly, I knew my parents' decisions were going to affect me for the rest of my life. My promise to be okay was flimsy; so much could still go wrong. Really bad things could happen, things I could only conceptualize with the mental shorthand "not getting into a top college," and even if I studied every minute of every day, I might not be able to stop them.

JUST AFTER CHRISTMAS, Colleen and Grandma Edna dropped me off at my mom's. They were on their way to visit Michelle, who had moved back to the Twin Cities.

Somehow, I cried again when I saw what used to be my home. I shook as I riffled through the medicine cabinet. I grabbed a pair of nail scissors, pulled down the waistband of my jeans, and sliced. Blood bloomed to the surface. I exhaled. My thoughts cleared enough to decide what to do: I'd sleep in the front stairwell that separated the upper and lower apartments.

I looked through my mom's collection of pills—mostly prescription painkillers in case someone had a menstrual cramp—and finally found what I was looking for: Xanax, an antidote to the Adderall beside it. I grabbed the ADD pills, too, just in case I'd need them sometime.

I took a pillow and blanket from my mom's bed and told her my plan. "You're crazy," my mom said. "There's no insulation. Give me a few hours to clear off the sofa."

"No way." In the front stairwell, still in my jacket, leggings, and jeans, I lay on the matted-down carpet. Wind hissed through the walls. Outside, the windchill was negative twenty. I knew my best bet to pass the time was sleep, but I was so upset my arms shook. I popped a tab of Xanax and rolled myself into a blanket, mummy-style.

When I squeezed my eyes shut, I had a vision of the hospital. Everything was warm—sheets, towels, showers. Everything white and clean and disinfected. How easy—a quick, hard cut and then calm, a bed, trays of hot meals I could eat or not.

I understood why I'd loved the psych ward so much, why I'd returned again and again before CRTC. When this house was all I knew, that had been paradise. But now I had another vision in my head of tall pines and arias, the laundry smell and vending machines and calculus homework and chocolate chip cookies, Charlotte sitting beside me. I took another pill and recited my incantation: *Michigan, Michigan, Michigan.*

I WENT TO SEE DR. WOODS. I told her about where I was sleeping and asked for a refill of Xanax. "Lay off the benzos," she told me, as if the pills hadn't been prescribed to me for situations just like this, when I might do something terrible. Dr. Woods suggested meditation.

"I don't think you understand my living situation," I replied.

She said I was free to send her photos and added a new medication, for anxiety.

I called Annette, embarrassed about the desperation in my voice. "There's no place for me here." I hoped she'd offer to let me stay at her big house by the nature reserve, though I wouldn't ask her.

"Look, I'll come over and help you clean a space." She seemed annoyed, like she thought I was being dramatic.

"No, no. It's okay. Don't come."

"I'll be there in an hour."

Annette pulled up in her Hyundai. She came to the front door, holding a sack of cleaning supplies. I wiped the snot off my face with the sleeve of my sweater. I led Annette into the stairwell where my blanket and pillow lay on the floor and opened the door to the living room. There was no path in this way, so Annette just stared inside.

My mom hummed, hunched over a pile of stuff. A Yorkshire terrier with matted hair stood at her feet, barking. "Hello, Annette!"

Annette's eyes darted around. I led her around the house to the back door, then she followed me through the detritus to my room, tiptoeing to avoid stepping in dog poop. After I inspected my bed to make sure the other woman was gone, Annette and I sifted through a heap of clothes. My mom came in to grab soiled toddler-size shirts out of the garbage bag.

"I bought Emi this great air purifier," my mom said and explained its many high-tech features. "What more could a girl ask for?!"

The fan blew the stench of mouse pee straight at Annette. Her face strained to stay neutral.

"Would you mind if Emi stays with me for a few days?" Annette asked.

"Of course not! That seems like a great idea."

I stuffed my clothes into my backpack and followed Annette out to her car in silence. She opened the trunk and set her cleaning supplies down next to a vacuum.

We both climbed in, streetlights making the snow glow all around us. The heater blew cold air as it warmed up. Annette shook her head. "I can't believe I was dumb enough to bring a vacuum."

*Twelve*

When I got back to campus, Charlotte and I went for a walk. I didn't tell her about my family or my break—I had no words, in any language. Instead, I talked about standardized tests.

After struggling through *Barron's* and *Kaplan*, I discovered *The Princeton Review*. It laid out a system: eliminate obviously bad answers, then plug in the rest. Finally, I had broken 700 on the SAT math section, the score I'd need to be a serious contender.

Charlotte pursed her lips. "Je déteste la strategie." *I hate strategy.* She asked me why I didn't just learn the math.

I tried to explain—I didn't have time. I'd devoted months to *1000 New SAT Math Problems* and it didn't help. If I insisted on doing things the *right* way, they'd never get done. Charlotte rolled her eyes.

Her judgment wilted me. It also drew me to her. I knew Charlotte would never plug in an answer. She didn't need strategy to survive. She seemed so pure, like I wished I could be.

I asked when she'd let me hear her play piano.

"Jamais," she told me. *Never.*

She dug her hands into her pants pockets. The snow crunched under our boots as we neared the edge of campus. Moonlight glistened on the pines.

Charlotte asked if I'd help her with a dilemma: her parents wanted her to attend one liberal arts college, where she'd get a big discount, but she had her heart set on a slightly more prestigious one where they'd have to pay full price. Agony shadowed her voice. "Qu'est-ce que tu penses?"

I sighed. I wasn't the only person worried about the future. But I wasn't sure what advice to give her. Her conundrum was my fantasy.

"Suis tes rêves," I told her, trying to sound certain: *follow your dreams.* She asked me if I really meant it.

I had no clue. It probably didn't matter where she went, but I didn't want to say that. Instead, I wanted to live, even vicariously, in a world where money didn't matter, where she could grow up and live in artistic poverty and only feel artistic hunger and never have to sell artistic sex because she had no profitable skills. Besides, it sounded like her parents would pay either way.

"Bien sûr." *Of course.*

Charlotte exhaled and threw her arms around me.


IN ONE YEAR, my college applications would all be turned in. That short window of time both consoled and terrified me. I camped out in the library's advice section, reading all the guides. My favorite was written by a celebrity consultant whose students called her Dr. Kat. She portrayed getting into an elite school as the central challenge of her protagonists' lives, which mirrored how I felt about my own, despite the fact that they had homes and enough money to hire an adviser who frequently appeared on television, and I did not.

*Rock Hard Apps* followed three students. One had subpar grades and a great application. Another littered his essays with red flags. Unfortunate circumstances had weakened the résumé of the third—which for her meant a few C's, two years of French club instead of three, and a boarding school drinking binge covered up by her father.

The book taught me that their futures—and mine—hinged on marketing. Each piece of the application, from recommendations to the personal statement to the résumé, contributed to the persona. Most important, you had to anticipate and answer every question the committee could possibly have about potential liabilities.

I was terrified. Compared with me, these fictional characters had simple histories. (And I thought even the weakest application was pretty good.) I had no idea where to start explaining my own life. I didn't talk about my family to anyone besides Dr. Woods and, occasionally, Annette. The truth was too complicated for me to understand and I couldn't do anything about it, anyway. The whole point of my college obsession was to free myself from that stress. Yet it appeared I'd need to package it first.

I clicked around Dr. Kat's website looking for pricing, hopeful I could scrounge up a few thousand bucks to work with her. Then I stumbled on a news article: her Platinum Package cost more than thirty thousand dollars.

After chastising myself for my naivete, I noticed that she did pro bono work. I Googled "pro bono" and learned it meant "for free." I burned my best photographs onto a CD and stuffed it into an envelope with some of my poems. In a fit, I wrote a letter begging her to take me on. I was never that candid, but Dr. Kat was a stranger, some lady whose book I found in the school library who would probably throw my sob story in the trash. If Dr. Kat responded, or if the admissions committees did later, I suspected that it would only be because I had seduced them with my words, painting a picture of someone worth assisting. I'd watched my mom do this—wooing doctors with her charm and the façade she put on—while I failed to effectively argue my side. I decided that to make people who'd never met me love me, I had to become an incredible storyteller.

I quizzed a writer who lived across the hall about the Interlochen nonfiction teacher. She said he was a man's man who loved Jim Harrison, fishing, and "adventure pants" that unzipped into shorts. And he always assigned an essay about gender.

On the first day of the spring semester, I waited outside the teacher's classroom with an Add/Drop form in my backpack. Acid burned at my sternum. I was afraid that I was going to get in trouble for manipulation and be punished—something swift and severe enough to break me. I feared my initiative indicated a character flaw, the way "strategic" often meant "dishonest" and "conniving."

But I wasn't Charlotte; I couldn't afford not to do this. How would I learn to write an essay that could seduce readers if not in this classroom? Students filed out in loose interpretations of the uniform, clearing out to reveal Bob Dylan smirking from a poster on the wall.

In the teacher's office, I detailed all the memoirs I'd read. He took a sip of coffee and did not seem impressed. I lowered my voice, even though we were alone, for my real sales pitch. "My parent is trans and I want to write the gender essay about it."

My stomach cramped as I said it, wondering if I was betraying Michelle by using her.

The teacher pursed his lips together and nodded in approval. "Sure, sounds interesting." He waved his hand, magnanimous. "Take the class."

NORMALLY, I hated how Michelle piqued people's interest. Most people assumed that either the transition "traumatized" me or I lived in a family with two smiling mommies, when the truth was far more complicated. But I didn't mind Charlotte's questions when I told her about it, as we walked close to each other on the narrow paths through the thigh-high snow. She never asked me, as strangers often did, how one surgically acquired a vagina (which I could answer in more detail than anyone cared to know).

I tried to sound as open as possible with Charlotte, but I held back. There were few openly trans people out there, and judgments were harsh. I wanted to protect Michelle, and I didn't want people to make generalizations based on her less than perfect behavior. It seemed unfair to bring up the harsh treatment of the "before" times, which Michelle later blamed on gender dysphoria. I also didn't want to dwell on the present, where my parent wouldn't talk to me or see me. Charlotte asked about Michelle's transition as if it were a miraculous transformation. In general, she believed that if people chose their personal truth over the values of society, things turned out okay. Her idealism charmed me; I didn't want to be the one to shatter it.

I promised to let her read my essay, though I had no idea what I would say. I poured out forty pages of memories, including many about the years Michelle had ruled the family as a patriarch, dictating to my mom and me what we could and could not do because of our gender. In the essay, I referred to Michelle often as "my father": the archetypal parent whom I feared and adored and adored because I feared, and also the stereotype of a parent who left. I used male pronouns. I felt conflicted enough about that decision to add a paragraph explaining that if I ever saw or spoke to Michelle again, I would use the correct ones, but that I felt justified in my error because it had been so long and because most of my memories with her were pre-transition.

I wasn't trying to be vengeful. More than anything, my choice was an effort to split my parent into two. I could assign everything harmful to "my father" and then hold out hope that there was someone else out there—Michelle's true self—whom I'd known only briefly but might one day meet again, who might be my second mother and give me everything my mom could not.

My workshop, when we discussed my attempt, was silent.

"It's alive," someone said.

"But does it make sense?" I asked.

The teacher waved his hand, indicating "not really," but he suggested how to edit my forty pages into a coherent seven. Charlotte was elated when she read it. She congratulated me too fast for me to understand as we walked, giant snowflakes twinkling.

A few days later, Charlotte finally asked if I'd listen to her play piano. She'd have to perform in a mandatory recital; just thinking about it had made her vomit three times.

Charlotte made me sit on the floor of the practice room facing away from her. I balanced my sketchbook on my folded legs, pen in hand. She explained it was a Debussy étude, which meant nothing to me besides that it seemed French.

She began. The melody built and fell. I drew loops with my pen, trying to show the way it made me feel: dizzy, circling, up and up and up. I craned my neck and peeked at Charlotte, her body loose, a river running over rocks, despite her terror. Facing away, I could feel her focus, her essence, transform into sound and fill the room. It was exactly what I loved about art. Exactly what I adored about my friend. I didn't care if she won national awards or if she got B's for "good effort." I cared about her as a human, a human who'd spent weekends locked inside, distilling herself into a song. When she read my essay, I hoped she felt the same way about me. That was the ploy of art: to trick people into listening to me when they'd otherwise disregard my perspective in favor of more convenient narratives.

MY ESSAY, "SCRAMBLED EGGS," got accepted into the campus literary magazine, *The Red Wheelbarrow*. Charlotte was even more thrilled than me. She sat in the second row at the reading, right behind the authors.

I stepped up to the microphone, the lights on my face. "I was everything Michelle wanted to be," I read. "At the Unitarian church's 'women's night,' complete with hot dish and drums, she whispered to me across the table, 'When you menstruate I'm going to throw a party and buy you a monkey.'"

Much of the essay was about my own experience of being female, which I primarily found banal. From my first understanding that I was a girl because I had "girl parts" and that was all being a girl meant, my family and community had layered arbitrary rules on top: that I had to cover my knees, that I couldn't play sports or percussive instruments, that I was gross if I wasn't thin. Only when Michelle transitioned did I learn that some people held deep convictions about their gender that rose from within themselves rather than being assigned. Both my parents still trafficked in stereotypes—Michelle called my mom "butch" and "a dyke" because she could wield power tools and refinish a hardwood floor, and sometimes used male pronouns when referring to her because she was not feminine in the ways Michelle valued. But Michelle's trans friends expanded my sense of who I could be: a six-foot-five museum curator; a twentysomething extremely cool blonde from whom I poached the name Emi; a trucker who told Michelle she needed to show my mom respect, at least in front of me (prompting her to throw cash on the Formica diner table and storm out). In an era of misguided help, they were some of the few people who showed me true kindness. They made me believe that I could re-create myself—no matter who disapproved or tried to stop me.

Over all of this hung a sense of peril about existing in a body like mine, accentuated by my mom's job as a crime scene photographer—with all the slain "girlfriends" and "prostitutes"—and by a film Michelle had me watch called *Boys Don't Cry*, in which a trans man is graphically gang-raped and murdered. She had made me see the completely age-inappropriate movie so that I'd understand what trans people went through. But I couldn't help but see the hate crime as not only anti-trans but also an act of aggression against anyone with a vagina.

It felt narcissistic to think the film, or Michelle's transition, had anything to do with me. But I couldn't help but think about them through my own lens. That was the condition of being an adolescent, or of possessing human subjectivity. Only when I was writing or making art did I feel free to express myself without someone harping on me to consider my parents' feelings, prioritizing their perspectives over my own. I clung to each gasp from the audience as they responded to my experience, in my own words, no one challenging or disagreeing.

"We hugged goodbye," I read. "'I love you, Mom,' I said. I talked to Michelle once on the phone, but I never talked to her again. A year and a half later, there were no drums for my first blood, no dances, just a trip to Rainbow Foods for pads."

Holding the audience captive, I felt a surge of power, perhaps the most I'd felt in my entire life, as I described being dragged into this world of womanhood that I didn't particularly wish to inhabit but that was my only home.

I STAYED WITH ANNETTE over spring break. I was taking extra AP exams, hoping it would impress colleges that I'd taught myself the material. Between practice tests, I stared off into space, thinking about Charlotte. I wondered if she liked me, if that's why she baked me stuff. My body felt full of sunshine, like nothing to hate.

When I went to see Dr. Woods, I gushed about my new best friend.

Dr. Woods leaned back into her chair. "Do you like boys, too?" she asked.

I folded my arms. "I don't know." I didn't see why it was any of her business.

"Maybe you should figure that out." She spun. "How's your mood?"

"It's fine. It's just . . . when I'm at my mom's house."

"Yeah, you can't live there. No one could." After I'd sent Dr. Woods photos during winter break, she stopped suggesting meditation. Annette had also emailed Ingrid, looking for a more permanent solution.

"Where could you live?"

"I got into a camp." My mom had suggested Stanford, of course, and they'd given me a full ride to study topology (some math thing).

"All summer?"

"Three weeks."

Dr. Woods shook her head. She picked up her phone and dialed a number from her computer. My jaw unclenched. For a second, I was sure she wanted to let me stay with her and was just calling to get permission.

"Hi," she said, "I've got a homeless teenager who needs to find housing." I felt so dumb for thinking she was about to take me in. I stared out at the parking lot so I didn't have to look at her. I hated that word, "homeless," and I felt it didn't apply to me. I was a boarding school student. "Go to this meeting," she said, gesturing to the Post-it with an address and a time. "Even if you have to spend your last twenty dollars on a cab."

I knew I wasn't going. Spending my break in government-provided housing would wreck my chances of doing something impressive. All the books said that this summer was the critical time. It was my one chance to do something worth writing my college essays about—and then write them.

Besides, if people knew about my mom's house, I suspected they wouldn't let me go back to Interlochen. If Child Protective Services got involved, I'd be stuck in Minnesota. Most of all, I was afraid of someone hurting me; being on my own felt safer than this weird program.

Instead, I made other summer plans. My mom took me to see a plastic surgeon. I hoped a laser would help get rid of the puffy red scars lining my legs from knee to thigh. "A laser's not going to help you," the handsome surgeon said. He called me "mutilated," which made me cringe, but then said it was a side effect of an illness, which felt like mercy. I imagined myself in eighteen months, wearing denim cutoffs, scar-free. A new beginning, the past literally excised. We scheduled surgery that summer. The doctor swore he'd make my insurance pay.

After my mom took me to get my driver's license, I asked for her cheesecake brownie recipe, grateful to want something from her that she could give.

"Even better. I'll gather all the ingredients before you go!"


ON THE BUS BACK TO CHICAGO, on my way to Interlochen, I slept with a soft-shell cooler between my boots: a box of Pillsbury mix, a pack of Philadelphia cream cheese, a film canister of canola oil, a baggie of powdered sugar, and two eggs swaddled in used paper towels.

Almost twenty-four hours after leaving Minnesota, I arrived on campus and checked out the keys to my dorm's kitchen. All they had was a cast-iron skillet, but it would do. I texted Charlotte on the flip phone I'd just gotten and waited for her on one of the benches in the corridor between classrooms.

We hugged hello and I offered her a brownie. We sat in an alcove, chatting about our breaks, eating. Charlotte leaned in and hugged me. She smelled clean, scrubbed with hippie soap. I didn't let go. She didn't pull away.

"Je voudrais t'embrasser." I said it: *I want to kiss you.*

"Pas ici," she said. *Not here.* She took my hand and led me to the end of the corridor. I followed her outside, through the narrow paths dug in the waist-high snow, past the chapel and the auditorium and the visual arts building, out into the Opera Field. We trudged in the snow to the center of the field. The brightness of the stars made me gasp.

I took her face in my hands and kissed her. Her lips seemed to melt into mine. We kissed again and again until Charlotte looked down at her watch. I'd be late for sign-in. I kissed her one last time and then ran back to my dorm.

INGRID WROTE TO my mom saying she had a "foster grandma" with whom I could stay during breaks and in the summer.

I was skeptical, but I didn't think it was the worst plan.

"You would lose your freedom," my mom wrote me. "And no matter how good they say people are, living with them is a different matter.

"It is apparent that Annette contacted Ingrid," she continued. "I was enjoying not having social workers or foster parents in my life (or yours). This dredges up memories of how difficult it was at Dave and Jan's."

Whatever joy I felt in the Opera Field evaporated: If my mom was mad at Annette, she could simply decide I'd never see her again. And I could tell from her tone that she was pissed.

"Mother," I wrote, defending Annette. "Try not to be angry at her. She is in such an awful position—in fact, so is Dr. Woods, and Kelly and most people who care about me—because of my living conditions. What good options are there for the summer? I don't especially want a social worker in my life, either, but what is the alternative? This is a bad situation for everyone involved, including you."

My email seemed to placate my mom; she wrote back, "Ingrid said that *if* she had favorites—you'd be the one!"

ON SATURDAY NIGHTS, Charlotte and I finished our homework and kissed. The snow melted. Grass shot up fluorescent green. Blossoms hung on the boughs of trees. One evening, we found a lake in the woods and lay side by side in the gold light before sunset.

I stopped caring so much about my body because, for once, I felt inside it. I ate the sweets Charlotte baked us, then tasted them again on her tongue. When we were together, the uncertainty that racked me fell away. I memorized an E. E. Cummings poem that made me think of her. It featured the line "kisses are a better fate than wisdom." I would have even blown off homework to see Charlotte more, but she had to practice.

Alone in my room, we lay on my bottom bunk. In its cave, I imagined a future, a home. For the first time, I could imagine myself as an adult. Charlotte and I would sit in armchairs beside a fireplace, silently reading. Maybe this was what Dave and Jan meant when they talked about "a normal life," as if it were something I could enjoy. As soon as I had someone, I couldn't believe how lonely I'd been.

I'D THOUGHT THE matter of the summer was settled: all my mom had to do was call the county and ask to have my case reopened. I didn't want to live in a foster home, but I knew it was better than the alternative: sleeping in my car.

Annette emailed me, following up. "I strongly believe you need a social worker, as your mother's difficulties to provide for you may at any time worsen further." She ended it in a boldface plea: "Please take my advice and convince your mother to call."

On the phone with my mom, during pauses between detailing her purchases, I asked her, "Will you call Ingrid?" My mom sighed. "You know I don't want to go to a foster home, but what choice do I have?"

My mom said she'd call later, when she was driving, but she didn't.

A MONTH BEFORE THE AP TESTS, Charlotte came to my room to do homework. She arrived at the door, holding two cups of red smoothie.

"Les cerises." *Cherries*, the Northern Michigan specialty.

My stomach lurched. When I'd tried to kill myself when I was thirteen, I'd passed out and woke up vomiting what felt like pounds of cherries. I'd avoided the taste ever since, even Diet Cherry Coke and flavored hard candies. But that was too much to explain. I thanked her and drank.

When we finished homework, Charlotte sat on my mattress. I held her face in my hands and kissed her. We both lay down. I rubbed my hand along her back and felt the outline of her sports bra.

Charlotte pulled away. She stared at the bunk above us. She said that her family was moving to Europe. She wasn't coming back to Interlochen.

I didn't believe it. It couldn't be real. I reached for Charlotte but she turned her back to me.

"Je ne sais pas qui je suis." *I don't know who I am*, she said.

"Ça ne fait rien." It didn't matter to me: I didn't care if she was gay or I was gay or if bisexuals existed.

Charlotte told me I didn't understand. As she spoke, she sounded farther and farther away as my stomach cramped. I pushed myself out of bed and ducked into the bathroom to puke: sweet, pink, acid.

When I came out, Charlotte stood in the door, wearing her backpack.

"Laisse-moi expliquer." *Let me explain*. But she was gone.


I DIDN'T SEE Charlotte for four weeks. She stopped coming to tutorial and the extra AP prep calculus classes. I heard she was sick, maybe with swine flu, but I didn't hear from her.

Without her, in horror, I realized everything I'd overlooked. One afternoon I stepped on the scale and saw an all-time high. I hadn't even remembered to hate my body. Now I had the figure of someone who ate warm cookies without guilt and reclined beside a lake reciting poems.

That was no longer my life. It was May, three weeks before the end of the term, and I still didn't know where I would live. I emailed my mom, again, who just didn't reply. I emailed Ingrid, who said my mom had to call.

I tried to line up places to go. Annette had offered to let me stay for two weeks, but she'd be gone all of August. I started applying to more camps, but even if I got in, I'd still have gaps between them. I didn't have the money to pay for lodging and, at sixteen, where could I stay alone even if I did?

Doing laundry one night, I bumped into a senior from AP Calculus. "What's wrong?" Isabel said, grabbing my arms.

My face must have given me away. I hadn't told a single person at school the truth about my living situation, not even my guidance counselor. (I couldn't get an appointment.) Next to the spinning dryers, my uncertainty spilled out. "Come stay with me in Virginia!" Isabel told me. "We can hang out!"

I pieced together a plan. My suitemate, Kayla, offered me a ride to Washington, DC. I looked up the East Coast on Google Maps: DC seemed close to Virginia. Two of the photo campers lived in Chicago. Out of the blue, an old roommate from the psych ward emailed me with the subject line: "I hope you're not dead." Courtney was one of the few people in Minnesota with whom I'd stayed in touch; I hoped she'd let me stay with her for a few weeks.

My mom was delighted by my resourcefulness. She finally wrote to Ingrid, describing whom I'd stay with and where, fleshed out with details that didn't exist. "This is prime college visiting time and Emi now has friends all over the country!" She said we wouldn't need the foster home, but that if anyone needed a French-speaking nanny, "They know who to call!"

I hoped I'd be okay if I kept moving.

## Thirteen

The day the dorms closed, the suitemate who was supposed to give me a ride poked her head into my room. I sat on the floor surrounded by the stuff I was trying to consolidate into my two bags. "Hey." Kayla bit her lip. "There might not be space in my car after all. I had more stuff than I was expecting."

In her room, a tower of boxes loomed over a stuffed laundry basket. Two suitcases leaned against the wall. Bosco Stick wrappers and old homework littered her desk, along with junk she still hadn't packed. All year, Kayla had been struggling; she wasn't coming back in the fall.

"When will you know?"

"When everything is in the car, I guess."

I rolled my eyes before I could catch myself.

"Don't you have anyone else you can go with?"

"No, I don't. I thought you could give me a ride. My mom lives eleven hours away." I felt irate, witnessing Kayla's nonchalance, but I also knew it was my fault for relying on someone so flaky. I offered to help Kayla pack the car, but she declined. She told me to just wait around. "The less stuff you have, the better." I sat down on my floor again, this time to consolidate everything I needed into my backpack: notebook, camera, test prep books, a stick of Mitchum deodorant. I spooled duct tape around my water bottle to peel off later. I ripped my towel down the middle and threw half in the trash.

Through the bathroom, I listened to Kayla's mom chastise her daughter for living in a pigsty. Part of me hurt for my friend, for whom boarding school seemed to have been a failure. (She'd repeat the academic year at home.) But her mom's criticism soothed another part of me: no one could say I was lazy, or that I melted down under pressure, or that I stress-ate. I rolled up all the clothes I'd wear that summer into a log, which could double as a pillow. Everything else would go into the trash. The tidiness of my bag almost canceled out the anxiety of not having the money to replace the things I discarded.

I heard a knock on my door.

"Come in!"

Charlotte slid in, wearing cuffed trousers and dangling a thermos, the picture of calm. We hadn't really talked since the night of the cherry smoothie. After the AP Calculus exam, she'd fled. "Salut," she said.

Charlotte eyed the packs of microwave oatmeal, bottles of shampoo, and art supplies piled beside me on the dirty linoleum. Shame flickered through me: Charlotte had told me that she was shipping all her books to Europe, even though she'd only stay a year. She would never be in my situation.

I stood up and rubbed my sweaty hands on my cutoffs. Face-to-face, I longed to reach out, to take Charlotte's chin into my hands and kiss her.

The world around us was silent.

"Fuck!" I yelled. I ducked into Kayla's room. Gone.

I hoisted my bag onto my shoulders. "À tout à l'heure." *See you later*, as if I'd be back in an hour.

"Adieu," she said to me: *goodbye*, as if she'd see me when we were dead.

I ran down the long hall, through the TV room. I spotted a minivan beside the loading dock, in front of a dumpster heaped with furniture. Waving my arms, I ran toward it. "Hey! Kayla! Kayla! Kayla!"

A woman rolled down the passenger window. Kayla hunched between her two sisters in the back seat, hiding.

"Hey, Kayla," I said, staring straight at her. "Do you have any room in the car?" I focused all my energy on the line of my mouth, curving it upward into a pleasant expression.

"Mom?" Kayla asked timidly. "If there's space, can Emi get a ride with us to DC?" My jaw clenched: Kayla hadn't even asked. I was so angry, realizing that my friend's offhand offer meant nothing to her, even as it was the foundation of my plan.

I shifted my eyes to Kayla's mom and fought to soften them. "Hi, Mrs. Adams. Kayla told me you could give me a ride to DC."

"Where are you going in DC?" Her hand rested on the window control, poised to roll it back up.

"I'm going to stay with a friend in Virginia." Kayla's mom grimaced. I wondered what face she would have made if she knew I only had an *offer* to visit Isabel, which might have been as insincere as Kayla's suggestion to give me a ride. "I'm visiting Virginia Tech. But I'd love to visit some of the great colleges in the capital. I heard Kayla wanted to go, too."

I smiled, this time authentically, eager that I could play the studious dream daughter, a role her actual daughter had failed. Kayla studied the calluses on her fingers.

Mrs. Adams looked behind her shoulder. "I think there's a little space in the back."

ROCK HARD APPS made it clear that the summer between junior and senior year was the critical time for college applications. As soon as I buckled my seat belt in the minivan, I extracted my notebook and started brainstorming essay topics. These two pages were my opportunity to show the admissions committee who I was, my true self. They could make or break my application.

"Let's watch *Lady in the Water!*" Kayla's youngest sister squealed. The three of them play-fought until they got the DVD in. Blue light splashed on their faces as they cuddled. "Mom, Daddy?" Kayla called up to the front. "Can we stop soon? I'm hungry. *Please.*" She must have known the answer would be no, but she still asked freely, as if there were no consequences for wanting what she couldn't have.

Kayla was only slightly younger than me, but so obviously still a child. From my vantage point, she had no discipline, no sense of urgency about her future. I doubted she'd even *thought* about college. In this sphere, at least, I had the upper hand. I told myself grimly that this advantage over her was what really mattered. Kayla's sisters would grow up. Her parents would die. When Kayla looked back, would she be able to console herself with a perfect SAT score?

While Kayla's parents didn't seem to espouse my extremist attitude, I could tell her mom was scared. Every parent said they just wanted their kids to be happy. But how could they be happy without a good job? Everywhere you looked, you saw people made miserable by the bad economy. The woods outside of Interlochen were filled with trailers and broken-down homes in foreclosure. All of Michigan seemed to be in a state of collapse. Often, I was reminded of my parents' separation seven years earlier during the dot-com bust. No relationship was safe from market forces.

When we got to Washington, DC, Mrs. Adams made Top Ramen for dinner. It seemed possible, even likely, that hard times had hit their family, too. Kayla avoided the rehydrated carrots and peas floating in the broth until her mom grew agitated and snapped. I slept on their fake leather sofa, my rolled-up clothes serving as a pillow. In the morning, I showered off the night's sweat and dried myself with my half towel.

I could tell my presence was barely tolerated: I was clearly not from a good family and possibly a runaway. (Kayla's parents seemed careful not to ask too many questions.) My only potential utility to them was to jolt Kayla into caring about her future. I suspected Kayla's parents would bring me up later to ask their daughter, "What's your excuse?" The question was sad—Kayla clearly seemed depressed—but I relished this strange power.

Upstairs, Kayla's mom yelled at her to get ready: we were going to visit universities. Eventually, Kayla hobbled down the stairs, hand over her face, as if she were hungover, even though I knew she'd just stayed up late watching *Hannah Montana*. Her mom led us and Kayla's two younger sisters to the Metro to visit George Washington University and Georgetown.

I took fastidious notes of the tour guide's anecdotes and drilled into the questions the college books advised me to consider in order to pick between thousands of schools. "Do you have a creative writing major? A minor?" I waved my hand in the air. "What is GLBT life like on campus?" Kayla's mom side-eyed me. Savoring the role of the student-consumer, a customer with infinite choice, I judged George Washington's maid service and Georgetown's excessively green grass.

I paid close attention even though I knew I wouldn't attend either institution. My choice was limited to the few dozen schools that would meet 100 percent of need without loans. I wasn't in DC to look at colleges at all; I just needed someplace to stay and kill time. But the fact that I was only there because my mom had refused to call the county depressed me too much to think about. With renewed vigor, I evaluated Georgetown's lawns.

THAT NIGHT, KAYLA'S mom asked me when I was going to Virginia. "Maybe in a couple days?" I offered, hoping Mrs. Adams would allow me to prolong my stay. I proposed touring some other schools.

The truth was, I hadn't called Isabel. We hadn't talked since the night in the laundry room when she offered to let me visit. I kept thinking about calling her, but the prospect of asking and potentially hearing no filled me with dread, so I didn't. Mrs. Adams pursed her lips, clearly unimpressed with my proposal to drag Kayla to American University, but not seeming to want to know the truth of my situation either. I feared that if I told her, she'd either chew out my mom or report us to Child Protective Services. Or both.

After dinner, I held my breath and called Isabel. Immediately, my phone died. The next day, it turned on, but Isabel didn't pick up. That night, it fritzed out again. I cursed myself for buying Target's cheapest flip phone. But I couldn't just ask the Adamses to borrow their phone: then they'd know that I didn't actually have a plan with Isabel. Making matters even worse, I had stored her number in my contacts but hadn't written it down anywhere.

The next morning, Kayla's mom drove me to the Greyhound station. We sat in the minivan.

"How is your mom okay with this?"

"I'm going to stay with a friend."

Kayla's mom narrowed her eyes at me, trying to figure me out. I knew she wanted me to say something to reassure her I'd be fine.

"I would never let my daughter be alone like this." I bit the inside of my mouth, resenting the implication that my trip was unsafe. My mom wasn't Kayla's. My life was what it was. I had to believe that everything would be okay.

We sat in silence for a moment and then Kayla's mom grabbed her purse and opened her car door. After I had my ticket, she told me, "Sit with the oldest woman you see on the bus."

There were lots of empty rows, with open window seats, but I sat next to an elderly Black lady with upright posture, who was carrying her handbag on her lap. Kayla's mom waited in the car until my bus pulled out and turned a corner, headed south.

———

For the first hour, I fiddled with my phone. No matter how hard I jammed the buttons, I couldn't get it to turn on. I'd have to plug it in in Blacksburg, in seven hours, and hope that did the trick.

I tried to swallow my anxiety. With each man who boarded, the bus getting progressively packed and thick with body odor, I was grateful for Kayla's mom's advice. Here on the bus, next to my neighbor, I was safe. I peered over her shoulder out the window and tried to do what my mom had advised: see America. To occupy myself, I wrote a letter to Charlotte that I knew I wouldn't send, telling her about the Confederate flags, which I assumed were ironic, and my disbelief that there was a town named Lynchburg. Most shocking to me were the mountains, lush and green: my midwestern imagination had cast the South as one scorched battlefield, cannons still smoking from the Civil War. In the early evening, the driver called my stop. I hesitated, suddenly unsure if it was better to be at my destination, without a plan, or on a bus, where I could keep going indefinitely. The doors threatened to close as I grabbed my backpack and ran out.

I clutched the straps of my bag, looking for a place to charge my phone in Blacksburg's tiny downtown. The scent of bread led me to a Subway restaurant, where I searched under the tables until I found an outlet to plug in my phone. I bought a bag of Baked Lay's potato chips for dinner, the cheapest thing they sold.

While I waited to charge my phone, I contemplated my options. I couldn't sleep at a hotel; no one would rent a sixteen-year-old a room. There were no airports nearby, at least none open all night. The closest person I knew was Kayla, a seven-hour bus ride away. Isabel's mom worked at Virginia Tech, so I decided I could go to campus and ask around until I found her office. But she and Isabel had different last names; I only knew Isabel's. Outside the restaurant, I saw a landscaped median and decided I could sleep there. Still, in this unfamiliar environment, I worried a wild animal might maul me. The humans definitely had guns.

Holding my breath, I tried my phone again. This time, the screen lit up with the red Virgin Mobile logo. I exhaled, relieved, then copied down Isabel's number so I'd never lose it again. I chewed my lower lip as I dialed. By now, my failure to call had become inexcusable. No matter how sincere my friend's offer had been, I knew I was violating every social grace by just showing up in her town. As I mentally whipped myself, Isabel picked up. "Hello?" she answered, voice bright.

"Hey! How are you? It's Emi." I made small talk, trying to hide my shaking voice. "Remember how you said I could come stay with you?"

"Yes, sure! When?"

I paused, as if I were studying my calendar. "Maybe like now?"

Isabel asked, "Where are you?"

"I'm across from the bus station in Blacksburg." I clamped down on my lip. The ocean roared between my ears.

"Okay. Let me ask my mom." During the minutes of silence, I berated myself for every misstep: I had lied to Kayla's mom. I had failed to make the plans I needed to make. Now I was going to be stranded here, in the land of men with aggressive belt buckles. Anxious sweat wafted from my pits to my nose. I smelled rank, an animal trying to convince predators I wasn't good eating.

On the other end, the phone rustled. "I'll pick you up in fifteen!"

WHEN WE GOT to Isabel's house, her mom hugged me. She was a tiny woman, a professor of material science, barely five feet tall in six-inch platform heels. "How long would you like to stay?"

I fiddled with my hands. I said my camp started June 22, but I could leave before that.

"Stay the whole time!" She opened the fridge. "Do you like steak?"

I hadn't eaten meat since leaving CRTC. "Sure!"

To my relief, Isabel's mom didn't ask about my family, or the chain of events that had led to me calling her daughter from the bus station. I wouldn't have known what to say. Instead, she just asked what we wanted to eat.

I couldn't believe that I wasn't an imposition. When I was growing up, I'd never been allowed to bring friends over for dinner, even after their parents had fed me meals assembled from food bank boxes. Once I got in trouble for sneaking a hungry friend a can of tuna. It wasn't about not having enough—my parents had plenty—but there was no joy in sharing and no obligation to do so. It shocked me to see a parent who had the space and time and money, who seemed to enjoy taking care of their children's friends.

It shocked me even more that Isabel would share her mom. But she seemed to feel no sense of scarcity, no fear of loss. My friend existed in a state I'd never known. I was a sidekick for her languid summer. I followed Isabel to interviews for summer jobs. When Isabel decided I needed to watch *Fight Club*, I watched *Fight Club*. If she wanted to go for a drive in the mountains, we went, blasting "New Slang" by the Shins on the stereo.

In my hosts' presence, I felt normal, as if I really could just step into their life and pretend to be family. They didn't ask too many questions, though I didn't sense Isabel's mom was scared of the answers. I had a place to sleep, and it was summer, and I was trying not to think about all the pieces of my college applications I had no idea how to do.

In between checking out frat boys outside Cold Stone Creamery one evening, Isabel took a bite of brownie-encrusted ice cream and asked, "What's so special about Charlotte, anyway?"

"I mean, she was mine. I don't know."

"You have to get over her. There are a lot of other people out there."

Isabel looked at me. "Take off your glasses." I did. "Wow," Isabel said. "Why don't you wear contacts?"

"I didn't want to have to carry the solution." Isabel clucked at me. "I want someone to like me for me. Not because I look a certain way." I was steadfast in this core belief. Part of why I loved studying so much was that getting into college seemed to have nothing to do with appearances.

"The world doesn't work like that," Isabel replied. She was beautiful, with rich skin and piercing green eyes. "You need a haircut."

Isabel's mom made an appointment for me at her salon. Because I was the guest, I had to go. The whole time I was nervous about what it would cost, but Isabel's mom paid.

To show off my new fashionable shag, Isabel had me put on one of her old dresses. She photographed me posing around her house. "You are so pretty now, Emi! Why didn't we take a before picture?"

I felt embarrassed, wondering how bad I had looked pre-haircut. It made me burn to be someone else's project, as if everything would be okay if I just got cleaned up around the edges. But Isabel and her mom were so nice about it. "Shouldn't Emi get contacts?" Isabel asked her mom, who nodded vigorously. Isabel took me by the shoulders and reassured me about the breakup: "You are going to find someone way better."

"Someone very special," Isabel's mom agreed.


When I arrived at Stanford, I looked around as if waking up in someone else's fantasy. For all my mom's aspirations, she'd never set foot on campus, but there I was among the stucco buildings and the ancient redwoods. My mom hoped my weeks at camp would help me get into the university, but I knew they wouldn't (despite my scholarship, these summer programs were largely cash grabs). Besides, I didn't want to attend college in the graveyard of my mom's crushed dreams.

But I had my own pressing expectations for camp: I was planning to write my college applications' personal statement about "topology," whatever it was. Since school got out, I'd taken notes on everything I could potentially essay-ize. But every topic I came up with was too morose: how drinking Diet Coke was the perfect way to stay full while spending minimal money, how I missed my mom during long bus rides alone, how seeing paint chips made me wish I had a home. Finally, I decided the prior sixteen years were just a warm-up for the life-changing experience of learning about knots and surfaces, which would illuminate my true, winning nature in a way institutionalization, foster care, and sleeping on sofas had not.

A few days before camp, I'd come to San Francisco to visit a senior who'd just graduated. I hoped she could help with this application-defining essay. Olivia had won the top Scholastic Art & Writing Award for her short stories—the Gold Key that came with ten thousand dollars and a ceremony at Carnegie Hall. She was on her way to Harvard. I was sure that she would tell me all her secrets. Yet when I asked her how she got into Harvard, it was as if the question, or the frantic anxiety beneath it, pained her. "Just be yourself," she told me. But I was convinced that was a bad idea: "being myself" in the presence of important adults only seemed to get me into trouble. I needed something more. But on campus at Stanford, it became clear my plan wasn't working out: topology camp had little to do with unlocking my deepest ambitions and everything to do with deriving mathematical principles from coloring sheets. Students were allowed in the computer lab only in the evening, which left me little time to prepare my applications. One night I checked my email before starting in again on my essay drafts.

I screamed before I finished reading the subject line: "You have been selected for an IvyWise scholarship."

The body of the email explained that Dr. Katherine Cohen—top college admissions counselor, author of *Rock Hard Apps*—had chosen me for "pro-bono services that value $16,775."

Five months had passed since I mailed in my sad envelope. I had written it off, assumed it was hopeless. But someone had found it in their slush pile, read my plea, and found me worthy. If IvyWise had, maybe the Ivy League would, too. And if I didn't get in, at least I'd know it wasn't because of my own ignorance, my one big chance blown by falling through the cracks.

THE DAY OF MY PHONE CALL with Dr. Kat, I jolted awake. Yellow light crept in around the shades. I grasped for my phone, checked the time, and then exhaled: it was still the middle of the night.

I drifted off, then startled up again, convinced the glow was the sun instead of streetlamps. Finally, my phone shook me awake. Outside where I wouldn't disturb anyone, pale dawn light filtered through the redwoods and made dew sparkle on the grass. I shivered in the gray cardigan I'd filched from a dorm lost and found and stared at my phone. It was 6:29 a.m., then 6:30.

My phone rang. I jumped.

"Hi, Emi, this is Kat." Her voice sounded scratchy, as though by 9:30 a.m. Eastern time, she'd already spent a full day telling people what to do. As Dr. Kat talked about the packet I'd sent her, fear of her importance tingled through me.

"What are you doing this summer?" she asked.

"Well, I'm at topology camp right now, at Stanford," I said, as if I knew what "topology" meant. "Then I'm going to AP Chemistry camp at Northwestern." I didn't waste Dr. Kat's time with any of the uncertainties, the unplanned in-betweens.

"Good, good." I sighed, relieved: I'd given the right answer.

Dr. Kat asked me about my first-choice schools.

"Columbia University in the City of New York," I replied, ready for someone to finally take me seriously.

"Columbia? Do you really want to study the Great Books?"

"The what? What 'great books'? Like Pulitzer Prize winners?"

"No, like *The Iliad*. The foundations of Western civilization." Dr. Kat sounded annoyed. "You spend your first two years studying them."

"Oh." Embarrassment flushed over me. I had my lucky T-shirt with the chipping decals, Columbia was my dream, and yet I didn't know anything about the actual school, as if on some level I'd wanted it to remain a cipher. "Well, can I just apply there and see if I get in?"

"No." Dr. Kat explained that I was going to apply to exactly ten schools: three reach, four targets, three safeties. Of all the essays I'd write, two documents were most important: my personal statement and a Letter of Extenuating Circumstances, which would explain my life story to colleges.

"Okay. But can I retake the SAT?" I wanted to get a perfect score, something objective that proved my qualification.

"What did you get?"

"2190," I said, wincing.

"You're not going to have time for that." It wasn't even 7:00 a.m., only my first time talking to Dr. Kat, and already it was clear: my fantasy wasn't going to look the way I'd imagined. I'd never wear my Columbia T-shirt on campus. I'd never attain a perfect 2400 SAT score, despite the years of slogging through prep books.

Dr. Kat's voice sweetened. "You're doing all the right things, but you're a little bit behind." I had to plan on finishing my essay and letter before senior year started in September. She repeated from her book, "This summer is the critical time."

Self-righteous anger sparked in my chest. So many adults had sworn

I didn't need to worry, but I knew better. Now I had just four weeks of summer not occupied by camp to do *everything*.

"If you want to work together, you have to commit one hundred percent to the process. Can you do that for me, Emi?"

"Of course," I replied, confused Dr. Kat would even ask. Nothing before this moment mattered anymore. I decided that no matter how many people and circumstances had hindered me in the past, if I couldn't produce good enough applications, I wouldn't get in and it would all be my own fault.

"We just want to tell your story," Dr. Kat cooed. "I'm glad I'm here to help, because it's not going to be easy."

Her warning, despite its warmth, struck me after I flipped my phone shut and leaned against a eucalyptus tree. Of course it wasn't going to be easy. Nothing had been easy. Of course my hopes were far-fetched.

But maybe they weren't so far-fetched anymore. The possibility of actually getting in, or failing to execute, pressed down hard on my chest. My actions mattered, now more than ever. And Dr. Kat seemed to be telling me that this wasn't going to be hard in a standardized-test way or even a finding-housing way, but in an all-consuming, almost spiritual way, a grueling task even for a celebrity college consultant.

## Fourteen

Annette let me stay with her in the week between camps. I loved her peaceful house, the yellow walls, the IKEA print of sunflowers in the living room, and how she tossed her salads with oil and vinegar (never ranch or blue cheese dressing from a bottle). When she got back from work, she found me sitting in the same position I'd been in when she left, putting together my list of colleges for Dr. Kat. "We should do something, Emi," Annette said. "It's too nice outside to waste. How about a bicycle ride?" She smiled—it was the perfect suggestion. Annette made me reapply sunscreen, then riffled through her hats. "Do you want a helmet?" she offered, then put it back. "We're just going down the block. It should be fine." She let me wear a baseball cap and took a huge floppy hat for herself, cinching the strap tight under her chin. We were headed down her block, toward the nature reserve, when a gust of wind whipped the hat off my head. I reached back to grab it and fell.

The next thing I knew, I was on Annette's back deck. Her husband looked into my eyes. "Do you know who the president is, Emi?"

"Obama?" I squinted at him, the world too bright, too green. "What happened?" I had to hold back tears, confused. "I just want to know what happened."

"You fell."

"When?"

"You fell off your bicycle and hit your head." The way he looked at me, forehead wrinkled with concern, I relaxed. For a second, it felt like a movie where I'd woken up in my real life, with my real family, everything before just a bad dream.

"Let's go, Emi," Annette said, purse slung on her shoulder. She was taking me to the emergency room.

"I'm fine," I told her, not wanting to cause trouble.

"No, your brain could bleed and you could die, like that skier." I wanted to assure Annette it wasn't a big deal; I'd hit my head plenty of times before. But I also savored the way she cared.

In the silent car, I shut my eyes to block out the piercing evening sun. The sound of the AC throbbed in my head.

Annette called my mom from Methodist Hospital's emergency room. After my CAT scan, Annette paced in front of my bed. Aware of the fact that my mom could prevent her from seeing me at any time, she was always worried about what my mom might think, despite my reassurances. "When is she coming? I would be so mad."

"I'm sure she's still at work. It's fine. She's not going to mind."

Eventually, a nurse let my mom into the room. "Hi, Annette! Hi, honey! I have some things for you in the car."

"Dawn, I'm so sorry," Annette cut in. "I can't believe I didn't make Emi wear a helmet."

"Oh, Emi's always been clumsy," my mom replied, waving her hand, telling the story of how I stepped on a glass Christmas bulb in her house and needed surgery to remove the shards of glass from my foot.

My mom was still talking when the doctor came in and sized her up. He turned to Annette, explained I had a concussion, and handed her my discharge paperwork to sign.

"Oh, I'm not her mom," Annette said, passing the clipboard.

My mom raised her hand, amused. "I'm the mom."

The three of us headed out to my mom's Buick. In the twilight, my mom sifted through boxes of oil pastels and bags of Twizzlers. The streetlights shimmered as I swatted off mosquitos, but Annette was too polite and too scared of my mom to pull us away.

Finally, I hugged my mom goodbye. "Bye, Dawn!" Annette said, voice tinny with fake sweetness.

In the car, Annette sighed, shoulders falling away from her ears. I thought about apologizing, but figured that might upset her even more.

"What do you want for dinner?" she asked me, finally, turning the keys.

"I don't know, what are you thinking?" I replied, feeling like—despite my best efforts otherwise—I took everyone who cared and wrung them dry.


SIX DAYS AFTER MY CONCUSSION, I started AP Chemistry camp at Northwestern. We were doing the entire year-long class in three weeks. This prospect had delighted me in the spring as I finished my physics final project (a book of poems). But when I got to Illinois, the words in the textbook blurred. In lab, I couldn't seem to pour the chemicals in the right order. Afternoons, college students shepherded us outside for mandatory recreation. I tried every excuse not to venture into the garish sunshine.

I didn't know what was wrong with me, not putting two and two together about hitting my head. Every morning started with a quiz; I pulled in C's and D's. I spent every free moment studying, not even working on the essay drafts I soon owed Dr. Kat, but nothing clicked into focus.

With one week left of chemistry, I got a Facebook message from someone I didn't expect: Michelle. She apologized for not seeing me when I was in Minnesota staying with Annette. Michelle wrote: "Since back when you quit talking to me I have had a hard time."

I felt like such a bad daughter. Often, I had this amorphous sense of being abandoned by Michelle, but now I was learning that she felt I had abandoned her. I knew it wasn't exactly true—I had been ten years old at the time—but what did that matter? For both of my parents, emotions created their own reality. It was up to me, as their child, to assimilate their points of view, even when they contradicted what I considered facts.

Michelle wrote about her hospitalizations and how she'd gained weight from medications, all of it starting after the divorce. I worried that I, or the guilt of my existence, had done this to her. She ended the note with: "I'm so sorry."

She hadn't asked anything about my life. She didn't know where I was, where I had stayed before this, that I was having surgery for my scars soon, or that I'd stay with my friend from the psych ward after. There was no offer of anything. Not even five dollars, so that I could pay for a few loads of laundry. Not two dollars for a Diet Coke.

I hated myself for reflexively thinking of money. I had been taught the virtue of unconditional love by adults who then failed to provide for my basic needs. Expecting anything made me feel manipulative and transactional, even though my life had started to revolve around making people like me enough to give me the means to survive.

After that morning's lecture, the students filed out of the auditorium and down the halls of the gifted children's camp. Suddenly, I felt the gap between my classmates and me. They all had married parents. Most of them went to private schools, ones with "Country" or "Day" in the name. One even rowed, explaining to me how he paddled boats down a river for sport.

I hated them: all the other students gossiping and talking among themselves. I hated their easy lives, the way that their parents had never just left, then sent a self-justifying Facebook message years later about how they'd never been fit for the task. I hated that they were better sons and daughters than me, that they didn't quit talking to their parents and send them to the hospital.

Near the front of the building, I passed an empty classroom. All the students were gone, but backpacks remained, slung on the backs of chairs. Hundred-dollar graphing calculators lay on desks.

Without thinking, I walked into the room and plucked them off, dropping them into my bag. Once I'd taken the visible ones, I started reaching into bags, feeling for the smooth plastic. I'd sell them all on eBay. Each would pay for an application fee, plus the price to send my test scores to one school. I imagined everyone coming back: the sweet, suburban kids finding their TI-84s stolen, crying. I'd break some part of them that had been broken in me for a long time. The power thrilled me as my backpack sagged with their weight.

I shut the door behind me and went to lunch. I sat down with the other students but couldn't eat. At lab, my hands shook as I mixed the chemicals in my beaker. I couldn't parse the teacher's instructions, his corrections of my mistakes.

I couldn't stop anticipating the announcement they'd make about the theft. They'd search our rooms. They'd say I didn't deserve to be there, that my desperation made me a liability—a fact I'd proven to be true.

When the others left for afternoon recreation, I hung back. "I'll meet up with you in a second!" I said. I hid the stolen calculators around the student lounge. One poked out of the sofa cushions, where I knew it would be found, kicking off the hunt. I told myself the whole thing would look like a prank. Just a shock, no harm, no foul.

I ran down to the elevator to catch up with the group, but I didn't relax. No one said anything. I jolted awake in the middle of the night, desperate to confess. Sticky with sweat, I had to swear myself to silence: one mistake like this could torpedo my future. *This isn't me*, I wanted to cry, breaking down to a sympathetic, imaginary ear. *I don't hurt people on purpose.* Maybe I was trying to prove myself bad, so that when I was treated poorly, it would be for a good reason.

———

Scar removal surgery was supposed to be a minor procedure under light sedation. (My mom suggested I see Dr. Woods right after.) Only Annette had misgivings. "A minor surgery is still surgery, Emi," she chided. But when else could I get it and have insurance pay? She didn't have an answer. She questioned if a friend's house was really going to be the right environment to help me recover, but I had nowhere else to go and she'd be out of town.

The day before my appointment, my mom snuck me into her office so I could scrub my legs with Betadine. (She hadn't showered at home in years; there was nowhere to put the stuff overflowing the tub.) That night, at dusk, I washed again in the backyard with a hose. I told my mom I was staying with a friend, but I slept in the Corolla, never leaving the alley.

The next day, I waited in a paper gown, plotting how I'd start editing my essays as soon as I woke up. The surgeon came in wearing green scrubs under his white coat, a little cap covering his blond hair. "Hello, Margaret." I blushed, too shy to tell him no one called me by my legal name. "May I?"

He extracted an extra-thick Sharpie from his pocket and pulled up the hem of my gown. From behind his glasses, he studied the red ropy scars. He circled the biggest and initialed it, then repeated the process for five on each side.

He took my hand. Goose bumps scurried up my arms. He held my fingers, delicately, as if about to kiss my hand or propose. Then he scribbled something on my skin and initialed that, too.

Covered in the surgeon's marks, I felt claimed. Soon, I would be changed, restored to the way I was before, my mistakes undone.

Then it occurred to me. "What will I do for the pain?" The surgeon was still holding my hand. The bite of Sharpie ink cut through the air.

"Don't worry. I'll give you something." The surgeon looked into my eyes. "You're very brave."

I couldn't help but smile, though I was scared: brave was often adjacent to stupid, but the type of stupid adults praised because it made their lives easier. In a flash, I sensed that any procedure requiring bravery or prescription narcotics was not a good idea at the moment.

The surgeon stood up and wished me luck in recovering. Almost immediately, a nurse anesthetist took his place and swapped the saline flowing into my IV with something else.

"Count backward from ten," she instructed, sounding jolly, "but you're not going to make it all the way."

I gritted my teeth, dizzy with regret. I was out by the time I said "six."

I woke up babbling to a nurse. "You're so beautiful," I told her, "I love you so much." She asked me to rate my pain on a scale of one to ten. "It's a miracle!" I declared. "I don't feel any pain at all." But she had to grab my arms to keep me from scratching and ripping the bandages taped over the wounds.

My mom led me, stumbling, into the parking lot. Sheets of gauze were taped to my thighs. She took me to a two-dollar movie theater so we could have air-conditioning for a few hours. When I got in the Buick, I immediately fell asleep.

I woke up in the morning in the passenger seat. My mom snored beside me.

I wasn't supposed to drive for twenty-four hours after anesthesia, but my legs were on fire and I had to get to my friend's house where I was staying so I could take Vicodin. The nurses had also warned my mom that I needed to take the painkillers on a schedule: once the hurting started, it would stay bad. But that proved infeasible. My friend lived an hour outside the city. By the time I got there I was desperate to scratch, shuffling from side to side as I waited on her stoop.

"Emi!" Courtney called, wrapping me in a hug. I exhaled in relief. Because we'd met in the psych ward, I worried Courtney would be unstable. But she seemed happy; she'd come into some money and bought her own place. "I'm so happy you're here!"

She opened the door. Smoke shimmered in the air. Two Chihuahuas ran around the living room, barking. Diet Coke and beer cans littered the floor between piles of dog turds. In the kitchen, Courtney introduced me to a man who sat at the table, smoking. "This is my boyfriend."

"Hi," I said, trying to hide my surprise; I thought she lived alone.

"Do you want a Diet Coke?" Courtney offered.

"Yes, please." Her fridge had nothing but pop in it. I winced, but I was a guest. I had no right to expect she'd feed me.

I fished out my Vicodin.

"What are those?" the boyfriend asked. He and Courtney both looked at me.

My heart sped up. He seemed like the kind of guy who'd want me to share, but I needed the Vicodin to ward off the fire ants colonizing my flesh. "Just ibuprofen," I said, swallowing two with a sip of pop.

"Sure," he said, calling me out on my lie.

I twitched, uncomfortable in his gaze, even as Courtney and I chatted. As the burning subsided, the room undulated. "Would you mind if I take a nap?"

"Of course." Courtney led me to a room with broken blinds and a mattress on the floor. "I know your mom's nuts. You can come stay with me whenever you want. Like I'm your home."

I jolted awake in the tired afternoon light. The Chihuahuas wailed, jangling their cage. I scratched the edge of the tape holding the gauze in place and whimpered. After I took more Vicodin, I hid the bottle in the bottom of my backpack.

I stood up and eased open the door. "Courtney? Hey?" My voice echoed in the empty house.

I knew I had to leave. Right then, while they were gone, before anything bad happened. I explained my unease to myself as *I can't write my essays here.* That was enough. I grabbed my backpack, took two Diet Cokes from the fridge, and left, leaving the front door unlocked behind me.

I HAD TO DRIVE FAST before the Vicodin kicked in. I didn't know the roads, but I knew my destination: the main library downtown. To calm myself, I recited my litany of a to-do list. A dozen achievable tasks erased the uncertainty of where I'd sleep.

I sat at a library desk staring out the window. I couldn't focus on my laptop screen. Colleges demanded to know who I was. Who was I? I was hungry; I hadn't eaten since the day before: a protein bar after surgery. Who was I? I wanted to cry. I didn't know. My other big task was no easier: the Letter of Extenuating Circumstances providing context for my life. But I had no context. I was still in the middle of it.

When security came to shut down the library, I sent my drafts to Dr. Kat, hating myself for how bad they were, and drove around looking for a parking lot where I could sleep. I needed somewhere quiet enough no one would notice me, busy enough that no one would try anything. A tornado alert interrupted Top 40 on the radio. I shut off the dial.

I drove through the lights of Dinkytown, the area around the University of Minnesota. It seemed filled with light and happy people. I imagined another version of my life, one where I had gone to Morris. I could have had a little apartment by now, a job. Tears pinched out of the corners of my eyes. I had to get into a good school. If not, what was all this suffering for?

Eventually, I pulled into a Rainbow Foods parking lot, near the back, under a floodlight. I put the silver sun deflector in the windshield for privacy, then climbed into the back seat. I stuck my JanSport under my head like a pillow and hugged my gray sweater. Curled up, I felt so dumb for leaving Courtney's house. I thought about her boyfriend, sitting at the kitchen table, eyeing me and my pills. He seemed like bad news. But that was a feeling, not a fact. Following that feeling had led me here, scrunched up in the car.

I shut my eyes and tried to sleep, to rest so that the next day I could be productive, but that just made the tears stream down. Why hadn't I planned ahead? I had left for the summer with such tenuous plans. Of course things fell apart. I had three weeks before school started—too long to sleep in my car, not long enough to do everything I was supposed to get done.

My legs burned.

I shut my eyes and imagined Charlotte, that the upholstery of the car seat was her body, pressed against mine, holding me.

I startled awake. A figure stood beside my window. Fear shot through me. I lay very still. Was it a cop telling me I'd broken a law, ready to take me to juvie? Worse, was it a man who wanted to hurt me? The shadow receded. I heard the trunk of a car opening, then an engine turning on, then the wheels on the pavement as it drove away.

Tears pooled in my ears. I scratched at the tape on the edge of the bandages more vigorously, wishing I could claw into the sutures that hurt more than any cut had. Hyperventilating, I did something I hadn't done in a long time. I prayed: *Dear Lord Jesus, finder of lost keys, granter of fives on AP tests. I'm so lonely.* My chest heaved with sobs. *Save me. Make me believe.* If I doubted, I was screwed. It was my responsibility, even then, to stay positive, convinced that the impossible would come to pass.

THE NEXT MORNING, I called Ingrid. "I know you're not my social worker anymore," I said, as I paced outside the library, trying to explain my situation. Just the fact that I was desperate enough to call her made me want to weep. "Do you think I could stay at that foster home you told me about?"

I didn't want someone to constantly watch me, cooped up with strange girls. But I needed a bed and food and Vicodin on a regular schedule. Grease matted my hair to my scalp.

"Actually, I just placed a girl with that foster grandma. She has an open bed."

I exhaled, relieved. That very night, I could be sinking into clean sheets, showered, fed. It might even have air-conditioning.

Ingrid said she'd talk to her supervisor. A few hours later, I dashed out of the reading room when my phone buzzed. "I'm so sorry." Because my case was closed, I couldn't stay in a foster home. My mom would have had to call as Annette had urged, and she would have had to do it months ago. I cursed myself for not being able to convince her. "I think you should go to a shelter."

I recoiled. At least in my car I was in control. The doors locked. It was a known quantity. But it wasn't conducive to writing.

When we hung up, I emailed Dr. Woods and asked what she thought I should do. She called me and asked, "What's the situation?"

"I'm really struggling," I told her, choking on my tears. "My essays— they are so bad."

"Where are you sleeping?"

"In my car. That's okay. It's just, everything I write is so shitty and this is *the critical time*."

"Look, I don't want to hear a single thing about the essays until you have a place to live."

Perhaps irrationally, I hated Dr. Woods for telling me my essays didn't matter and, by extension, my dream didn't matter either. But when she started giving me names of shelters, I dutifully wrote them down. "Will you go?"

"Maybe."

I wasn't going to go. How was I going to do my applications there, in some facility? The applications were the true solution, the only thing that would get me out, make all this struggle worth it.

After I hung up with Dr. Woods, my phone rang again. This time the number started with 212.

"Fuck." I'd figured out 212 meant Manhattan. Dr. Kat. I flipped my phone open.

"Hi," I said sheepishly, thinking of the awful drafts I'd sent her.

"Hi, Emi," she said, raspy as usual. "What's wrong that you can't finish your essays?" The traffic on Hennepin Avenue fell away. It was just me and the terrifying woman on the phone, my only hope, who now seemed ready to drop me. "What do you think is the problem?"

"Look. I'm sorry. I'm trying. I just had surgery, and now I don't have anywhere to go, okay? I've been sleeping in my car." I tried my hardest not to sob, but I did. I clenched my eyes shut to hold back the tears.

"What? What's going on?" Her voice softened.

"I haven't lived at home since I was fourteen, remember?" I sucked the snot back into my nose. "I ran out of places to go during break."

"What are you going to do today?"

I knew the right answer. "I'm going to start over on my essays."

"No, that's not what I mean. You said you slept in your car; where are you going to sleep tonight?"

"I'll sleep in my car again."

"Go to a shelter. There's got to be a shelter or something like that." I wanted to scream. "Did you call the school?"

"What?"

"Have you called Interlochen? Did you tell them what's going on?"

"No." That never would have occurred to me. "Do I have to?"

"Yes. You do," Dr. Kat said, sounding irritated. "Go to a shelter. Call the guidance office right away from the shelter. Explain the situation. Tell them everything. You need to leave a trail."

I shut my eyes and clenched my jaw: Dr. Kat wanted me to have a place to sleep, but she also wanted me to collect evidence. The last thing I wanted was for people to see me in this state, to witness the lowest moments of my life, record them, and trot them out later. The whole point of college admissions was to make my problems disappear, but now I was learning that I'd have to use my problems to get in. The evidence that a shelter could provide might even make the difference between acceptance and rejection, a golden ticket out or more years struggling. The idea made me so upset that I trembled.

"Do you need my assistant to look up a shelter for you?"

"It's okay. I know where to go."

"Let me know how it goes." As if she knew just how to console me, she added, "You can fix your essays once you're there."

I PARKED OUTSIDE the Bridge for Youth building and sat in the car, stalling. I kept looking at my phone, trying to figure out a way to disobey Dr. Kat. But unlike anyone else, she wanted what I wanted: my admission into an elite college. I'd do whatever she told me.

I got out and stood in front of the door, my backpack slung over my shoulder. I reached for the buzzer, then retracted my hand. Sweat circled the pits of my Columbia University T-shirt. I stank. I'd worn the same faded-brown running shorts since the surgery—the only thing that didn't make me itch. I was disgusted with myself and had no idea what I'd say.

Before I gathered the nerve to ring the bell, a white lady with dreadlocks opened the door. She took me to an office and offered tissues. I told the story, feeling better as I cried.

"Will you consider going home?" she asked me.

"I can't." I put my hands over my eyes. "I've tried so hard, so many times, but I can't live with my mom." I'd dodged that truth again and again. But finally, sitting in that office, I knew my mom was not an option. She'd support me when she wanted to, but I couldn't rely on her for the basics. I felt proud of myself for seeing reality, asking for help.

"I'm sorry," the lady said. "But you can't stay here." She explained that the shelter was only for youth who were willing to reunite with their families.

"What?" Fire balled up in my stomach and bloomed through me. "I haven't lived with my mom in three years. She has no room for me. Her house would be condemned if anyone saw it. Can I just stay here tonight while I figure something out?"

"We can talk, but you can't stay." Every shelter had a different policy. The Bridge was so named because it connected runaways with their parents. She handed me a list of other places I could try.

It was twilight by the time I trudged back to the Corolla. I sat in the driver's seat, stunned, and stared through the windshield. I wanted to bang my head against the steering wheel. What did it take to get help? I was supposed to be honest, but sometimes honesty closed doors. I'd fall through the cracks if I didn't ask for what I needed again and again; I'd get punished for manipulation if I did.

I reminded myself that anger at the arbitrariness of the system served no purpose. Methodically, I went down the list of shelters, calling. The Lutheran Social Service shelter was full. So was the Native American shelter and the one for sexually exploited teens. Avenues for Youth had no more beds.

I felt so ashamed of myself. What was I going to do? Call Dr. Kat and tell her that not even a shelter would accept me?

Then it dawned on me: all I had to do was lie. No one cared if I was willing to go home, if I *could* go home. They just cared what I said. "Play the game but don't believe it," my mom had told me, and I hated that she was right, grinding my teeth as I gathered up my stuff and walked, defeated, to the door. I wanted so badly to be a person of my word, always honest, always kind, always understanding.

"I changed my mind," I told the white woman with dreadlocks. "I'm willing to go home."

"You're lucky," she said, opening the door. "We have one more bed."

I WAS GRATEFUL Dr. Kat hadn't told me how far behind I was; I already knew. It took three days on a schedule of Vicodin for my legs to stop hurting. Then I was too doped up to do any work. The other teenagers and I mostly sat in the common room, listening to KDWB. Every hour, the song of the summer came on, "Best I Ever Had," where Drake serenaded a girl who looked most beautiful barefaced in sweatpants—our exact aesthetic.

I'd always assumed I was different from kids who stayed at shelters. No matter how bad things got, my family had maintained our superiority by looking at people worse off than us and saying, "We're not like them." But once I was at the Bridge, I saw that I was just like the other guests. We were a diverse group, but a lot of us had been in foster care, then returned to our parents, only to stay with other relatives, couch surf, and sleep in cars. As far as I could tell, none of us had spent the night under an actual bridge.

"I just can't stand my mom," one of the girls said, squeezing her eyes shut in anguish. No one corrected her, saying she should be able to. It was understood: there was a reason behind what she said. Despite the demand for beds, the counselors didn't moralize or tell us we were to blame for our situations. I appreciated that, even though I felt responsible, sure that I wouldn't have wound up there if I'd just planned better.

After five days, it was time for my mom to come to the Bridge and make a plan. I worried that she'd be mad, saying I should have come home and making me feel guilty, but instead she was impressed by the facilities. "They even have central air!" Compared with her house, it was a luxury resort, complete with a functioning kitchen, trial-size shampoos donated by do-gooders, and fresh underwear you didn't have to wear inside out the second day.

I wanted to scream at my mom. I was in a homeless shelter and she still couldn't see.

The caseworker had me make a list of every possible place I could go. I knew two photo campers in Chicago. Interlochen agreed to let me arrive a few days early with the international students. My French teacher could give me a ride. I had to call Grandma Edna and ask if I could stay with her that night. She was sick and incontinent from bladder cancer but relented, so the Bridge discharged me. I understood: they only had fifteen beds. They had to make space for someone else who was in immediate crisis.

I packed up my clothes, now washed, and the bag of hotel toiletries that served as a farewell gift. I knew I was supposed to be grateful for a few days of peace, sleep and food, and postsurgical recovery, but I was heavy with the knowledge that I was couch surfing before and I was couch surfing again, in the exact same situation, just with less time.


THE NIGHT BEFORE MY BUS to Chicago, my mom bought a twenty-foot tarp at Home Depot. We laid it out in the backyard. My mom dragged out the covers from her bed. A lime-green quilt covered the blue plastic. I curled up under a down comforter. It smelled like mouse pee and mold. It smelled like home.

"Now, don't use my buckwheat pillow," my mom said. "I'm going to go in and do my bedtime routine." I knew it would take a while for her to get through all of her inhalers.

"Okay. Good night." I lay back on her buckwheat pillow, the husks rearranging under my skull, and stared up at the gray-blue sky beyond a tangle of power lines. Cars swooped past at the end of the block. The apple tree sagged with the weight of hundreds of wormy fruits. My childhood playhouse lay collapsed beside the shed.

I woke up to my mom stroking my hair. "You stole my buckwheat pillow. It's okay. I let you have it. It's time to get up."

My mom's affection hurt. I knew she loved me with her whole heart and that love wasn't enough. I wondered if it was even possible for her to recognize there was a problem, or if all the people who witnessed her behavior and didn't intervene just confirmed in her mind that it was normal.

She cleared a space for my backpack in her trunk. I drove us to the parking ramp where the Megabus picked up. My mom pulled out a cooler full of mini Ben & Jerry's ice creams she'd gotten on sale. We ate them for breakfast, then hugged goodbye.

I waited all day for a bus that didn't come. By the time I boarded, it was evening. Relief mixed with fear: I had one more sofa to sleep on, one more ride to hitch. Then the summer would be over. The crucial summer, the critical time. Nothing was done, besides bad drafts I balled up and threw in garbage cans. I looked at my face, twisted in the reflection of the bus, superimposed on the skyline of my hometown.

As the freeway scrolled past, I longed to forget the whole summer. But I knew I'd need to discuss it again and again on my college applications, prostituting my sorrow for a shot at joy. That fact seemed the saddest of them all.

## Fifteen

My mom emailed me while I was sleeping on someone's couch in Chicago: "I found a crumpled up copy of your Letter of Extenuating Circumstances." She'd discovered it on the floor of her Buick. I cursed myself for leaving evidence of my failed drafts somewhere she could find it, no matter how unlikely it was that she'd clean her car.

I hadn't involved my mom in any part of the application process; I hoped she'd stay out of it. After all, I wasn't asking for anything—no extra money to pay for test fees, not even a place to live. But she took it on herself to help, writing, "I am composing a simpler letter entitled 'How (and why) Emi took tenth grade three times.'"

"DON'T BOTHER with the letter," I wrote back. "I love you, but the letter is mine to write. Colleges want to hear my version, not yours."

I was embarrassed and ashamed about the whole issue of the letter: ever since I'd sent Dr. Kat the first draft, she'd kept telling me I needed to be clearer. Because my garbled threats to blow up a hospital had been presented as the reason I went to residential treatment, I tried explaining CRTC and foster care as "I did bad things, paid the price, but have now recovered and repented"; Dr. Kat seemed annoyed and said that made no sense. She wanted me to say things that no adult had put so baldly: that my mom was a hoarder with mental health issues, that her home was uninhabitable, and that my environment was a direct cause of why I'd struggled. I protested, citing my own mistakes, but I couldn't explain why it was so important to me to take responsibility. Not until my mom read my draft and claimed it was all wrong.

In her email, my mom replied to my version of events:

> *Attached is a rather unemotional letter.*
> *Overcome victimhood.*
>
> > *Love,*
> > *Mom*

I put my hands over my face and dug my palms into my eye sockets. *Overcome victimhood.* Was I doing the opposite? Letting victimhood overcome me?

In the email attachment, my mom explained my life to me. "As a transition from residential treatment, Emi was placed in foster care." She said I'd spent my summer attending camps and visiting friends, erasing my vulnerability and desperation. It took me right back to after the divorce, my mom telling shrinks I was ungrateful and spoiled. I'd spent summer break traveling—what was there to complain about?

I deleted the file, but the note lingered in my inbox, my mom's disapproval hovering. It didn't matter if the admissions committees were small groups of strangers, thousands of miles away, whom she'd never meet. It didn't matter if she'd eventually get to wear a YALE MOM T-shirt and buy a matching navy license plate frame. She would never admit she had a problem. After all, she'd let me be homeless all summer instead of calling the number to open my case as everyone had urged her, giving me a place to stay at no expense to her.

It occurred to me to fear that my mom might contact my school guidance counselor or, God forbid, colleges, to "set the record straight," as someone had with Interlochen. If she did, who was going to back me up? I didn't even believe Dr. Kat would trust me over her—despite all the evidence on my side—because no one had listened to my version of events when I was younger. What reason did I have to think they would now?

KELLY SHUT THE DOOR to her office. "I heard you had a rough summer."

"You could say that." I fixed my gaze on a brochure for Indiana University. I was waiting for an apology.

"I had no idea." Her freshly cut bob fell around her face.

"I tried to tell you last year." I folded my arms. "I couldn't get an appointment." Kelly told me it was "my turn" now that I was a senior, but she was self-righteously skeptical of Dr. Kat, telling me I needed to be careful. After we picked classes, she asked what colleges I was thinking about.

"An Ivy League or a women's college." I could have rattled off my list, in order—Yale, Brown, Penn, Johns Hopkins, Wellesley, Barnard, Smith, Harvey Mudd, Mount Holyoke, and the University of Wisconsin—but my heart was now set on Yale, "the Gay Ivy." I'd made peace with not applying to Columbia. Dr. Kat was right; I didn't want to read the Great Books. In hindsight, my decision seemed juvenile and T-shirt oriented: the fixation of a child who had never even been on the College Confidential online message boards. Meanwhile, Yale had a great arts program and was close to New York. It was almost as prestigious as Harvard, but I'd never had a teacher I despised drink from a Yale mug while wearing a Yale lanyard. People wouldn't think I'd chosen it for status. Also unlike Harvard, it had early action admissions, which meant I'd hear back by winter break, with a boost in my admission chances for promising to attend if I got in.

Kelly reached for a brochure. "Have you thought about Kalamazoo College?"

My cheeks stung. The suggestion of the local liberal arts school, which could offer me little if any aid, felt like the ultimate vote of no confidence. Then she added, "I think Ball State would be another good option."

I wanted to lash out at Kelly, but even though I had Dr. Kat, I'd need a recommendation letter from her.

"Thanks," I said, narrowing my eyes as I stood up, refusing to touch the pamphlets on the side of the desk.

BACK IN MY DORM, I went into the bathroom and locked the door. I took a long shower, cupping my hip bones in my hands, fingering my ribs, the hardness that the summer had brought out.

The adhesive on my bandages softened. It was time. In the steam of the bathroom, I peeled one sheet back. Gray gunk flanked pale, pruney skin. On top of the field of scars, five wounds gaped, bigger than any cut I ever made myself. They weren't going away.

Nothing would be redeemed, I realized. The past wouldn't be erased. Some pains, like the surgery, would amount to nothing. Whatever future was in front of me, I'd go into it with scars from my groin to my knees.

I ran the water so my roommate wouldn't hear me cry.

THAT YEAR, I lived with a girl from French class named Jane. I didn't tell her or anyone else about my summer, but I knew neither of us had finished our college applications yet, although she'd been at home in Palo Alto while I was comparing people's sofas.

"Do you know Palo Alto?" she asked me, snapping a bracelet against her wrist.

"Yeah, it's right by Stanford. I went to camp there."

Jane shook her head. "Yeah, but do you know what it *means*? My old high school was a pressure cooker. Interlochen is nothing compared with Paly. Kids were always jumping into the Caltrain," she said.

"Only suicidal people attempt suicide," I replied, considering myself a subject-matter expert. "They must have had some underlying condition."

"You don't understand," Jane said. I wasn't sure how I was supposed to pity rich kids for the "pressure" they faced, because their problems were the near opposite of mine—too many opportunities, too-high expectations. Wasn't pressure just the reality of living in a winner-take-all world? What was the supposed cure: for all of her classmates to get into Ivies, leaving me no chance?

But there were a lot of things about Jane's life I didn't understand, like how she confided that she'd inherit a bunch of money when her grandparents died. In fact, initially I had no idea why she'd want to hang out with me, or why she'd jumped at the chance to live together. Then I remembered: I was skinny.

In the past, I would've gloated about my appearance, but now it felt almost sad. Without trying, I'd shed the softness I gained while falling in love. When people weren't feeding me over the summer, I'd subsisted on cartons of yogurt, or cups of Diet Coke with unlimited refills so I could kill time in fast-food restaurants.

"You're not fat," I told Jane when she came back after dinner, confessing that she'd broken her tofu-lettuce-hummus diet with no-bake cookies. Her greatest wish, along with getting into conservatory for flute, was to find a boyfriend and have her first kiss. "You're not single because of your weight, Jane. You're single because there are ten straight guys on campus and they all think they have golden dicks," I told her. But even as I reassured her, part of me basked in the way she looked up to me. I had life experience; Jane had never even done her own laundry.

We turned our shared desk into a shrine. I taped up a photo of a dorm sparkling in the twilight, a newspaper cutout I'd scrounged over the summer that quoted Oscar Wilde ("We are all in the gutter, but some of us are looking at the stars"), and Post-its scrawled with motivational quotes like "I WILL WIN THE GAME."

When my jaw felt as if it would crack from clenching, Jane said, "Hey, Emi, can I show you something?" She pulled up a red-and-white website called YouTube and loaded a music video for a Trace Adkins song, "Honky Tonk Badonkadonk." By the third replay, we knew all the words. When Jane snapped her bracelet extra fast, nervous, I got her attention and said, deadpan, "Slap your grandma." We both broke down in giggles.

At night, we lay side by side a foot apart. The closet wouldn't open, but we were seniors and would no longer tolerate the indignity of a bunk bed.

"Isn't it weird?" Jane asked me.

"What?"

"Us. That we're such good friends."

It certainly surprised me. I'd wanted to room with Jane hoping we'd only speak French together. (She nixed that idea right away.) I hadn't expected us to dance, or hang out at the Melody Freeze, or eat dinner with her goody-two-shoes friends. "Why would it be *weird*?"

"Because we're just so different."

I felt a pang of rejection in the middle of my chest that I knew Jane hadn't intended. Still, she was right. We *were* so different. Jane meant superficially, like that I had masturbated and knew how to drive. But the distance ran deeper than that.

TWO WEEKS INTO the school year, I got an email: my tuition hadn't been paid. My mom instructed me to call my cousin who managed my college fund and replied to the school: "Emi knows more about this than I do."

Of course there was going to be an unforeseen crisis; Dr. Kat's assistant was preparing a six-page spreadsheet of all the application tasks I had to finish before November began. As my cousin's phone rang, I wondered if I'd get extra overcoming points for getting kicked out of Interlochen. I already knew the answer was no. How could I possibly thrive at Yale if I couldn't even sort out my familial logistics? My cousin didn't pick up. I left a message.

Two days later, I got an email from Michelle. I'd written her back a month ago, while I was at the shelter, apologizing that things had been so hard for her. I flickered with hope that her reply was news about my tuition. Maybe my cousin had died and that's why she hadn't responded.

I opened the email. Her only question or comment about my life was in the second line: "Are you cutting?"

Rage surged through me at the invasive question from someone who was essentially a stranger, but I quickly felt awful to be mad—Michelle wanted me to be okay. Wasn't that good? But it felt as if she were the latest in a long line of adults caring about my "mental health" but nothing else about my life, as if the two were unrelated. She didn't know my stomach hurt from worrying about what I'd do if I couldn't get ahold of my cousin.

The question seemed to ask for absolution: if I said, "No, I'm fine," Michelle could tell herself she hadn't really hurt me, that she had no responsibility for my situation, because I was so strong. I responded, "I wonder why you ask me that and not, 'What are you reading?' or 'How's school going?'"

Two weeks passed. By the end of September, I still couldn't reach my cousin. I had no idea where I'd get the thousands of dollars I needed, or where I'd go if I couldn't find the money. Live with Dave and Jan, or another version of them? Go to a group home?

Even though Michelle was closer to my cousin than to nearly anyone else in the family, I couldn't ask her to call; I worried that if I even mentioned it, she'd accuse me of using her and might never write back. As much as her emails upset me and as tart as I could be in response, I hoped they would get better if I could prove that I was a good daughter, selfless, not just keeping in touch for my own financial benefit.

At the end of the month, I got another email from Interlochen: still not paid.

Finally, my cousin responded and put a check in the mail. A few days before I turned seventeen, Michelle wrote me, "As your birthday approaches I have been working on reading your email. I have decided that what I need to do is come up with a plan in case what you say is negative, angry, and rejecting." She wrote about her psychiatric resources and her latest diagnoses. I felt I couldn't be upset about her lack of curiosity about my life: Michelle was mentally ill. Not sick in the way I'd been sick, where on some level I could choose to act okay, but really ill. Grandma Edna supported Michelle financially, paying for her rent, a cleaning service, and grocery delivery. I tried not to resent that: Michelle had needs. But I had needs, too.

And it was hard to be mad, because she included an apology: "There is so much that could have been done differently in bringing you up and I must apologize for all the dumb mistakes I made."

I didn't respond. I just ate a bowl of cereal for dinner, then threw up. When Jane asked me what was wrong, I said it was my personal statement; I still didn't have anything decent written. I told myself that that was the most fucked-up thing about my life.

On my birthday, I got a short message from Michelle full of clichés. She called me the "brightest" person she knew and signed it "Michelle (who wishes she were your bio mom)." I wondered if that would have made things better between us, but it wasn't as if my biological mom was supporting me either.

———

"WAIT, explain it to me again," Dr. Kat said. I paced outside so that Jane wouldn't hear me. "Start at the beginning."

I exhaled, trying to keep everything straight and be clear. "So my parents separated when I was in fourth grade." I went on to detail fifth grade, sixth grade, and the first half of seventh grade.

"What about the second half of seventh grade?" she asked.

"There was no second half," I said.

I knew my transcript would be a mess; I couldn't bring myself to look at it until Dr. Kat made me. Even then I couldn't understand the mélange of grades listed as transfer credits on the Lakeville South letterhead. In the years before Methodist Hospital, I'd gone to a charter school, done an online homeschool program, been in day treatment, and attended a Minneapolis public high school. Plus I had credits from the hospital education program and the school at CRTC.

"Look, if I don't understand, there's no way colleges are going to," Dr. Kat explained, meaning that if they didn't understand, I wouldn't get in. My chance at upward mobility relied on the appropriate marketing. Without context, my credentials were good but not spectacular. Every successful applicant to the top schools had a shtick: legacy, recruited athlete, lone student from an unrepresented state, organ player. Mine was my past, the tremendous things I'd overcome. But I hadn't exactly "overcome" those circumstances: they were ongoing.

Providing context required distance that I lacked. No one besides my mom had ever narrativized my life for me, but her cheerful glossing over of my darkest days and instructions to "overcome victimhood" haunted me.

"You have to be extremely explicit," Dr. Kat continued to coach. "Otherwise no one will understand how bad it was."

But how bad *was* it, spending my summer at camp and staying with friends? I'd never been beaten. I'd never slept on the sidewalk. My whole life, adults had forced me to take responsibility for any problems I had. Now Kat was urging the opposite. She wanted me to list everything that had happened, including my diagnoses and hospitalizations, as if they proved something bad about my life, instead of something bad about me.

Dr. Kat wanted the facts. But what were facts? Anything that negated my agency, that framed me as a helpless child tossed on the rough seas of neglectful parenting and the child welfare system, felt like a lie, or like I was refusing to acknowledge that others had it worse.

"What about your horrible foster parents? Why don't you talk about that?"

"I don't know if they're *horrible*. Misguided, maybe. They're Minnesotan."

"You don't have the word count for that." Dr. Kat sighed. "Save the rest for your memoir."

AT THE END OF OCTOBER, a few days before my early action application to Yale was due, Dr. Kat called me. "'Scrambled Eggs' is your personal statement!" I'd sent her my creative writing, trying to put together a supplementary portfolio, but she liked the essay too much for only a few English professors to see it.

"What? That's not my story," I said. The personal statement was supposed to be my chance to show colleges who *I* was; I'd spent so many hours agonizing over how to summarize my entire personhood in two pages. The self I'd written about in "Scrambled Eggs" was so much younger, secure in a world long lost to me. After the events of the summer, even the girl who'd written it six months prior felt alien and naive. And over and over in my life, it felt as if I were defined in relation to my parents; I didn't want to repeat the pattern here.

"It's one part of your amazing story," Dr. Kat said sweetly.

I sighed. I was going to do whatever she wanted.

"The only problem is it's kind of long," she said. We'd have to cut my original essay in half, removing most of my reflections about my own gender but keeping what felt like the most titillating details: choosing Michelle's lipstick, Michelle burning our furniture in the backyard, getting my first period on Father's Day.

I asked Dr. Kat what pronouns we should use. Having gained marginally more awareness than I'd had when I first wrote it, I thought I should switch to she/her pronouns in the essay to refer to Michelle after her transition.

"If you do that, you're going to confuse people. No one will understand." As always I bowed to Dr. Kat's assessment. It seemed accurate, anyway: no one in my orbit, besides Charlotte, seemed able to comprehend Trans 101. Of the many teachers who'd read my essay, none had suggested I reconsider the pronouns. In real life, if someone didn't understand, I'd have a chance to explain. But there was no such chance in the applications: confusing the reader meant not getting in.

A younger me might have refused Dr. Kat on principle, just as I'd refused to comply at Methodist. But I'd learned the consequences of pride, or principle, the hard way. *I am a whore of my sadnesses*, I wrote to Charlotte in French, my emails always longer than her replies.

As soon as my Yale early application was in, I frantically sent in submissions to writing contests and then scoured fastweb.com for scholarships. True to her usual breeziness, my mom always acted like free money was there for the taking, but I only qualified for two major programs: the Ayn Rand essay contest (which required reading a 753-page book) and the Horatio Alger Association of Distinguished Americans. The latter was named after a prolific nineteenth-century novelist whose protagonists' virtue invariably leads to their success. They awarded twenty thousand dollars to 104 lucky scholars for "overcoming adversity."

"Can you believe this?" I told Jane, laughing, as I showed her the red, white, and blue website.

"Are you sure it's not a scam?" she asked.

"Wikipedia says it's a real-life nonprofit organization."

I wrote an essay comparing myself to Distinguished American Buzz Aldrin, second man on the moon. Then I completed a checklist of hardships, which I called "adversity bingo." I laughed while reading the categories aloud to Jane, who snapped her bracelet nervously. Thanks to everything, I scored highly. The game was so ridiculous, I felt no guilt in playing.

Still, I couldn't help but notice the tragedies they omitted. There was one checkbox for abuse and no bonus points for sexual assault. Even for an organization that rewarded triumph over misfortune, common tribulations were still unspeakable. Kids transcending poverty were a hot commodity, but certain adversities just made people squeamish.

Every time I had to "sell myself," the distinction between what produced revulsion versus what prompted praise weighed on me. I tried not to think about what I was losing, only what I could win. I stuffed manila envelopes full of my traumas and submitted them for the judges' consideration. When the facts themselves didn't depress me, I felt high on the hope that I might cash in on my sorrows.

"Is it wrong for me to pursue conservatory?" Jane asked me one night after lights-out. "Even if I become a professional flautist, I won't make much money. But I know I'll still be comfortable." Distress tightened her voice. "I feel so guilty. Like I don't deserve the life I have."

I looked up at the ceiling. I wondered if I was the reason why she felt bad, a living example of "it could be worse," despite trying to shield my roommate from my tribulations.

"You didn't choose to be born into a wealthy family. Just like other people didn't choose to be born broke. You don't have to feel bad about it," I said. Hearing Jane agonize, I felt grateful my dilemmas weren't so existential. Unlike her, I could want a better life and not feel bad about it. "You just have to be a good steward of what you have."

"I feel bad about that."

"You have a different set of cards. You play yours, and I'll play mine."

"What are you going to do for the holidays?" Jane asked.

"I don't know. I don't want to think about it."

"Come home with me. My dad has a bunch of miles. I bet he'll get you a ticket."

"Thanks." Relief washed over me, followed by a fresh worry. If I ended up at one of my safety schools, would I still not have anywhere to go over breaks? If I didn't get into a school that could give me a full ride, how long would it take me to claw my way out of the student-debt hole? I imagined myself in a shitty apartment with beige carpet, working shifts at a grocery store, dating an older, sugar-daddy type. How many years would pass like that? How long could I hold on until things finally became easy?

I told myself not to think about it. Jane breathed long and shallow as she fell asleep. My Yale application was in; the others were written already in case I was rejected. There was nothing left to do but wait and see.

## Sixteen

"The van is going to be here any minute," Jane said. She stood next to the door, flanked by suitcases filled with dirty laundry. I hunched over my computer, pounding refresh on my email, waiting to hear back from Yale before we left on winter break.

All the muscles in my neck were tensed. Within seconds, my life could change forever. I could be accepted to Yale, going to Yale, wearing a Yale navy sweatshirt all of spring semester (gloating). I'd be wanted. I'd have finally proven myself. I could throw away my nine other applications, rejecting all those schools before a single school could reject me.

I hit refresh again. There it was. My cursor shook as I hit the email. My eyes scanned. "We regret to inform you."

I gasped. Rejected.

"Emi," Jane said, her eyes wide, scared. She reached out for me.

"Just give me a second," I said, biting my lip as I shoved my way into the bathroom and shut the door. How could this have happened to me? How could I have been stupid enough to believe I'd get into Yale? I riffled through the medicine cabinet and found my X-Acto knife. I cut two lines on my left wrist in the shape of a Y. I held my arm as dots of blood rose to the surface, outlining the letter.

I exhaled. Everything slowed. I shut my eyes and leaned against the door, the tension draining out of me. Stillness enveloped me.

Then I felt like such a loser. The cut was ridiculously melodramatic, even for me. I'd gotten my hopes up, grown attached, and now I felt like a spurned lover. I tried to will myself not to care, even though this rejection was not only a rejection: it meant three and a half more months of agony, waiting.

"Emi?" Jane said, on the other side of the door. "The van is waiting. We have to go."

I dug through junk in the medicine cabinet and found some knockoff Livestrong bracelets to obscure the wound. I threw open the door. "Okay," I said. "I'm ready."

DR. KAT EMAILED ME, calling me her "shining star," and said that she was "shocked" and "stunned." I thought there was nothing to do except hope for a better outcome in the regular admissions round, but Dr. Kat leapt into action, making me ask Kelly to call Yale, then querying her network. I sat in Jane's backyard while Dr. Kat filled me in on her reconnaissance efforts. After several high-profile campus suicides, she surmised that they ran psych evals on people's applications. I'd probably failed mine.

"I don't understand it. It's so common," Dr. Kat said, telling me about her students with eating disorders, depression, anxiety. "I don't know how they can hold it against you.

"We just need to tone it down," she added, matter-of-factly, as if my suffering were a stereo and we just had to select the right volume.

"But isn't that dishonest?"

"Look, would you feel like you had to disclose cancer?" Dr. Kat asked.

"No, but . . ." It just felt different. If I had leukemia, no one would have said the illness was my fault. My treatment wouldn't have focused on confessing my wrongs, taking responsibility for my condition, and changing my behavior. As a cancer patient, I would have been an object of pity or an emblem of courage, not a cautionary tale of a teenager gone off the rails. "It was just TMI," Dr. Kat said, sounding pleased with herself for knowing the acronym for "too much information."

But I wasn't convinced; I was too used to hearing that I had erred and now I needed to suffer the consequences. Even apart from the way my mom closed her eyes to my struggles, I was coming from years of other adults telling me I had chosen to be sick and created my own misery, from residential treatment's insistence that taking responsibility was a moral imperative to Dave and Jan's view that my ambition, not my circumstances, made me depressed. Whenever Dr. Kat suggested otherwise, it baffled me. She was offering me an opportunity to go easy on myself, but I wasn't sure I wanted to take it. In blaming myself, I had agency. In owning up to my mistakes, I could claim whatever integrity my life afforded.

I still wasn't sure if I should follow her advice when Kelly emailed me: she'd talked to Yale. "They did not feel that the overall power of the academic program was there." Most applicants had similar test scores and grades, but my file "did not seem to hold unique academic qualities." I cursed myself for not retaking the SAT: at least if I had a perfect score, they couldn't hold it against me. Yet, I suspected that wouldn't have made a difference; a perfect SAT score would hardly make me "unique." I had taken every hard class, begged to be let into APs, studied on my own for extra exams, slept wherever I could during breaks so that I could go to boarding school and camps—but it wasn't enough. I suspected they wanted a homeless child who'd also won the Intel Science Fair and started a global nonprofit.

Feeling awful about my mediocrity, I kept reading Kelly's email. "Regarding the past issues, the list was daunting. The readers did not feel a sense of reflection or your 'success story.' They wanted to read more/learn more about how you have overcome."

I'd get no points for merely surviving while getting grades and test scores that put me in striking range. My past was a liability unless it made me stronger and more interesting. According to Yale, I had failed to reach that threshold.

Kelly ended the email abruptly, with no sign-off—no "their loss," no "best," only her name. I interpreted this as a display of her disdain.

I hated Kelly. I hated her so much. I knew it wasn't her job to take care of my living situation or my feelings and that she was stressed and overworked. But I couldn't help but see in her every adult before her who had told me to be realistic, to settle on a goal that would check me off their list (even if it set me up for a rocky future), as if they could predict the outcomes of my life far better than I could.

I would've done anything to prove her wrong.

In this flush of emotion, no matter how misguided the target—a guidance counselor who was simply a messenger—I felt, for the first time, the conviction that I'd been held to bullshit standards. I couldn't understand why the adults in the Midwest were so punitive and Dr. Kat was so forgiving (though I suspected it had to do with her being rich and living in Manhattan), but I was finally willing to accept her version of the story. I had two weeks before my applications were due. I could be a fucking success story. I could be the picture of triumph, of overcoming, just as I'd been in my application for the Horatio Alger scholarship. How dare they suggest that I wasn't?

Horatio Alger had given me the template: what adversities people admired and which were red flags. I studied the applications I'd prepared. Who was making me mention the hospitals? No one. No diagnoses. I wasn't going to tone down my mental illness; I would excise it.

The only problem would be my year at CRTC, all the academic credits earned there and at Methodist. But when I scanned the transcript

Interlochen would send out, there were no documents from any schools before Lakeville, just a list of transfer credits. There was no mention of treatment. I didn't have to say a word.

I changed my two-page timeline-focused Letter of Extenuating Circumstances to half a page, concentrating on the buzzwords: foster care, homelessness, my mom's hoarding, Michelle's absence. In my list of schools, I left out CRTC. In the explanation, I wrote, "I began high school in the Minneapolis Public Schools. After ninth grade, I went into foster care." It wasn't a lie. I scoured my nine application drafts, searching for any reference to treatment I could cut.

Dr. Kat had been clear that I'd apply to ten schools, no more, no less. But Harvard had snuck onto my list, if only because it had an easy application: no extra essays, no "why do you want to come here" suck-up prompts. And it was even more prestigious than Yale. I transferred all my hope onto this new target. At least in private, I was no longer shy about the size or starkness of my desire.

When we spoke before I hit "submit" on the applications, I told Dr. Kat, "At least I can still apply to Harvard."

"You have to," she said. "I think you've still got a good chance."

I EXPECTED TO feel relief when all my applications were in: for three and a half years, college had been my near-exclusive focus. I'd envisioned relief, an unburdening. Instead, I looked up at the orange trees in Jane's backyard as dread settled over me. I tried to take deep breaths until I couldn't stand it any longer and checked the clock on my computer. Five minutes had passed.

During those years, I'd had something to ponder in any spare moment. With my ambition, I was never alone. I never realized how comforting it was to always have something to do—even if it was just mentally reciting a poem I'd memorized in French—until there was nothing to be done. I lived in a flat world, where getting into college was the horizon. After that, the earth dropped off.

Within a day, I became obsessed with my appearance. I stared into the mirror at Jane's house, my face frozen into a grimace of permanent concern. When I wasn't in my school uniform or clothes I'd taken from the lost and found, I wore the shirts and jeans that a counselor at CRTC had bought me with county money. I'd always ignored my self-presentation in favor of more pressing concerns, but now I wondered how I could ever move forward into my new life if I still looked the same on the outside.

On New Year's Eve, I headed into downtown Palo Alto with my backpack and found the American Apparel store. I swooped up youthful, impractical clothes—a floral lace bralette, shiny black "disco pants" that zipped all the way up and down the leg, a REPEAL PROP 8 NOW! tank top—and took them to the dressing room. There were no plastic tags on the clothes, no metal stickers to trigger alarms. I shoved it all into my pink-and-purple backpack. My pulse pounded as I left the dressing room, half expecting a clerk to stop me, but I walked out of the store and down the street and straight back to Jane's house. I felt no guilt, though its absence rankled me: it was as if my actions no longer mattered unless the admissions committee got wind of them.

Next I turned my attention to completing my outfit for the college alumni interviews. I had no idea how many interviews I'd have, if any, but that didn't stop me from agonizing over my footwear. Dr. Kat promised me that these exchanges didn't really matter—I just had to seem personable and interesting—but I didn't trust her. I had witnessed the transformative effects of a makeover too many times. Whether it was washing my hair in residential treatment or getting a shag from Isabel's mom's stylist, these changes affected the way others saw me more than they'd admit. I was always suspicious that people helped me because I looked like them. Most fancy people could look at me—white and blonde with a nice bone structure, if a bit wide-faced—squint, and see a stereotype of success. And I'd ascertained that no matter how progressive elites claimed to be, they appreciated a certain aesthetic. My clothing would communicate shared values—classy, practical, effortless beauty—and serve as my strongest argument that, if accepted, I'd fit in. The creation of this mirage did not include pleather loafers from Target.

Every morning, I begged Jane to come shopping with me in San Francisco. Besides two walks around the block, we hadn't left the house unchaperoned. Jane refused. (She later told me her mom forbade it, convinced I'd persuade her daughter to get a tattoo.) Eventually, I went by myself. Jane's mom drove me to the Caltrain station a mile away, clutching the steering wheel and warning me to be careful in the big city. I did little to assuage her anxiety, but I did promise I'd be back on the 7:00 p.m. limited-stop train.

In the San Francisco Bloomingdale's, I noticed a pair of black patent leather flats. I flipped the shoe over. My size: eight. Dior—my eyes widened. They cost two hundred dollars. At 80 percent off, they were a great deal, but I had only four hundred dollars in my checking account. I put them back.

A saleswoman came up behind me. "Just try them on."

I didn't need much encouragement. They slid on, hugging instead of pinching. A sturdiness I'd never felt—"arch support," the woman called it—embraced my feet. As I walked across the floor, the tap-tap of the soles announced my arrival. When I looked down, I imagined the store's carpet transforming into the marble mosaic of a grand library.

I took them off. It was stupid to spend half my money on a pair of Dior flats.

*But what if I bought them,* I wondered, *and got in?* For a moment, I imagined a future where I wore *only* two-hundred-dollar shoes. This was just the first pair, ensuring I made the right impression, my gateway to those shoes and that life.

"You can always return them," the saleswoman offered. I handed her my debit card.

I spent the day clutching my Little Brown Bag, trying on knockoffs, but by the time I got on the train, I was sure I'd found the right footwear for my future. Even if they seemed painfully expensive now, they were a leap of faith. With them, I could let myself believe that I'd get in, that I'd be okay, like I'd become the kind of person the Dior flats suggested.

Mission accomplished, I relaxed. I slid my bag under my seat so I could sketch the other passengers. When the train reached Redwood City, I called Jane's dad to tell him I was ten minutes away. At Palo Alto, I stepped off into the chilly night, invigorated and proud.

As the train pulled away, I realized I'd left the bag. I wanted to run after the train, shouting, but I couldn't move except to fold in half at the waist.

As I waited for Jane's dad, a Baby Bullet train arrived. I called out to the conductor who stood in the door. "I forgot something on the last train. How can I get it?"

"Get on this. You can meet the other one in San Jose."

I turned back to the parking lot and saw Jane's dad's headlights. Jane's parents were my hosts; I couldn't just be late. "It's okay," I croaked, and went to the car.

I told Jane's dad I left something on the train, too embarrassed to admit how much they cost. I hoped he would offer to drive me to San Jose to get them, but instead he suggested I try the lost and found hotline. The next day, I called again and again. I left a message, then another. In my heart, I knew I'd never find the flats. Suddenly, I regretted stealing the clothes from American Apparel, afraid that this loss was my first helping of karmic justice, fearing I was cursed. In my nightmares, I stood on the platform watching the train pull away again and again, with my shoes and the future they represented.

I ONLY HAD ONE INTERVIEW THAT WINTER, for Harvard. Ever since I'd put together my list of colleges, I'd pretended that I'd be happy at any of them. But when I was honest with myself, I wanted the best—and that was Harvard. I wanted the prestige with its attendant security and riches and acclaim. But I knew that kind of baldness charmed no one. Before my interview, I scoured the College Confidential message boards looking for "acceptable" reasons to want to attend: the upperclassman House system, freshman-only seminars, grants to study abroad. On the scheduled afternoon, a counselor drove me into a Traverse City law office, where I waited with my ankles crossed in borrowed pleather flats, a size too large.

A man in slacks and a sweater led me to a wood-paneled office. Tomes filled his bookshelves. Diplomas presided on the walls. My interviewer sat down on the other side of his big desk and asked me to tell him about myself.

"Well, I grew up in Minneapolis," I began. "My family was Evangelical Christian. I was the state Bible memorization champion in fourth grade." I listened as my story slid out of me. What had once been so sensitive, stuff I couldn't even admit to Dr. Kat, now was polished. I even knew the moments—discussing homelessness—where I could shed a few neat tears, if required. My tale of obstacles and overcoming, tragedy and triumph, charmed even me. I was a good girl who loved learning: eager, enthusiastic, with a few slight humblebrags. As far as this interviewer was concerned, I'd never been sick. I had no dark secrets. No messy past. No scars under my opaque tights. The banter came easily: having an educated adult act interested in me was something I'd craved for a long time.

When I stood up and he shook my hand, I was surprised to see our hour-long appointment had stretched into two and a half hours. That was a good sign, I consoled myself, looking for any omen other than my shoes, which slapped against the floor as I walked.

"I had a great time chatting," the lawyer said. I beamed. He then explained that last year more than a hundred students had applied from my district of Northern Michigan, and only two had gotten in. Most years, no one did. The local odds were far worse than Harvard's most recent acceptance rate of 9 percent. "It's a shame," the lawyer said, shaking his head. "But I'll put in a good word for you."

I sighed and thanked him profusely.

"Though I don't think it matters." He chuckled. "These interviews are just to keep the alumni busy."

He shut the door to his office. I stood in the lobby, looked down at my cracked footwear, and forced myself to breathe.


THAT WINTER, I was plagued by memories. I poured out hundreds of pages about my childhood—Michelle punishing me for trivial missteps, my mom's self-absorption during the divorce, the sexual assaults of sixth grade and their lingering effects. It was as if unearthing and packaging traumas for my applications had brought up the deepest ones.

By mid-February, I was fielding emails from colleges every day. Because I'd filed the federal financial aid forms as an independent student, instead of my parents filing for me, they wanted to know if I was an orphan or a ward of the courts. Each individual school needed to verify my story. Just thinking about it made my mouth hot with bile.

One afternoon, hanging up the phone with an admissions office, I rummaged around the bottom drawer of my desk until I found the bottle of Adderall I'd filched from my mom's apartment. Little beige pellets danced in the capsule. I swallowed it dry. All afternoon, I felt normal. I read, able to think about things other than the future that one wrong move could jinx.

Within a few weeks, I was running out. I emailed Dr. Woods for a refill, expecting her to chastise me and tell me to knock it off, but instead she suggested I visit someone local. I went to see a family practice doctor in town, wearing my college interview outfit: "I was diagnosed with ADD when I was eleven." I told him Adderall had helped. He wrote me a prescription for ninety pills, administered from the infirmary.

IN MY NIGHTMARES, admissions officers interrogated me. They led me to a fluorescent-lit conference room with a one-way mirror along the wall—a replica of the first office where I'd gotten therapy. My interlocutors sat around a big table, lobbing questions.

"Why did you threaten to blow up Methodist Hospital? Why didn't you put *that* in your application?"

"How many schools did you really attend? What about your sophomore year?"

"Does sleeping in your car really make you homeless? Isn't it true your mother gave you a 1992 Corolla?"

"Why did you lie to Dave and Jan in Lakeville? Why should we accept a liar? A liar and a thief?"

"Why did you cut yourself when you got rejected by Yale? Why are you taking Adderall? Why did you start throwing up again?"

My interrogators asked me about everything I left out, forcing me to account for all of my imperfections. It seemed deeply unjust that I could omit the ways I'd fucked up when others could not—I assumed the other applicants were completely forthcoming with their tribulations and mistakes. Otherwise, wouldn't their parents tell on them? The idea of adults shielding kids from their mistakes seemed bizarre. On the contrary, I figured everyone else's parents were busy airing grievances with their children, too. That, or my errors were especially egregious.

"Don't you love your parents?" the officers asked me, questioning my goodness as a daughter. "Then how can you throw them under the bus?" Like the counselors from CRTC, they demanded that I take ownership of my actions.

"Why did you use the wrong pronouns for Michelle? How can you care more about people 'understanding' than about her feelings? Don't you have values?"

As the dream accusations pelted me, I tried to summon the composure I'd found at the Harvard interview, but the committee invariably found a hole in my story. Not a success story, they ruled. A fake. A fraud. A liar.

In other nightmares, I stood in front of the one-way mirror. I had to anticipate what the adults wanted to know and confess independently. If I failed to adequately skewer myself, I'd go right back to sleeping in my car.

I woke up in a clammy sweat, pulse throbbing in my wrist. Light crept through the windows. Jane lay three feet away, fast asleep. All I could do was crawl out of bed and take an Adderall. I couldn't defend myself from myself. The nocturnal admissions officers were right: I wasn't the perfect overcomer I presented in my applications. I wasn't the worst-off person in the world, and I wasn't yet okay. Those facts made me feel like a lie, a sham, undeserving of the security I craved most.

Six weeks before decisions came out, my mom wrote the required parent letter for my application to Smith. Dr. Kat annotated my mom's draft, detailing in all caps what my mom needed to add. She ignored her, refusing to confirm my situation. Dr. Kat decided I needed more support. Annette agreed to write a recommendation, in which she recounted my adolescence in her typically frank manner. Dave and Jan had given away my spot "for financial reasons" and now, between breaks, I was homeless. It startled me to see my life written up so plainly: "I have been in her mother's house, and it is not possible for Margaret to sleep there. The place is filled to the top with garbage, and everything is covered with mouse and dog excrement. There is no bathroom, no warm water, and no central heat."

Even if I'd had that level of perspective on my situation, I could never have been so blunt. The description would have sounded negative coming from me; burdened with the task of "overcoming," I couldn't have a bad attitude. No one required that from Annette. She was an objective outside observer who could sign at the end with her professional titles—not just my mentor, but a medical doctor with a PhD.

Annette's pedigree shined on me in her final paragraph: "Margaret is the most amazing girl I have met. She is highly gifted, extremely creative, and a very hard worker. She is also a very sweet girl with a great personality."

I couldn't believe someone would call me "a very sweet girl"—that seemed like the antithesis of what I was. I hadn't known that Annette thought my life was so bleak. Ingrid had made it clear that my mom loved me far more than her other clients' parents loved them, which heightened my guilt at exposing her failures. But Annette wrote that I never gave up, despite "the complete lack of support from her parents." When Annette sent the letter to schools, I wondered if the support of a trustworthy, distinguished person would be the deciding factor, more important than anything I'd done.

At night, I lay in bed next to Jane. She breathed deeply, but I was wired and itchy, caught in Adderall's chemical jet lag.

In a way, Annette's letter gave me relief; it could only help me, and I was touched that she'd written these details without being specifically prompted. But her witnessing also made my situation real. It was not something I could wish away or adjust my attitude to fix. I really was screwed. I'd been counting on a top school to rescue me, but it was hard to accept that I actually needed saving.

My vulnerability haunted me, along with the fact that I'd lost a lot of weight on Adderall. I knew it wasn't good for me, but I couldn't stop.

I squeezed my eyes shut and imagined the relief of a teacher's door clicking shut. I wanted to admit to someone how much it took out of me to pretend to be so successful, to act as if I had figured everything out. I longed to go to Mika, the head of the Writing Department, and collapse into her chair, to feel a soothing hand on my shoulder.

Yet I couldn't. My applications hinged on my having a clean bill of mental health. I feared that if I told anyone about my struggles, seemingly omnipresent committees would find out. Still, the only way I could sleep was by promising myself that I'd talk to someone the next day. The thought lulled me until I passed out.

I woke up to the sound of my sobs in the darkness.

"Emi? Are you okay?" Jane asked.

I willed myself to stop crying. "Yes. Just a little stressed."

In the morning, I got up and saw Jane at her desk, eyes wide. "I didn't know you cried. You're so . . . so hard."

"Thanks." I remembered an AP English vocab word that defined the state I'd aspired to: "sangfroid," from French, meaning cold-blooded, unfeeling. But maybe, I realized, I was too hard for my own good, though I knew of no way to be softer.

That day, I went to class as normal. I didn't talk to anyone.

RIGHT BEFORE SPRING BREAK, Mika approached me in the Writing House. Her eyes darted around. "Can I speak to you after the department meeting?"

I could feel the sweat begin, ready to soak through the pits of my baby blue polo shirt. "Sure," I said, voice strained. As soon as we were alone,

I was sure Mika was going to say, "I've noticed you're not yourself. I'm concerned about you." She would ask what was wrong.

Terrified, I twitched through the announcements, the collection of money for communal coffee and hot chocolate, the next deadlines for the campus literary magazine. I kept studying the clock, counting down the minutes. One part of me ached for release; the other kept screaming that I couldn't afford a breakdown.

When the group split, Mika came to me. "Are you ready?"

"As ready as I'll ever be."

I followed her upstairs to her office. The door clicked shut. I sat down in the big chair across from her desk. My pulse thudded along. I forced myself to exhale. I reassured myself it would be okay. This is what I wanted: Her arm on my back. Tears on my cheeks, no longer trapped alone in my body.

"I have someone on the phone."

I wondered if it was the school nurse, or my mom, or Dr. Woods.

Mika handed me the receiver. I wanted to drop it on the floor and bolt, but I knew I had to answer. "Hello, Emi. Is now a good time?" I heard the warm voice of a stranger. Had Interlochen contracted a service that staged phone interventions?

"As good as any," I said. I feared I was going to pass out. Suddenly, the idea of fainting consoled me: Mika would scream, scared for me, then summon help.

"I'm calling from the Scholastic Art and Writing Awards," the voice on the other end said. She explained that I had won one of fifteen Gold Key Portfolio Awards, the highest honor. "Congratulations!"

I still couldn't breathe. I looked at my teacher, searching for a clue of how I should respond. She beamed. But I couldn't.

The woman from Scholastic explained that I'd won one of the most prestigious contests for young writers and artists, following in the steps of Sylvia Plath and Andy Warhol. I would be celebrated at a ceremony at

Carnegie Hall and receive ten thousand dollars. I already knew all the details—I'd wanted the prize since Miss J.'s photo class, when she helped me pick some photos to submit.

"You sound surprised," the lady on the phone said.

"Yes. I am." When I passed the phone back to Mika, my hands shook from nerves or Adderall. Mika was still smiling after she hung up. I buried my face in my hands, and the world collapsed into darkness around me. My sobs blocked out every other sound.

I felt Mika's body perched on the armrest of my chair. She laid a skinny arm on my back.

When I could speak, I said, "I've wanted this for so long. I thought I'd never have it." I started crying again.

After a while, Mika asked me what was wrong.

"I don't know." A few weeks earlier, staff had caught a dozen students smoking marijuana. I'd watched one of them, a writer, go in and out of teachers' offices, her face swollen from crying. The teachers' intervention saved her from expulsion. Sometimes I spotted the girl whispering with the adults. They seemed to care about her more for having seen her at her weakest. Sitting in Mika's office, I longed for that solicitude, even though I finally had what I'd wanted.

I looked up at Mika. "Why don't I feel happy?"

She turned toward the window looking on the trees starting to bud. I studied her face. I tried to imagine her younger, in my chair. She'd gone to Interlochen, too, and as a high school senior she'd won a Gold Key Portfolio Award, so maybe she would know.

"Success is hard," Mika said. "It doesn't always make you feel the way you think it will."

This answer satisfied me. I took the tissue she offered me and we discussed the logistics. Until the news was public, I had to keep it quiet, even from Jane. I could tell Harvard, maybe one other school—but that was a risk.

I stood up to leave.

"Emi," Mika said, stopping me. "Have you lost weight? You look thin."

Reflexively, I answered no before I could stop myself, even though it was the question part of me craved. I almost said, "Actually," and sat back down. But by winning, it felt like I'd missed the chance to be loved without regard for my accomplishments, even as I stood right there in Mika's doorway.

## Seventeen

M y mom invited me to join her in Seattle over spring break. I was
not a fan of her motivation for the trip—she was interviewing
for a graduate program in Christian counseling—but I was eager not to
spend the time alone, especially in the terrifying days leading up to college
decisions, which came out at the end of break.

I booked my flights early, with the monthly allowance my mom gave
me, and then plotted our trip. My mom wanted to see Vancouver, so I
researched what we'd need to cross the border and bought bus tickets.
After casting my mom as a villain in my college applications, my efforts
felt like penance. I hoped that travel would bring out the best in us, even
if only for two weeks in a cheap hotel.

I kept reminding my mom to buy plane tickets. By the time she finally
looked—one week before my arrival—she declared it was too expensive. Luckily, she came up with an ingenious solution: she'd take the
train. It took four days each way, but my mom saw that as a perk. "I'll
be seeing America!" But she only had so much vacation time, and I already had my ticket, so instead of our spending most of my break together, I'd arrive before her and then, after five days together, she'd go
back to Minneapolis while I went to Vancouver by myself. I'd be alone
when I learned where I got into college.

It was too late for me to change course, though I hadn't cared where we went, I'd just wanted to see her. In Seattle, I wandered through the city studying printed-out directions. On the streets, I saw mirror images of myself: grungy teenagers carrying backpacks. I crossed the street when I encountered them. They spooked me.

When I found the hostel, the man at the front desk studied my driver's license and then told me I couldn't stay. "You're a minor," he said, as if the reason were obvious. I kicked myself for not thinking about this possibility, even though it hadn't occurred to my mom either. In the end, I'd be the one sleeping on a bench or begging some adult to break their policy, while she was on the train, seeing America.

I had to think fast, because I suspected I wouldn't get another chance to stay there. I asked if the man could call my mom and get permission, explaining she was on her way but running late.

The man sighed but picked up the phone. I heard my mom's distant, cheerful voice on the other end. Of course her daughter could stay there, my mom said. She was used to taking calls like this one, giving her permission.

I was so relieved when the man gave me a key that I wasn't even mad at my mom. And when she arrived, the city transformed. Alone, it was a place full of street kids and men talking to me. Together, it was filled with art museums and open studios. My mom had a list of everything important in Seattle. We toured the Theo Chocolate factory, gorging ourselves on samples instead of eating dinner. After the divorce, my mom and I had played a game where we pretended to star in a reality TV show. The trip felt like that again, from the morning when the man making pancakes asked my mom for my hand in marriage and she pretended to take his offer seriously, quizzing him about himself, to when we fell asleep on the hostel's full-size bed (so we didn't even have to pay for two spots, just one). Despite everything, sharing a bed with my mom made my body relax. The two of us together seemed like the most natural thing in the world. It hurt me to even imagine being without her again.

AFTER TWO DAYS of exploring the city, my mom had her info sessions at the graduate school. I wandered around trying to kill time, the days before I heard back from colleges feeling endless.

I agreed to meet my mom at the end of a happy hour for her program. Most of the people around the table, with beer mugs and plates full of food, seemed to be in their early thirties. A lady who reeked of "administrator" greeted me warmly. I glared at her and sat down next to my mom.

"Do you want some?" My mom offered me a carrot stick from her plate of chicken wings, which I suspected was the cheapest thing on the menu, our dinner. I stung with pity for her: she seemed uncomfortable in this restaurant that wasn't McDonald's or the mall tavern at home with half-price appetizers and free birthday pizzas.

Reflexively, I resented the younger applicants. I scorned the school for selling dreams to people like my mom, who wanted a second chance after working her whole life in a menial job to take care of me. I took the carrot stick and tried to make my mom feel comfortable, chatting with her neighbors about their excitement for their future. Once my mom and I got on the bus back to our hostel, I told her, "This program is stupid. It's way too much money."

My mom frowned. "I don't tell you *your* dreams are stupid."

"I'm your daughter! You *have* to believe in me. But how are you going to pay for it?"

I knew this parent-child conversation usually happened with the roles flipped, but if she retired from her union job early and took out one hundred thousand dollars in loans at age fifty-seven, with no guarantee of a job as a Christian counselor after graduation, the outlook for both of us would get bleaker than it already was.

For the rest of her stay, I dedicated myself to convincing her grad school was a terrible idea. With each criticism, I saw her face flinch in pain. I willed myself not to care. When I dropped her off at the train station, she didn't seem all that sad to leave without me.

I HAD FIVE DAYS left before I heard from colleges when I got on a bus for Vancouver, the trip my mom and I were supposed to take together. When I got to the border, the immigration officer questioned me. I didn't have a passport, just a driver's license and a notarized letter from my mom saying it was fine with her if I left the country. I exaggerated and told the officer I had a few thousand dollars in my checking account on top of the thirty US dollars in my pocket.

He asked me how he knew I wouldn't stay in Canada and sell my body.

I pondered this. It seemed like a valid question.

"I have to find out if I got into Harvard," I replied. With this stranger, I could admit my real desire. But not wanting to jinx it, I added, "And if I got in anywhere else."

He let me through.

But as soon as I got off the bus in Vancouver, my debit card was gone. I had a hunch it had fallen out of my pocket on the bus. I hated myself for being so irresponsible. Following my printed-out map, I trudged past even more strung-out people than in Seattle, looking for my hostel. I called my mom at 10:00 p.m. and hoped she'd pick up. She was probably somewhere in Wyoming, chatting up a fellow passenger on the train. When she answered, I exhaled in relief. I explained the situation and asked if she'd pay for the hostel over the phone. She agreed but didn't offer to wire me money, and I didn't ask.

Bus fare would have cost more than my six-dollar daily budget, so every morning after the hostel's bread-and-cereal breakfast, I walked two miles to the library, telling myself I wasn't hungry.

On my long walks back, the wind off the Pacific whipped through my thin gray cardigan. One afternoon, I wandered into a department store selling leftover merchandise from that winter's Olympics. I tried on a hat with earflaps and a fuzzy lining that declared CANADA across the forehead. Even on sale, it cost twenty dollars. If I bought it, I'd only be able to afford one more yogurt before I got back to the United States and could visit a bank.

I shoved it into my backpack. As I was leaving the store, just before I passed through the alarms, I realized that I could get arrested. Arrested, deported, and booted out of college before it even began—proving the mean border patrol agent right, and more. This hat could be my undoing.

I walked out of the store. No alarms went off. I power walked two blocks away and then hid behind a wall. My heart pounded in my chest hard enough that I was no longer cold.

I put the hat on, tugging the flaps over my numb ears. No amount of guilt could negate its warmth, the small muscles in my face softening, protected.

ON THE BUS BACK TO SEATTLE, I sat next to the oldest woman. There was a whole clique of them: empty nesters on a girls' trip. My neighbor let me borrow her laptop to check my email to see if any colleges had gotten back to me early. On the bus's wi-fi, it took a minute for Gmail to load. I saw the message from Johns Hopkins and wanted to throw up in anticipation as the bus lurched along.

I clicked on the email and waited for the decision to load, gnawing on my fingernails as the text appeared on the screen. Rejected.

I slammed the laptop shut and offered it back to its owner.

"What did you hear?" she asked. Four ladies turned to me.

"I got rejected." I didn't want them to look at me.

One of the moms cooed. "Oh. Was it your top choice?"

"No," I said, embarrassed to admit that I was so upset to be rejected by a school I didn't even want to attend. But if Hopkins, a target school, rejected me—what hope did I have for my reaches?

"You're going to be fine!" another woman told me. "All of my kids went to the University of British Columbia and they have great lives!"

I wondered if her children were in foreign countries wearing stolen hats.

AT 2:50 P.M. on April 1, I sat in front of a computer at the Seattle Public Library, with ten minutes to go before college decisions came out.

The armpits of my shirt were Rorschach prints of perspiration. I'd applied deodorant twice in the hostel that morning, but I still had the special stench of anxiety. At least I couldn't smell myself over the body odor of the other library patrons.

2:53 p.m.

I looked around at the men with matted hair and the women with plastic shopping bags. I looked up at the ultramodern building, all glass and steel. I looked around for trash cans, anywhere I could puke if I needed to.

2:55 p.m.

If I didn't get into a top school, I could take the bus to San Francisco and jump off the Golden Gate Bridge. Both Seattle and San Francisco were on the West Coast—the bus ride couldn't take that long. I Googled directions. *Fuck*, I thought: it was much farther away than anticipated.

2:58 p.m.

I pounded the refresh button.

Two new emails popped up. Penn and Wellesley.

Penn. *In.*

I exhaled.

Wellesley. *In.* Wellesley was good! Secretary of State Hillary Clinton had gone there. If it was good enough for her, it was good enough for me. I wouldn't jump off any bridges.

*Maybe there's a chance.*

Refresh.

Refresh.

Refresh.

The anxiety wrapped around me like a boa constrictor.

At exactly 3:00 p.m., I read in the subject line: "Your application to Harvard College."

My cursor shook as I clicked.

> *Dear Ms. Nietfeld*
> *I am delighted to inform you that the Committee on*
> *Admissions and Financial Aid has voted to offer you a*
> *place in the Harvard Class of 2014.*

I saw the word "delighted" and screamed. My voice echoed across the library, bouncing against the glass walls. Light filled my chest, my torso a hot-air balloon. My legs took off, past the disheveled patrons at computers, down the escalators, out into the drizzle, where I screamed, "Yes, yes, yes!"

And in a moment it was real. After so many months, years, of bracing myself for a "We regret to inform you," my body went loose. It could so easily have been a no, but I had been chosen.

My life was going to be easy now. No more wondering where I was going to sleep. I'd never steal another hat, another calculator, another sweater from the lost and found, like this one that was getting wet. My future seemed to unfurl in front of me: a home with rugs and plants, art in frames on the wall behind glass, piles and piles of books—new ones I'd never read. An armchair. Someone else in another armchair. I was going to bike down a street in New York, a canopy of ginkgoes, brownstones flanking me, skyscrapers, bodegas, sidewalks filled with friendly people like me who loved art, who believed in dreams, who once longed to escape a life that didn't fit them and now congregated in celebration.

My arms tingled. I breathed in again and again, my mouth open, as if I could exhale my old air of desperation and replace it with new oxygen. Everything was going to be different. I'd drink a Frappuccino every day, I'd have air-conditioning in every room, a jacket so warm I'd never feel cold, boots that didn't leak, brand-name jeans with ornate stitching on the butt, highlights I didn't give myself from a box.

Soon, people were going to look at me and see a "Harvard student" instead of a greasy-haired teenager who stank of nervous sweat. The shame of my past would be erased because I *meant* something. A group of people had chosen me, selected me as worthy. All that work, the Quiet Times, the evenings at the kitchen counter in Lakeville, working toward a goal I couldn't see, something so far off—my closest thing to faith— had paid off. It was redeemed.

My life would become inconceivable. I'd buy sandwiches on baguettes and vacation in Paris. So many wonders, things I couldn't even understand yet, far from my old life of constant crises and budgeting for stamps. Entire vocabularies of happiness, unknown.

When they heard the news, Kelly would be shocked, Dr. Kat and Jane and Annette thrilled. Dave and Jan would be ashamed—humiliated—that they ever doubted me. I'd be treasured and adored. At school, the other kids would wonder why they underestimated me, how they didn't see.

I jumped up and down, screaming. People stared, but I thought, *Fuck you all*. I slumped against the wall of the library entryway, sweater damp, exhausted and finally satisfied.

## Eighteen

My mom didn't pick up when I called her. I tried a couple of times and then left a message, just saying that I had news. Dr. Kat called me almost immediately and was elated. We only spoke for a few minutes as tears rushed to my eyes, happy I could make her proud. When it was over, I dialed Annette.

"I got into Harvard," I told her, wondering how many times I'd say it before it felt real.

"Emi," she said, "that's wonderful." I thought I would never stop smiling, eyes burning from the tears pooled at the edges. It seemed possible my face was stuck like that, permanently. We talked about my plans—yes, I was going to go, I said, was it even a question?—before Annette offered, "I have to admit, my husband and I thought you had no chance."

I stopped smiling. I was still sitting on the floor of the library entrance, hand cupped around my phone to mask the sounds of revolving doors. "What?"

She said she'd always known I was smart, "but it's just so hard to get in. For anyone."

*I thought you believed in me,* I wanted to tell her. To me, the only way to believe in me was to think that no matter the odds, I would defy them. At that moment, anything other than praise felt like criticism.

Annette asked me about financial aid, which would come later. The question seemed to advise me not to get my hopes up: I could have gotten into Harvard and then still not be able to go.

"I should go," I told her. "I need to see where else I got in."

I went back inside but found myself locked out of my computer. I went to the librarian to ask for another visitor code. "There's one code per day," she told me.

"But I had to leave," I said, "to make a phone call." I leaned forward toward her and whispered, "I got into Harvard."

Those four words couldn't help but make me happy again, realizing all over that what was a distant possibility ten minutes ago was now reality.

But the librarian did not seem impressed. She said that she'd seen me there before and that the visitor codes were not for people from out of state; I was lucky to get them at all. She warned me that it was the last time, that I should not expect to use their computers tomorrow.

She spoke matter-of-factly, as though this were a speech she gave all the time. Suddenly I understood the way I looked to her: my rumpled T-shirt, my grown-out hair. I was just like any of the other homeless teenagers who killed time at the library, Harvard or no Harvard. I had never felt categorized so swiftly or so harshly, at the time I least expected it.

She offered up a code and I accepted. "Thank you," I said with all the "fuck you" my voice could bear.


A FEW HOURS LATER, my mom called. I picked up and she answered, "You got into Harvard!"

"How do you know?" I snapped. "Who told you?" Could Annette have already called her? Dr. Kat? Did Harvard email parents?

"You didn't seem sad on the voicemail! Your mom's not stupid, you know."

"Why didn't you let me tell you?" I had wanted to tell my mom that I got into Harvard. I'd gotten in, but I wouldn't get to say it to her.

"Do you remember that when you were in fourth grade, you were already reading at the college level? And Ms. King at Lakeville was so impressed. She said a lot of college students struggle with *Pilgrim at Tinker Creek*. But you read it just for fun!"

I wanted to scream. My mom's praise wasn't the acknowledgment of shared reality that I'd wanted. To her, everything was perfect: of course I had gotten into Harvard. To her, my feat was almost obvious. But I was standing alone in the rain, in my cardigan, without an umbrella, still upset from the librarian's brusque treatment. *Don't you get it?* I wanted to yell at her. *Do you have any idea how hard this was? And how much harder you made it?*

Before, I would have raised my voice, but in a matter of hours, my position had shifted. I was no longer just the daughter annoyed or wronged by my mom, or an underprivileged person in a sweaty T-shirt. Now I was the beneficiary of unbelievable good fortune. As my mom monologued, it dawned on me: from now on, others might expect me to live up to a certain standard of behavior. When people weren't judging me for the ways I was unpolished, they would expect me to be gracious and self-aware, cognizant of all of my advantages.

I did not feel up to the task.

After I hung up with my mom, I sought validation. I posted "Crimson" on my Facebook wall. I emailed Charlotte. Besides Jane, I wondered who else cared. I told the barista at Starbucks, who said, "That's nice," as if it were my half birthday. The man at the hostel who'd asked my mom for my hand in marriage looked offended when I told him.

I FELT RELIEVED to get back to campus, where phase two of my acclaim could begin. On the first day of class, I lingered after each hour, waiting for the teacher to pull me aside and congratulate me. I had my reply planned: "I'm thrilled! I'm still in shock. I couldn't have done it without your help." I packed up my pens one by one. My French teacher was still erasing the whiteboard as the next hour's students started filing in. I sighed and dragged myself to my next class.

My peers weren't congratulating me either. Only seven people liked the Facebook post I made about Harvard (the single word "Crimson"), including Jane. ("It was a little cryptic," she explained.) Dining hall gossip still centered on the valedictorian organist who had gotten into both Harvard *and* Yale. Every time I heard his name I fumed. Whenever the opportunity arose, I vindictively cited his unfair advantage: every fancy school needed someone to play their organ so that it didn't get frigid. My classmates rolled their eyes. In our room, I asked Jane, "Do people even know I got into Harvard?"

"Of course they know," she said. She snapped her bracelet against her wrist. "They're just jealous." It was a tough year for college admissions: the first chair violin hadn't even gotten an audition at Juilliard. Jane had only gotten into one conservatory.

I tried to bring up financial aid at every opportunity. "I would have gone to Wellesley!" I said, when my social studies teacher asked us to share where we were going. "But I didn't get enough money." Everyone could see through my lie, but it was true that finances took away any pretext of a decision. Harvard had offered me a full ride, including fees and books and plane tickets. Wellesley, Smith, Mount Holyoke, and Penn all wanted me to pay ten thousand dollars a year. I'd get reciprocal in-state tuition at the University of Wisconsin, but that still made it the most expensive option—except for Harvey Mudd, which offered me two hundred thousand dollars in student loans.

Even though my classmates didn't know about my dire home and financial situation, I tried to imply that everyone else was lucky, not me. In fact, I was jealous of my classmates who just picked where they wanted to go without considering cost or future job prospects. I wouldn't trade my school for theirs, but if it were a package deal, I would have traded in my whole life. As I watched others go around campus in their University of Michigan and Eastman School of Music and Kalamazoo College apparel, I wouldn't feel comfortable wearing a Harvard sweatshirt—it would seem like bragging. Besides, I didn't have a Harvard sweatshirt.

When I got to our room, a care package lay on Jane's bed, with a T-shirt from her new college.

I sat down at our desk. "Why isn't anyone happy for me?"

"I'm happy for you," Jane said. I met her eyes and knew she meant it, even though she was sad about her own rejections.

I smiled. At least in this one tiny room on campus, I belonged. I asked Jane, "Do you want to get married on Facebook?"

"I thought you'd never ask!"

THERE WAS ANOTHER WINDFALL that spring: I won the Horatio Alger scholarship contest. In order to go to the mandatory conference, from which I'd travel to Harvard's prospective students weekend (Visitas), I needed to get permission from my teachers to leave. It felt like a final chance for them to congratulate me, though I'd mostly given up hope.

The last teacher to sign was Mrs. Z., my calculus teacher. She knew more about my life than almost anyone on campus, because she'd written me a recommendation letter for the adversity-dependent scholarship.

Mrs. Z. pulled down her glasses and squinted at the paper. She looked up at me. "You shouldn't be missing school."

"I'm not even missing multivariable." I'd miss one hour of class, total.

"Why do you need to go to this if you already know you're attending?" she asked. The hostility of her tone shocked me. Why did I need *anything*, now that I had gotten into Harvard? Mrs. Z.'s question seemed to call out my failure to be immediately satisfied, as if she could see right through me and tell I was upset no one had sent me a sweatshirt.

"The financial aid office already bought me a plane ticket," I offered.

Mrs. Z. looked into my eyes and told me her alma mater, a state school, was a good college, too.

"I never said it wasn't."

"You could have at least applied there."

"I only got to apply to ten schools!" I replied, frustrated.

"Well, I only applied to one." Mrs. Z. signed the form and held it out for me to snatch away.

I wanted to beg Mrs. Z. to tell me what I had done wrong. She had always been good to me: teaching my independent study, urging me to join the math team, taking me to dinner at her house. Later, I found out that she'd offered the same cold treatment to the girl who'd gotten into Harvard the year before me. The institution held a strange power to make someone who knew me and cared about me suddenly turn sour.

And how upset could I be about it? I had worked so hard to pretend that I had transcended circumstances that were still unfolding. It seemed like I had fooled everyone. Everything Harvard promised me in the future seemed to make me unworthy of compassion in the now.

I WAS GRATEFUL to get off campus to attend the Horatio Alger conference. It felt like, finally, the recognition I deserved: up to twenty thousand dollars—whatever Harvard didn't cover—and a free trip to Washington, DC. They put up the 104 scholars in the Fairmont, a confusingly nice hotel. We spent the first day learning table manners. Then we had a meet and greet with a Supreme Court justice, Clarence Thomas, who hugged all the girls and then lined up with us for a group picture in rented gowns and tuxedos. Condoleezza Rice stood in the center.

I had no idea what was going on. It all made me feel uneasy; the hairs on my arms perked up. After the group photo, we were ushered into the balcony of an auditorium. Below us, the donors dined. This was the induction ceremony for the new Distinguished Americans—eleven men and Condoleezza Rice—whose biographies they'd sent us in advance and assigned us to study.

After the lights dimmed, the national anthem played. At the peak of the song, a live bald eagle soared across the auditorium to rapturous applause. One of the MCs, Lou Dobbs, announced the special guests in attendance: Newt Gingrich and Rush Limbaugh.

In a flash, I understood: these were conservatives. The men onstage introduced the "deserving scholars," of which I was one. Fifty thousand students had applied for 104 scholarships. We were proof that anyone could do it.

While they lauded us for overcoming tremendous obstacles, there was no sense that those obstacles were unjust. In fact, the teenagers sitting in the balcony were evidence that no one needed a social safety net— because we had made it out.

I looked around to see if anyone else picked up on how they were using us, but the other teenagers sat with hands neatly folded in their laps, just as we'd been taught. I wanted to say something, to do something, but what? I needed the money. I disagreed with the "pull yourselves up by your bootstraps" talk when it applied to the other scholars, who were clearly still children, mesmerized to fly on airplanes and leave their home states, often for the first time. But I agreed when it applied to me: I had to be "deserving" in order to be worth a chance at a better life. And was I? Was I more deserving than the kid to my right or the kid to my left, kids who weren't going to Harvard?

As we sat ramrod straight in our rented finery, there was nothing to rage against besides indolence and sloth. All we had in common was our incredible individual powers of will, which made me feel so lonely.

———

BREAKFAST THE NEXT MORNING was at the Ritz-Carlton. I sat at a table with the midwestern donors, who acted like they were meeting celebrities. A well-preserved lady asked the table, "What were your adversities?"

We went around the table, naming items from the checklist we'd filled out six months prior. Embarrassed, I said, "I was in foster care."

At lunch in a State Department dining room, a boy gave a speech about growing up in shelters with his single dad. The twenty thousand dollars made college possible for him. I had to wipe my eyes with my cloth napkin. His desire for a better life was so pure. *He* deserved it. Not me. I lied. I stole things. At the conference, I puked viennoiseries in bathrooms that had washcloths rolled up next to the sink.

The speaker sat down at my table. The donors complimented him, then asked where he was going to college. He'd start at community college and then transfer. "What about the rest of you?" a donor asked. My heart gathered in my throat.

I paused, choked, and said, "Harvard."

"What will you study?" a woman asked just me, excited. A businessman overheard and took down my address in order to send me a five-piece set of luggage for all the traveling I'd surely do. A gray-haired Minnesotan asked me, "Have you ever had a mentor?" When I said yes, her family's foundation gave me an additional scholarship. They would send me care packages full of snack-size Chex Mix, chewing gum, microwave popcorn, with printouts of platitudes to cheer me up. They'd also buy me a Harvard sweatshirt and take my picture in front of a red-brick building for their promotional catalog.

All the attention complicated my disdain about the ceremony the night before. These people were so kind. They genuinely wanted to help me. They saw me as a hero for pursuing my selfish dreams and selling out in my applications. After not getting the validation I craved from my teachers and my mom, I was eager to be honored, even if it felt dehumanizing. Despite the fact that the scholars were there because bad things had happened to us, the conference was a celebration. Each handshake reminded me of the heartbreaks that won me the award. But there was no room to acknowledge the bad things: we had already triumphed.

After the conference, Dr. Kat introduced me to one of her friends, a financier in New York whose West Village townhouse spanned two addresses. I went to visit her before flying back to school. The banker's butler greeted me, then she whisked me up in an elevator to her terrace, where she offered me bottled water from a special bottled-water fridge. We sat down, I told her my carefully rehearsed life story, and she wrote me a check for the most money I'd ever seen in my life. She'd sponsor me in college, she offered, sending me spending money every month. "All you have to do is pay it forward someday," she said.

I walked to a park holding the check, stunned. I told myself I was crying out of gratitude, but it was more. Finally lavished with gifts, now that I'd proven myself, I thought about how much I needed, how desperate I'd been. *That's over*, I told myself. *Now I'm a Harvard student.* But somehow the heaviness lingered.


When I got to Cambridge for prospective students weekend, I was surprised to learn that the admissions office consisted of a well-appointed suite with wallpaper and rugs—far from the interrogation chamber of my nightmares. They handed out T-shirts at check-in, and then my admissions officer shook my hand. I was stunned. I couldn't believe she was a real person who recognized my name.

In a caravan of prospective students, I walked from one event to another. A boy asked the group, "Where are you deciding between?" He wore faded red shorts that made him look like his social worker hadn't taken him shopping in years.

"Yale," a blond guy answered. The two of them wore the same ugly slip-on shoes made of tan leather that someone called "Sperrys."

"Princeton or Yale," a brunette said. A single pearl rested in the hollow between her collarbones.

"I'm definitely going to Harvard," a girl in a sundress said. Another girl, wearing a scratchy-looking half-zip sweater, nodded. I nodded, too.

The boy who posed the question added, "Well, I'm thinking about MIT."

The students who'd gotten into other schools that mattered followed Mr. Maybe MIT to discuss their very important decisions, ditching me and the other two girls.

I tried to hide the sting.

"Where are you from?" the girl in the sundress asked me. I looked down. She wore the Sperrys, too. My all-black Converse were held together with black duct tape.

"Minnesota."

"Oh my God!" the second girl said. "I'm from Minnesota, too! I go to Blake. Where do you go?"

I wasn't sure what to say: *Between three and six different high schools, depending on how you counted?* Then I remembered my out and felt relieved. "I go to boarding school."

Sundress girl perked up. "I go to boarding school, too! In Massachusetts."

"It's crazy; we have so much in common," the Minnesotan said.

I braced myself for one of them to ask for my SAT score, now that we were all friends. I felt ashamed of my 2190 (out of 2400). It was just about average for Harvard, but that average included a substantial group of recruited athletes.

The Minnesotan walked closer to me. "So how did you get in?" she asked. "What was your *thing*?"

I froze.

How did I get in? I felt like I had prostituted my life story while conveniently leaving out all of my mistakes. It seemed like the price I paid for my new future. It had never occurred to me that my fellow students would *ask*.

I had an idea. "I did creative writing."

"What did you write about?" the girl in the sundress asked.

"My dad had a sex change," I blurted out. As soon as the indelicate explanation was out of my mouth, I wished I could unsay it, worried the girls would be too interested.

"Wow, what a crazy story!" she said, politely, then turned to the other girl. "What about you?"

"I started a nonprofit in Africa."

"Oh my God, I did too!"

The two of them sped up and walked side by side, leaving me behind.

I wanted to throw my new water bottle with a funny mouthpiece into Garden Street and scream. Why hadn't I started a charity in Africa? What had I been doing all through high school? What the fuck was wrong with me?

The Minnesotan and the boarding schooler stood close, already looking like fast friends. From a distance, they resembled slightly healthier girls from the Methodist Hospital Eating Disorder Institute. My future classmates weren't all intellectuals interested only in books, as I'd expected. Instead, they had a social code that I couldn't understand, involving "boat shoes," necklaces that looked like rotated four-leaf clovers, and liberal use of "Nantucket red," which apparently referred to a vacation island. School hadn't even started, yet the hierarchy seemed just as brutal as the application process had been.

But then I got to the Quad, where the activity fair was held, and saw the fluorescent green grass—just like a postcard. I walked up and down tables advertising the hundreds of clubs and student organizations. I could write forty hours a week for *The Harvard Crimson* and walk onto the rowing team and join the Premedical Society, the Global Health Forum, the French Club, *and* the Francophone Society. I wrote down my email again and again.

Each time I signed up for a mailing list, I felt hope: the void that college applications had once filled would vanish again. In a few short months, I'd flit from class to meeting to dorm. I could become the type of person they wanted, that I owed them to be, for taking me and giving me this chance.

I learned quickly. By the end of the weekend, when students asked why I got in, I replied, "I won a national writing competition. What about you?"

My Facebook marriage to Jane got more than a hundred likes—an all-time high. We were officially a duo as we danced outside the Melody Freeze to Miley Cyrus's "Party in the U.S.A." and memorized all the lyrics to a YouTube song called "Show Me Your Genitals." We were both weirdos, but we were weird together.

Shortly after, I got an unexpected post on my Facebook wall. Somewhere in the blaze of college applications, Michelle had sent me a friend request. I'd accepted. Now she wrote for all of my 378 friends to see: "I hope that your profile is incorrect in indicating that you are married."

Our last interaction had been in January—I'd invited Michelle to a livestreamed *Red Wheelbarrow* reading. I signed my message "Love" but got no response.

Anger flared through me. I'd been so disappointed by all the people who hadn't acknowledged my feat that until I got that message on my wall, it hadn't occurred to me that Michelle should be proud.

My fingers pounded my keyboard. "Nice to see you comment on that and not on the fact that I'm going to HARVARD."

I wished that she had never reached out. I would have preferred radio silence. For years, I'd held out hope that my remarkable accomplishments would eventually rouse adults into caring. But now I had pulled off the greatest possible coup, to no avail. No other dreams glistened on the horizon, promising me the love I craved. That reality was crushing.

A week later, I got a long message from Michelle. "Dear, I have loved you since you were born," she started, then explained that she thought she was sterile. I knew the story from my mom—Michelle hadn't wanted to become a parent but hadn't insisted on birth control either—but it stung coming from the source. Michelle hadn't wanted me. Now she was using that to justify why my childhood had played out like it did.

She apologized for the "many mistakes" she'd made, without specifying what those mistakes were. Still, it was more than I could hope for, and made me think the rest of the note might be the acknowledgment I craved.

But then Michelle wrote that she was "deeply traumatized" by losing custody and expressed her pain that I "wouldn't" speak with her after that. She listed the times I'd hurt her: when she tried to visit me at school, against court orders and without my knowledge, reminding me that I'd stayed home. I hadn't used an email account that my teacher was supposedly going to give me but didn't. "You were everything to me yet you rejected me." She wrote that I had broken her heart and it had never healed, that she knew logically that because I'd been a child, she shouldn't blame me, "yet emotionally I feel abandoned and betrayed."

"I'm seventeen years old. I'm still a child," I wrote back. I told Michelle I was unfriending her and willed myself to be strong and do it, although I felt guilty.

I read Michelle's message to Jane, snickering. "Isn't this ridiculous? There are no congratulations about Harvard. Nothing."

That was what stood out to me, everything in my life orbiting the fact of my acceptance.

Jane stopped snapping her bracelet. "Emi, are you okay?"

"Yeah, of course I'm okay." How could I not be okay? This note had proven to me that the only people who would love me had a stake in my perfection. I'd made that bargain in my college applications and doubled down at Horatio Alger. "I'm just grateful to have one crazy parent in my life instead of two."

"I'm so sorry."

"Whatever," I said. "At least I'm going to Harvard." I knew that it wasn't enough, but it was all I had.

EARLY ONE MORNING, Scholastic called me. The woman on the phone seemed nervous. She wanted to confirm that they could put my essays up online with the other winners'.

Sensing this wasn't a routine call, I asked, "Why?"

"Well, they're very personal."

*Of course,* I thought, *that's why they're called "personal essays."* In addition to "Scrambled Eggs," I'd submitted one called "Speedbird" about my relationship with Adderall, and a third about my mom's job as a crime scene photographer and how it influenced her response when I was assaulted in middle school. While I didn't feel comfortable talking about these topics in real life, I'd tried to transform these experiences into art. I was proud of my craft, not ashamed about the substance. But even after Scholastic confirmed and had my mom sign off, they decided not to include the piece that referenced sexual violence. Someone explained to me that it was "sensitive." Shame bloomed over me each time I thought about the situation. Even though that essay helped win the ten thousand dollars, I wished I'd never written it. From now on, I knew to keep my mouth shut. A few weeks later, before I spoke to the first of the reporters calling about the Scholastic awards, Interlochen's publicist urged me not to bring up my family or what I wrote about. "Stick to the awards." I nodded, having internalized what I should and should not discuss.

"If you smile into the receiver you'll sound friendlier," the marketing guy said, handing me the phone. A *Traverse City Record Eagle* reporter was on the line, ready to make me into a human interest story. I gushed with appropriate gratitude and then blabbed about the latest thing I'd won: three thousand dollars to excavate Roman ruins in Northern England. With that and some money from Scholastic, I'd spend the summer backpacking in Europe, where no one would turn me away from hostels for being underage. On my first stop, I'd visit Charlotte in Germany.

For fifteen minutes, I successfully avoided mentioning my family and my past. I wondered if it would be best to avoid those topics for the rest of my life.

When I read the bland write-up that resulted, running with a photo of me posing in my lucky gray cardigan, I stopped worrying so much. I talked to more reporters from other local papers. Then I got a frantic email from my mom, whose coworkers had sent around an article from the *St. Paul Pioneer Press*. I had no idea what she was talking about: I'd stuck to the script.

But from the latest article, I learned that I had written about "struggling with a prescription drug addiction." Apparently, this reporter had actually read my essays. I was unbelievably embarrassed that she was calling it "a prescription drug addiction," especially because I had taken an Adderall that morning.

My skin crawled as I trudged back to the dorm. I swiped the scissors off my desk and went into the bathroom. I leaned over the sink and snipped my hair close to the roots. I was sick and tired of acting like a goody fucking two-shoes when I wasn't one at all. I was duplicitous and they had exposed me. I grabbed handfuls and sawed.

If I wanted to be happy, to be deserving, it was going to take a lot more than just smiling into the phone. I had to change. I had to become someone worthy of the amazing gift I'd been given. Wasn't that the bargain I had made when I first wrote to Dr. Kat? I'd cemented my commitment with each college application I'd sent in. Yes, I hadn't understood what I'd done at the time—I had been so young, just barely seventeen—but now I was seventeen and a half, on the cusp of adulthood, and I had to own up to the fact that I owed people.

I decided I'd quit Adderall as soon as I graduated. I had to at least try to be an overcomer, the person I'd pretended I was and that I'd promised to be.

## Nineteen

After the awards were publicly announced, I became more popular on campus. With my short bleached hair and bony physique, I resembled the rapper Eminem. I won "Biggest Hipster" in the yearbook. On the senior trip to Mackinac Island, I convinced Jane to ride a tandem bike with me. I steered, assuring her everything would be fine, before we crashed in a laughing heap. On MORP night, Interlochen's backward version of prom, we danced in a water park's ballroom and then went bowling. I wore my American Apparel leggings that zipped up all the way, with my hair spiked and no bra.

Annette flew out for graduation. My mom tried to crash her hotel room, until Annette booked my mom her own. I kept persuading Jane to wait to pick up our gowns until the only ones left were XXL and comically large. We posed for selfies in our room and danced one last time to "Show Me Your Genitals."

After the ceremony, I thrust myself into Jane's arms. I didn't expect to miss her so much, but I did. We were normal. She was my best friend, my Facebook wife, with me through college application turmoil and my renewed self-destruction. I'd no longer have her sleeping within arm's reach.

"You know where to find me," she said. And I knew—whenever I needed her, she'd be sitting at her kitchen table, snapping her bracelet and frantically sending Facebook messages.

I STAYED WITH ANNETTE during the two weeks before the Scholastic ceremony. Without Adderall, I felt like an electric toothbrush running out of battery. I slept for twelve hours a night. Oblivious to my chemical comedown, Annette took me on brisk walks and fed me Weetabix cereal. As each day passed, I felt less like a fraud.

Annette insisted that I look great for the awards. She took me to get my hack-job haircut smoothed out and then drove me to every mall in the southwest metro area, hunting for a dress. For someone who didn't care about fashion, Annette had a very high bar: nothing too matronly or too childish, nothing black, nothing too short or too prudish. I had to look young and radiant. Finally, we found a green Calvin Klein sheath dress on the clearance rack. There was only one left.

"Try it on," Annette said, handing me the hanger.

We both stood in front of the mirror and stared at my reflection. The dipping neckline framed my neck and my clavicles. It hugged my waist, skimmed over my lower body, and stopped at my knees. I stood on my tiptoes and felt very tall. I ruffled my hair so it stood on end.

"It's perfect," Annette said. I looked the way I imagined in my fantasies of success. "Now you just need shoes." At the Mall of America, I held up six-inch platform stilettos. Annette shrugged. "You're young. They're fun. And I don't want to shop forever."

I flipped the shoe over to see the price on the sole.

"Don't be silly, Emi," she said, grabbing the box, the decision made.

That night, I sat on the floor of Annette's den. I divided my things between the backpack I'd take with me and what I would leave behind.

"I wish you wouldn't go," Annette said, standing in the doorway.

"I've always wanted to see Europe." I rolled up a T-shirt. "Plus, there's nowhere for me here." I waited for her to tell me what alternative I had. I couldn't stay with her; she was hosting her in-laws during July. As a seventeen-year-old, I couldn't exactly rent an apartment for three months. Hostels abroad wouldn't care about my age. I'd save money *and* see the world.

"It's not safe. A girl? Alone?"

"They don't have guns there like they do here. Besides, I'm visiting a friend. Then I'm going to excavate the Roman fort near Hadrian's Wall."

Annette folded her arms and watched me. When I finished packing two boxes of my journals and sweaters, she put them deep in one of her closets. "Your mom is crazy for letting you go," she told me.

Even though my mom was coming to New York, too, Annette insisted on driving me to the airport so I wouldn't miss my flight. At the check-in desk, she handed me five hundred dollars in twenty-dollar bills.

"It's nothing," she said. "Get yourself something nice. You're going to look great in the dress. Be safe."

We hugged goodbye, just our shoulders touching. I teared up as I watched her go, before she turned and told me, "Call me to tell me if your mom makes it on the plane!"

IN OUR FANCY HOTEL ROOM, my mom and I were a family reunited. She took my picture around the city. I got to tour *The New Yorker* and read my poems at Bryant Park. We went to Macy's in Herald Square—"the world's largest department store," my mom remarked seven times—to buy a shirt she could return after the awards ceremony. Even Dr. Kat was coming.

I bowed onstage at Carnegie Hall. When a judge hung a gold medal around my neck, the weight of it completed me. An actor read from

"Scrambled Eggs," my essay about Michelle. When the audience sighed and laughed and clapped, it felt like it wasn't for my words—it was for me.

At the after-party for the donors, I gabbed while smiling effortlessly. I gushed about my summer plans backpacking through Europe to a reporter from *The New York Observer* and told him about the books I planned to write. A man in a suit came up to me. "I read your stuff," he said. "It's brave."

"All I have are my secrets," I replied. Secrets soon to be anthologized in *The Best Teen Writing of 2010*. We shared a laugh. He gave me his business card and offered to help if he ever could. When he left, I looked at it: he was the CEO of Scholastic Books. I looked across the room and saw my mom gesturing wildly, probably bragging about her "brilliant" daughter. She played the proud mother so well. And in that dress with the medal around my neck, I was finally the right daughter.

FIVE DAYS LATER, I wrapped my gray cardigan around me, shivering, as the plane crossed over the Atlantic. I couldn't sleep, I was too excited: I was finally going abroad. All my stuff was in my backpack, as usual, but now that made me an intrepid backpacker instead of a homeless minor. I had a note from my mom that said I was free to do as I pleased. If anyone needed confirmation, they could call her employer and ask them to search the office intranet for "Dawn's daughter wins prestigious award."

In nine hours, I'd see Charlotte. How many times had I shut my eyes and imagined her? The smooth skin of her face, her fluffy hair, the way she looked off into space as if reciting a poem to herself. We'd only have four days together, but that seemed like enough to rekindle what we'd had before she left Interlochen. Now I'd finally tell her everything: about my mom and her hoarding, about how I thought about her on the

Greyhound bus or when I woke up on people's sofas or fell asleep in my car.

In the Freiburg train station, a girl with shoulder-length hair stood in front of me. Then I recognized a familiar old sweater. "Charlotte!"

"Tes cheveux," she said. *Your hair.* I touched my head self-consciously. I'd hoped Charlotte would love my new look, my way of coming out, though I wasn't sure as what. I noticed her hair—long and conventional—and wondered if this meant something, too. We hugged stiffly.

I couldn't believe I'd imagined us making out in front of old churches.

In the morning, we set off for Berlin. The Franglais that had flowed between us was suddenly stilted. Within an hour, we'd lapsed into English. It felt weird, wrong. Suddenly, now that I could understand everything she was saying, the mystery was gone.

"Don't let anyone hear you speak English," Charlotte whispered to me. "They'll know we're American."

"Why are you ashamed of your country?" I asked.

"They'll think we're ignorant." She folded her arms. I judged her for caring what a bunch of strangers thought. Even if they were cool European strangers and I cared, too.

When we got to Berlin, I was in awe. "It looks just like IKEA except the signs are in German. All the words are super long."

She shook her head, disapproving. "I can't believe you'd say this whole country looks like *IKEA.*"

"I *love* IKEA." When the big store opened across from the Mall of America, my mom and I would spend weekend afternoons in their air-conditioning, gawking at the square footage of the tiny apartments, pretending to live in those immaculate boxes. My mom loved their Swedish meatballs.

"You're ignorant, too," Charlotte said.

Of course I was ignorant. Did Charlotte look at me as I'd looked at

Dave and Jan? In a flash, I hated her, just like I'd hated the Methodist girls. I resented her liberal arts college and her life, with parents and a home and boxes of books she shipped over to Europe.

"You don't know what it's like to need money," I spat out.

"At least I'm not going to school with the capitalist pigs," she retorted. I hated that Harvard automatically made me the oppressor. But I worried it was true. After all, I'd been plotting how to live in a glass box in the sky, clean and perfect like one of those IKEA apartments. I wasn't pure like her, dead set on dedicating my life to art while subsisting on baguettes and Brie. She had values, I decided, and I didn't, which is why I had adored her.

We walked back to the hostel in silence.


In Berlin, I got an email telling me about a gap year internship at Disney. My admissions officer knew that, in my attempts to go abroad, I'd applied for a State Department program to study language for a summer or a year. They'd rejected me, but the opportunity made my admissions officer think of me, in case I wanted to defer college.

"Guess what?" I told Charlotte. I bubbled with excitement that the officer remembered me and my interests and believed I could work somewhere so prestigious.

Charlotte made a noise from the back of her throat. "Disney? I can't believe you'd even consider working at an evil corporation. Do I know you at all?"

"Did I ever know you?"

"I'm going to bed."

As I watched her walk away, I wondered how much of our shared language was misunderstanding. That night in my bunk, almost two years prior, she'd said she didn't know who she was. I'd replied that I didn't care. Maybe that was truer than I meant: I just didn't want to know. That way, I could pretend she was exactly who I needed.

At the end of our four days, I felt relieved to say goodbye. She reminded me of all my desperation, the way I'd overstepped boundaries by showing up at Kelly's office, sending my teachers emails, inviting myself to stay at people's houses.

As Charlotte's face got small in the window of the train, I exhaled in relief: I knew how to be alone.

I WANDERED AROUND EUROPE, marveling. To save money, I ate bread and sometimes cheese. I drank local beers, which were cheaper than bottled water. I only threw up two or three times.

Every few days, I emailed my mom, but she didn't care where I was going. She knew I'd be fine. A few thousand dollars wouldn't last the summer in France, so I took a sleek red train to Munich, then a Soviet-era train to Prague. One week after saying goodbye to Charlotte, I watched the Danube shimmer outside the window of my bus to Budapest. I believed that my life, from then on out, would be a parade of wonders, each more fascinating than the last.

My eleven-dollar hostel was in an old, empty building, through a courtyard and down a dark, crumbling hall. I found it hopelessly charming. The two men who worked there sat in the kitchen smoking. I dumped my stuff on a bed in the otherwise-vacant dorm room and then went to see *The Road*, the film based on Cormac McCarthy's novel.

I nursed a beer while a man and his ten-year-old son trudged through a post-apocalyptic wasteland. When the father began coughing, I started to cry: it sounded just like the cough I'd had for a year in middle school. The pair's only hope was to reach the ocean, where maybe they'd survive. The father wore a gun tied to his waist, with two bullets left—a visual reminder of suicide's temptation. That made me cry harder, thinking of the bleak years, how I'd wanted so badly for the pain to stop.

At the end of the film, they reached the ocean. Then for ten long minutes, the father died.

I covered my face. I couldn't watch. The boy's loss felt familiar: losing the person who cared for me, again and again. My body racked with each inhale. My knees drew up to my chest. The story seemed impossible, a tragic ending with no way to turn it around.

Then, in the final five minutes, a dirt-covered man showed up. Terrified, the boy pulled his father's pistol. But the man invites the boy to come with him.

"How do I know you're one of the good guys?" the kid asked.

"You don't," he said. "You'll just have to take a shot." Hope bloomed through me. In the final two minutes of the movie, the boy met his new family: brother, sister, dog. The mom touched his face, said they had been following him, watching, hoping he'd join them. The kid was scared and heartbroken, but had his chance to start over and be loved.

The credits rolled. People around me stood up and left, but I kept crying as a man came to sweep popcorn off the floor. Faith in humanity overwhelmed me as I walked back to the hostel, tears blurring the streetlights: any situation could seem desolate and then suddenly light up with hope. Like my own life. I was off Adderall. I hadn't cut myself in nine months, since the dumb Y. I missed Charlotte, but I was living up to the person I'd said I was in my applications. The future spread out in front of me—my new start as a Harvard student, when my past wouldn't matter anymore—and it felt like mercy.

I DIDN'T SEE any other guests at the hostel, so I sat down with the two men in the kitchen. My chair was in the corner, wedged between a bookshelf and a dining table.

"Do you want a drink?" the blond guy offered.

"No thanks. I already had a beer at the movie." We laughed: I was such a goody two-shoes.

"You sure?" the dark-haired guy said. I shook my head. The three of us chatted, relaxing, before the blond stood up and said, "I'm going to buy cigarettes."

Across the table from me, the man said he was thirty, from Serbia. I thought about some of Annie Leibovitz's photographs of the war, from the exhibit I saw with my mom.

"Did you grow up during the war?" I asked.

"Yes," he said. He pulled a cigarette out of a pack on the table. "You want?" I shook my head. "You want a drink? Beer? Weed?" The man told me that his family had fled the conflict when he was a child. The light from the ceiling fan cast shadows under his eyes. It made him seem handsome and mysterious with his thick accent. "What about you?" he asked. "Your story."

I felt flattered. "I'm going to Harvard in the fall," I said. Joy rushed over me, giddy about my future.

The man smiled at me. He ground out his cigarette. "Kiss," he said. It sounded like half of a question.

I felt nervous, but couldn't pinpoint why. Dr. Woods had questioned me if I liked guys. Maybe that was it. Even though my hair was short and I was wearing men's jeans and Birkenstocks—the queerest outfit I could come up with—I wasn't sure myself. I took off my glasses and leaned across the table. My lips rubbed against the man's stubble. He smelled scorched.

I recoiled.

He stood up and started undoing his belt. "Let me clean myself, I'm very dirty," he said, smiling.

Panic shot through me. "I don't want to do much more than this."

He stood right in front of me, over me, his pants down. "Why?" he asked, exposing his gnarled teeth.

I heard myself say, "I'm a virgin," voice shaking. I searched his face for any pity, any emotion that I could appeal to.

He reached for me.

My chair banged against the wall as I tried to get away. The table blocked me in. Even if I somehow pushed past him, he'd catch me before I made it through the unlit hall and down the stairs; then he'd be angry. I decided that if I did whatever he wanted, I'd be okay.

The man grabbed my head and yanked me toward him. He forced himself into my mouth.

His stench overwhelmed me. I fought not to gag at his unshowered skin. *I'm choosing this*, I told myself, trying to stay calm. *I'm choosing this.*

The man thrust into my face, banging the back of my throat. Pain shot through me. My hands flew up to his hips, bracing him, but he ripped them away, and pulled me to the front of my chair. His fingers pried into my scalp, gripping my head as he shoved harder, punishing me.

I could no longer pretend I was in control. *You're such a fucking idiot*, I told myself, *signing up for this*. The impact turned everything into starbursts, blinding me.

He jammed himself into me and held me so all I could see was the black of his pubic hair. He started yelling at me: lines from porn, in a perfect American accent. I was so startled I couldn't process what he was saying. Calling me a bitch, telling me to swallow his cock. He seemed to get angrier and angrier. I wanted to cry and beg him to explain, that I'd do what he wanted if he just stopped hurting me. But I couldn't breathe. He clutched my skull, holding me completely still. Saliva covered my nose until I was suffocating.

He pulled himself out just enough that I could take one breath. As I gasped for air, he shoved himself into my throat.

I writhed, desperate to get away. He pushed farther, groaning. I had to stop moving. If I didn't stay still, he'd rip open my windpipe. Or he'd get upset and kill me on purpose. But I couldn't control my body. The echo of his pleasure filled the room.

*He talked about a war and I said I was going to Harvard*, I thought. *You deserve it, you fucking bitch. This is my comeuppance.* Nothing had ever seemed more right, more true. I held still.

As if sensing my submission, the man let me take another breath.

Then he pried me open again, moaning as I gagged. My mind cut in and out, berating myself and feeling nothing, then pain tearing through me. Taking one breath at a time, I couldn't get enough air. I was going to pass out, the kitchen getting dark around the edges. *God*, I thought, *take it: Horatio Alger, Scholastic, Harvard. Anything to make it stop,* until there was nothing left.

Then the man started jerking off over me. Fear electrocuted me: he was mad I hadn't gotten him off. He was going to rip open my jeans, drag me onto the floor, rape me again. I felt myself get wet, the arousal making me sick, as he twisted my breast through my cardigan, my T-shirt, my sports bra.

He put himself back into my mouth. I couldn't take it anymore. I wasn't going to be able to stay calm. I imagined my body bloated with water, floating down the Danube. Then the man started to come. He pulled out and kept coming on my clothes, my lucky sweater, the one I'd worn in the newspaper.

I studied his face, all I could see. His expression was the only thing that mattered in the world. He opened his eyes. His brow seemed twisted, in rage. I hadn't pleased him. I stared at him and swallowed. Our eyes locked and I lifted my arm to my face and licked his semen off my sleeve.

He shook his head and snickered, suddenly relaxed. He reached for a box of tissues on a shelf behind my head and cleaned himself off, buckled his pants. He stuck the box in my face. "Sorry," he said, in a childish voice, like he was mocking me.

I didn't understand. Why was he saying sorry? Was I obligated to accept his apology? I took a tissue and wiped the spit and snot smeared across my face. When my hand grazed my cheek, I realized I was crying. How long had I been crying? I willed myself to stop, but I couldn't. His cum on my jeans, the taste in my mouth, tears streaming down my face—I felt so humiliated. No matter what I had achieved, I was still at the mercy of another adult.

The rapist lit a cigarette, still standing right over me. He took a drag and blew out smoke. "What's your name again?"

The question eviscerated me. I wished I'd killed myself when I had the chance.

The rapist laughed and ashed his cigarette. "Just kidding, Emi."

I clenched my fists. I wished I'd fought this man and let him kill me. Once, I had fought. At Methodist, I'd struggled.

The man said, "Kiss," and leaned down. I kissed him.

As if on cue, the other man came back in. I wiped at the cum on my jeans, frantically. The rapist stepped back to let his friend see me. The two men looked at each other, knowing.

I stood up and pushed past them, to the dorm room. I put the pillow over my head and prayed they would leave me alone.

FROM MY BED, I Facebook messaged Jane. "I seriously want to shoot myself right now. . . . I said to him, 'I don't want to go much further than this.' But he unzipped his pants. . . . And turning away of course didn't help. God, it was horrible. God awful." I told her how much my throat hurt.

Outside the dorm room, the men talked and laughed. I was too afraid to leave because they'd see me.

Jane was typing. I imagined her sitting at her kitchen table, her mom in the corner, just like winter break. I would have given anything to go back exactly one month, when we sang "Honky Tonk Badonkadonk" together in our dorm room.

"Emi Emi Emi . . . I love you, I hug you, and I am NOT judging you. I just have a silly question I want to ask." If I thought I might be a lesbian, why did I kiss him?

I shook in the dorm bed, the sheet pulled over my head. Glass clinked on the other side of the door.

"I don't really know who I am," I wrote. I hated myself for ever thinking I might be gay, for cutting my hair, for dressing like I did, in men's jeans and sports bras and ugly sandals, for falling for Charlotte. The idea that I was bi was even worse, because it carried with it the idea of promiscuity, something I felt I had just confirmed.

"I'm really sorry that happened to you, but I guess it goes to show you can't kiss every interesting guy you meet, cause you didn't really know him at all!"

Then she tried to reassure me. "It's another experience. . . . I promise everything is going to be okay."

I said we should Skype soon, but Jane didn't reply. The last thing she wrote was "I just wish I had a boyfriend."

When I woke up, my throat hurt so badly I worried I'd never speak again. I pulled my laptop out from under my pillow and slid out of the hostel to McDonald's. I wrote a frantic email to Dr. Woods, asking for advice, worried I was injured.

Then I couldn't find the key to my locker. Inside it was my pink-and-purple tie-dyed backpack, my passport, my clothes. All I had on me was my camera, my computer, a little bit of money. I wandered the city, stunned, checking my inbox again and again. Horatio Alger requested financial aid forms. A high school literary magazine called my poems "tremendously powerful" and requested line edits. A businessman's secretary asked for the right address to send a five-piece set of luggage. For whatever reason, Dr. Woods didn't write back.

I made a plan: I'd go back, find the key, get my stuff, and leave. If I didn't speak to anyone or go into the kitchen, I'd be fine. I walked up the stairs in the eerie building, flinching at the echoes my footsteps made. Just before dusk, the hallways were already dark. I eased the hostel door open, then stepped into the dorm room.

I felt him behind me. My stomach rose into my throat as I smelled him. My rapist had been just inside the door, waiting for me.

His calloused palm slid under my dress onto the bare skin of my butt. I blacked out.

I WOKE UP the next day in a hostel a mile and a half away. I had no idea how I found it or how I got there. All I had was an email asking me to leave a review, and a photograph from 11:30 the night before of a man— my rapist—smiling while he broke the lock on my locker.

I canvassed Budapest, trying to call my mom from pay phones. None of them worked. I kept needing more money, more coins, taking out cash from ATMs, buying Diet Cokes just to break the bills, holding the cans to my forehead, crying. I spoke to no one, my throat scraped raw. I couldn't email my mom, I couldn't Skype her from McDonald's—I had to be alone. Finally, I got through.

"I'm so lonely," I cried. I couldn't tell her what happened. I was trying to make myself say it: "I miss you. I want to go home." But then the stern lady came on, telling us in Hungarian that we were out of time. I had no more coins. My mom emailed back suggesting I call 800 numbers. I could go to the airport and hold up a sign reading DO YOU SPEAK ENGLISH?

The next day, desperate, I scoured the city again. Finally, I reached my mom, then the story spilled out. My mom said reassuring things while the cars in the road blasted by on the other side of the booth.

I shoved forints in until I ran out. In our final minutes, I told her I'd been planning to go to Venice next.

"I heard Venice is beautiful," my mom said, characteristically optimistic. "Make sure to buy some Venetian glass."

A FEW HOURS LATER, my mom emailed me. The subject line read "I LOVE YOU!!!" She thanked me for sharing my "awful experience." I felt relieved that she wrote "I am not saying this was your fault." She said the man "violated" me. But as I read, more self-blame set in. "You were just a kid who didn't know what to do," she wrote, advising me that going forward I should make up mind "to say NO and walk away." She told me to "say no" four times total and kept bringing up the beer I had at the movies. I hadn't even thought to feel bad about that.

It seemed like she had a point: I hadn't said the exact word "no." I hadn't walked away. Sure, I was trapped in the corner of the room, with no time to respond, but what difference did that make? I'd learned that it didn't matter what other people did to me, only how I responded. I felt like I'd failed the biggest test of my life. I had been given this amazing opportunity, to be a Harvard student, and I had fucked it up. Where had that girl gone who had fought the nurses at Methodist? Who thrashed around so she wouldn't look like a loser?

I hated myself for my submission. I hadn't fought him. I let him do it. It didn't matter that he grabbed me, used force, held me so I couldn't move, and choked me nearly unconscious. He knew what he was doing: his English was so perfect, his lines rehearsed, the fact that the other man came back in at the end. It didn't matter that he waited for me the second night, that I had no memory of what happened then.

And it didn't matter that he could have killed me. Two men, one girl— it would have been easy. If I had been brave, strong, the person the newspapers said I was, I would have let him kill me before he humiliated me.

My mom seemed to forgive me: "This certainly was a learning experience." She offered me a way forward. All I had to do was stop drinking, even beers at movie theaters, and pull myself together. "Stop acting that way. Remember who you are!" she wrote, paraphrasing from a superhero film, *The Incredibles*. She provided a list of my accomplishments, proof of why I had to cheer up.

"You are an overcomer." I flinched, thinking about the man masturbating over me. "You will overcome this. Get your bearings and grit back. Take back your power." She quoted Marsha Linehan, a famous psychologist who invented the acceptance-based therapy I'd received: "Don't make it worse!"

Barely forty-eight hours had passed since I left the hostel. It still hurt to swallow. But apparently it was time to get over it. My mom was already writing about how, one day, my story would help others, implying that it was all for the best.

I went for a walk in the night, pacing the city. On the famous chain-link bridge, I stared down at the Danube. I pressed my belly against the railing. Someone had told me that if you fall far enough, all the bones break at once. Then I remembered the donors and Annette and the admissions officer who'd signed my letter and wrote in longhand, "I hope you'll join us."

Obligation overwhelmed me. I stepped away.


THE NEXT DAY, I stood in a plaza, rubbing the foil eagle on the cover of my passport with my thumb.

My mom and I had emailed back and forth. She offered suggestions: go to the police, but wait, don't, because they'd assault me; gargle with salt water and see a doctor in three days if I was still in pain; stay at a convent. She recommended I beg Charlotte to take me in. Visiting the embassy was the only reasonable advice. I approached the guards with machine guns slung over their chests.

"I'm seventeen without my parents," I blubbered. Just that was enough to whisk me through security. A woman came to meet me and threw an arm around me. I gasped for air. "A man shoved his dick down my throat."

I sat down in a chair and wept. I felt young, like a child, which I hated. My face was swollen, my eyelids so heavy it hurt to lift them, all my things in the backpack at my feet.

A man in a suit came out and reached for me. I flinched. He took me to his office. Two framed photos hung on the wall: President Barack Obama and Secretary of State Hillary Clinton. I gave him my mom's phone number. I dug Dr. Woods's card out of my bag of toiletries.

"The police are worse than nothing," the man explained, after introducing himself as Dan. Later, I learned that the State Department provided very little help for crime victims. If *I'd* raped someone, they'd assist me in jail. But even if the laws in Hungary had been more favorable, the embassy wouldn't have helped me translate with the cops. At the time, I took this all to mean that what that man did wasn't serious. It was, like my mom seemed to suggest, a mistake that could have been prevented if I had said "no" loudly and clearly.

All the embassy could do was send me to the doctor, then take me to the airport the next day to go home. In my shock, I didn't even think about how there was no home waiting for me.

On the way to the hotel where I'd spend the night, the consular officer took me to get dinner.

"You don't have to," I told him. "Go home."

"I have to eat anyway." We were sitting at a sidewalk café while he ordered doner kebab for us. I flinched.

"Are you okay?"

"The hostel is on this street." The entrance was three hundred feet away. "It's okay. It's okay. We can stay."

Dan's jaw clenched. "In a way, I'm glad I don't know what it's called because I would be so tempted . . ." I wanted him to keep going. Maybe then I would have understood that what happened was wrong. In one of her emails, my mom suggested, "Maybe someone's brother or father would want to take justice in his own hands." This was the best I could hope for, a stranger wanting revenge, showing me compassion.

Then I realized: the embassy had never even asked for the name of the hostel.

THE CONSULAR OFFICER made me promise I wouldn't leave my room until he came to get me. I wasn't going to leave. I stared at the phone and thought about who I could call. The only place I came up with was Interlochen. I left a message on the voicemail of the dean of students, then felt dumb—what could she do for me? I no longer belonged to Interlochen.

I took my camera to the bathroom and photographed myself in the mirror: my face pulled tight, my ribs, the small breasts that didn't seem to fit on my body. Then I put my camera on the floor, knowing that I'd stop taking pictures, stop making art for a long time because everything I'd try to create would come back to that room.

I leaned over and reached down my throat. But when my fingers grazed my esophagus, pain sparked through me. I gagged, once, then folded in half, sobbing without tears: it was too much like the rape.

Suddenly, I understood that my self-harm was violence, too. I'd never be able to do it again, not really.

I clung to the sink as I sat down on the floor. I rested my forehead against the wall, overwhelmed. Even my old coping strategies, harmful as they were, had been taken from me.

I knew it would look like a kind of triumph. That someday, if I ever told this story, someone would say, or think, that my rape had a silver lining because it made me get my act together. Adults never seemed to recognize that there was a big difference between hurting myself and other people hurting me. But from then on out, I had to take care of myself; I had to stop causing my own pain. I was so broken down that, otherwise, I wasn't going to make it.

THE NEXT DAY, the consular officer drove me to the airport. I sat in the passenger seat of the black car and stared out the window at the wide, open road. It was a Saturday, Fourth of July weekend, and I knew he wasn't supposed to be working, let alone wearing a suit.

He talked the entire time, telling me a story about his last assignment, when he'd been in a bad car accident that killed everyone in the other car. His family was fine, but, he said, "for a year I was destroyed by guilt that we survived." I was grateful to him for the story, although it felt as if a plate of glass separated us, separated me from the rest of humanity.

"Of course it's not like what you went through," he said. Through his eyes, I sensed the gravity of what happened. Even though I'd try to take back the attack, to forget it, to rewrite it as an accident, my fault, a parable about privilege—in that moment it was real, irrevocable.

"One day," Dan promised me, "you will wake up and feel like yourself again." He said my life would go back to normal.

But he didn't understand that my life had never been normal. It was never going to be the same. My future would never be what it could have been. I'd worked so hard, clinging to the faith that my efforts could redeem the past, make me happy and keep me safe. That story was over.

Dan stood beside me at the Delta counter where I bought a one-way ticket for $1,200. The sum made me shiver. My mom had offered to pay, but I knew she wouldn't. Fresh guilt washed over me about the money from Dr. Kat's friend and Scholastic, squandered.

At departures, Dan talked to a security agent in Hungarian. "I asked him to go easy on you," he explained: my last-minute ticket triggered red flags. They'd frisk me again and again, inspect each pair of my underwear, and confiscate all my souvenirs.

"All you have to do is three things." I clutched my itinerary. "Get through security, get on the plane, and establish armrest superiority. And then it will be okay."

I nodded, trying to be brave. In my head I was sobbing, choking on my tears. I didn't want to get on the plane. I wanted to beg the man in the suit not to make me go. He was so kind. I didn't want to have to say goodbye to him, too.

"Just don't let anyone take the armrest, okay?"


IN FRONT OF HER LAUNDRY ROOM, Annette asked me, "What were you expecting?"

My mom had called her, chipper as ever, asking if I could stay. Annette agreed to let me come for a few days, even though she was hosting eight of her in-laws.

"Eastern Europe, Emi? Really?"

I balled my fists and stared at the carpet. I knew she hadn't approved of the trip. But what was I supposed to have done? Be homeless in America? She was right; it should have happened sooner: someone's boyfriend or father, anyone, could have attacked me anywhere, in any airport or guest room.

It seemed that as long as I succeeded, I exemplified triumph. Then when someone hurt me, I'd be held responsible for the vulnerability I'd had all along. My clothes rumbled in Annette's washing machine. When the load was finished, I'd fold the sweater, the T-shirt, the bra I'd worn during the attack, to wear again and again. Was that resilience or just desperation?

I looked up at Annette's face, pursed with anger. Years later, she told me she felt guilty and responsible, blaming herself for letting me travel. But all I felt was my own failure. I just knew I couldn't defend myself to her, because I needed a place to stay.

I WENT TO see Dr. Woods. I flinched when she leaned toward me, expecting her to blame me, too.

"I'm sorry," she said instead. "It's the worst to see you like this."

She asked me if I'd considered suicide.

"I won't," I said, each word hurting. "I owe too much to too many people."

"Good. I'm glad." We talked about where I would go next. At the end of our half hour, she said, "Look, it's probably not going to help. But if you want I can increase your Cymbalta."

As SOON AS I arrived in the United States, my mom never brought up the assault again. Annette's house was full, so after a week, I had to find a new place to stay. I got on a bus to Chicago, stayed with a photo camper, took a bus to Milwaukee, boarded a flight, stayed with a girl from topology camp, and then flew back to England, because my mom insisted I go on my archaeological dig as planned. I couldn't handle being with kids my age, so I wrote a note to Harvard deferring for a year and took the gap year internship at Disney in Los Angeles, where I filed expense reports and tried to pull myself together. I lived in an extended stay hotel, then in a house with up to thirteen men, and two other places, before finally moving in with a twenty-seven-year-old I met on OkCupid. My boyfriend, Leo, was exactly what my mom wanted for me: tall and rich and, most important, a man. He also controlled everything from my diet (vegan) to my hair (dyed in bright Manic Panic colors). He told me sternly that he would always pay for dinner, but I always, always, had to thank him. It seemed like progress for me to engage in an adult relationship. I interpreted every bad feeling I had about him as an overreaction, a response not to his actions, but to my past.

Even though I was desperate for comfort, I knew what was expected of me: to smile, to pull myself together. There was no room to grieve, to fall apart. My mom emailed me all year, praising my resilience and resourcefulness.

## Twenty

I showed up at Harvard with two suitcases, my tie-dyed backpack from foster care, and blue hair. Campus cops directed Subarus and Porsche SUVs into makeshift parking spots. Skinny moms and sporty dads flitted in and out of doorways, carting plastic bins. No one was fat. The word "Connecticut" wafted through the air, a state I had never before considered but which suddenly seemed essential.

On the far edge of campus, I found the long, fluorescent-lit hallway I'd call home. After their parents cleared out, my neighbors and I gathered on the carpet between our rooms. Almost all the freshmen lived in suites with roommates in the historic Yard. In our class of sixteen hundred, there were only thirty or so single rooms, with a few left open in case students flipped out midyear and had to be sequestered. This gave our dorm the nickname "the psycho singles." Everyone laughed. (I worried I'd been quarantined.)

We speculated on why we'd been selected for such an honor. "I think it's because we're so independent," an a cappella singer volunteered, citing the high prevalence of gap years and Israeli Defense Forces service in our dorm. The others nodded as I bit my lip: to an eighteen-year-old, "independent" was supposed to be a compliment. I, too, had longed for freedom and seen college as the path there. But now that I'd arrived,

I felt acutely what I'd missed: a period where I didn't have to rely on myself.

Luckily the other girls in my "Pod" were disarmingly nice, with all the diversity of an admissions pamphlet: a Greek girl, a Black girl, two Asian Americans, one girl from Hong Kong (whose parents had flown across the world to move her in), one girl who said she was from New York but, after questioning, was quickly revealed to be from New Jersey, and me, the girl with blue hair. In our group of nine, there were also not one but *two* Manhattanites.

"Both of you?" I asked. They sat cross-legged next to each other.

"Oh, yeah. We know each other," the blonde New Yorker said.

My mouth fell into an O. What were the odds that, out of nine people at Harvard, two would know each other?

No one else seemed surprised. The two New Yorkers leaned against the wall at ease, as if everything in their lives had pointed toward our hallway. I looked around and wondered if anyone had a background similar to mine. If they did, they didn't let on. My richer peers—the one-percenters who made up 40 percent of our class and the slightly less wealthy plebeians who filled it out—set the social tone. While there were folks from more modest means around somewhere, I didn't know how to find them. My boyfriend had discouraged me from joining the pre-orientation Dorm Crew scrubbing toilets or getting a work-study job, advising that the whole point of Harvard was cavorting with VIPs. Remembering this, I tried to wipe the shock off my face and make a good impression.

I perked up when a girl said she was from Idaho, a state I knew solely for potatoes. "Which part are you from?" I asked, as if coming from flyover land meant we were neighbors.

She replied, "Oh, I went to boarding school." When asked where I was from, I took the hint and added the same caveat, pleased with myself.

———

I FELT GOOD about my performance the next day when the brunette Manhattanite, Victoria, invited me into her room. I complimented her elaborate configuration of plastic organizers and sat down on her bed slowly so that I wouldn't mess up her duvet.

"This is the perfect setup," she said. I nodded, pretending to agree. "It's private, but we still have each other across the hall." Victoria said "private" as though she were a celebrity who needed to be hidden behind hedges, protected from paparazzi.

I pushed a strand of cobalt hair behind my ear. "I like the way your decor coordinates." My decor consisted of a suitcase exploded across the floor and a towel spread over my mattress in lieu of sheets.

"Thanks, love." She smiled a big white smile. She opened her closet and looked in.

"Your clothes match, too."

"I basically order the J.Crew catalog every season."

"What's J.Crew?"

"It's just a clothing store." Victoria sat on the bed next to me and played with a single pearl on her necklace. Pearl studs glimmered in her earlobes. As she moved on to fiddling with a wedding band on her right hand, Victoria confided in me that she was a descendant of a disgraced public figure. In high school, a newspaper had written a hit piece on her. I nodded, understanding this feeling of exposure from the article that had called out my "prescription drug abuse." I could already tell we were going to be friends, united by our media tribulations.

But before Victoria had finished telling me about getting hassled every time she used her debit card and people saw her last name, I noticed her nails, glossy like little shells. Sitting against the frills of Victoria's pillowcases, heat rushed over my skin, sickening me, as I flashed back to semen on my clothes. I could never tell Victoria about Budapest. Maybe if I'd never walked into that hostel, I could have recited the simplified, stripped-down version of my circumstances from my college applications: "I was in foster care and then I was homeless. And, yes—I am incredible!" Perhaps I could have convinced myself that this was a noble, or at least intriguing, story, the way people seemed to think it was. But instead, the rape had become a metonym for everything before that had happened, everything gross: the stench of my life, my unwashed clothes, my stolen hat, the constellations of scars lacing my legs, the neediness that emanated from my sweat glands. Anyone who knew one thing, I feared, would know it all. I was sure that they would then see me as permanently disfigured, frozen in my most pathetic moments. For all the reveals of my application, Harvard was a place of discretion. The only way forward was to forget.

"I need to go choose classes," I explained, although I knew I'd probably just end up Skyping my boyfriend. "Bye."

"Wait," she said, as I stood up. "Can I have your number? We should get a meal." Her teeth twinkled when she smiled. I was stunned that maybe she wanted to be friends.

I sighed with relief when I left her room: I'd made it through twenty minutes without exposing any shameful secrets. I only had seventyish more years to go until I could take them to my grave.

THE CLASS OF 2015 gathered under the chandelier and vaulted ceilings of Sanders Theatre for convocation. Harvard's largest auditorium was supposedly an important venue: Winston Churchill, Theodore Roosevelt, Martin Luther King Jr., and Mikhail Gorbachev had all delivered addresses on its stage. (I was proud to recognize two of those names.) I scanned the pews, looking for celebrities. My peers included the children of infamous politician Eliot Spitzer, Al Gore, and Xi Jinping, a man I'd never heard of but who was apparently so important that his daughter attended Harvard under an assumed name and identity.

An administrator paced across the stage. "College," he told us, "can be a rough landing." He explained that my average classmate had been president of three clubs, captain of a sports team, and high school vale-dictorian. Horrified, I sat on my hands, trying not to gnaw off my re-maining nails. He explained that the laws of math dictated that precisely one half of us would be below average. Heads turned as students sized up their neighbors. I stared straight ahead, confident that the bottom half would include me.

"It's normal to struggle," the administrator concluded. As we filed out, I pondered this phrase: four simple words that acknowledged suf-fering while minimizing it. I was learning that New Englanders seemed to embrace this credo, as effortlessly as they carted Le Pliage tote bags instead of backpacks, canvas duffels instead of wheeled suitcases. Eschew-ing plastic rain ponchos, they donned waxed cotton jackets in hideous greens and browns. ("Good for pheasant hunting," a classmate explained, which seemed like an even worse hobby than hiking or sleeping outside on the ground.) For exercise, they grunted down the Charles in absurdly expensive boats. Every time I saw a man in a sleeveless vest, I thought: *Aren't your arms cold?* In this new world, winning smiles hid family mem-bers' addictions, high-profile suicides, and financial scams. Very thin girls never said a word about how they stayed that way (and whatever they did, it was normal). No one at Harvard would pathologize my ambition anymore. On the flip side, the attendant pain would be par for the course, quotidian.

That night, the professor who lived in my dorm's basement (and was ostentatiously titled our "proctor") parroted the same line. So did the troupe of three upperclassmen in fluorescent green T-shirts who formed our Peer Advising Fellows. Upon repetition, orientation's unofficial slogan began to seem more sinister. When I most needed a pep talk, everyone was telling me not to get my hopes up, that the next four years would be very, very hard.

There were lots of other truths they could have told us, like "the hardest part of Harvard is getting in." The median grade was apparently an A; the mean an A−. What we learned in class would not matter nearly as much as the people we met, often by chance. It was nearly impossible to flunk out. "Failure" meant a future as a well-paid SAT tutor. But those weren't things people talked about; they were unspoken, and I wasn't in the know.

ALTHOUGH MY FANTASY of getting to college and finally finding the place I belonged wasn't surviving contact with reality, I eagerly awaited meeting my hand-selected adviser. In addition to teaching freshman composition, he was a poet, so I figured that a dean had remembered the Scholastic awards and assigned me an artistic mentor. I met the handsome poet in the writing program office. Like a startling number of people in Cambridge, he was uncomfortably good-looking. He slid an essay across a heavy wood table: I recognized it as my placement exam from the at-home test that summer.

"Do you notice anything about this?" he asked.

I looked at it and shook my head.

"I'll just give you a moment to look it over."

In the middle of my timed exam, I'd gotten a call from the local dental school offering me a last-minute appointment to remove my impacted wisdom teeth. I'd had to finish writing right afterward in a haze of Vicodin, mouth metallic with blood, at my desk at Disney, during breaks between filing expense reports. As soon as time ran out, I'd emailed the writing program office, explaining, requesting to retake the test during the makeup session. They said no.

"Anything?" the man asked, not unkindly, his green eyes sparkling.

I shrugged: there were a lot of things to say. Helpfully, my adviser observed, "It ends in the middle of the sentence."

"I emailed," I explained, knowing that didn't matter now. Because this was Harvard, they wouldn't *force* anyone to take remedial writing, my adviser clarified. It had to be my decision. But, he confided in me, "This is one of the worst essays we've ever seen."

My chest seized at the use of "we": the faculty had discussed me. Harvard was designed to make students believe the world was open to us, but hearing that sentence made a door slam shut. My reputation preceded me, not as one of the nation's best high school writers, or even as "the girl with blue hair," but as one of Harvard's worst freshmen writers of all time.

My adviser explained that many students took remedial writing, "especially students with nontraditional backgrounds." A "nontraditional" background, I was learning, meant anything other than the world's top high schools (plus an alumnus parent for good measure). The absurdity of this definition did not weaken my sense of inadequacy.

I studied my adviser and told myself he was just trying to help. I scolded myself for feeling attacked, and wondered if I was just resistant to his efforts, hardened by my past. My adviser proceeded to list all the reasons I should take remedial writing until I felt surprised I'd ever managed to string words into a sentence.

"Why couldn't I just retake the exam?" I asked him.

"It's too late for that now. But based on this?" he said, holding up the paper. "It's impossible to say."

I shut my eyes, pressure rushing into my forehead. My wisdom tooth situation wasn't extraordinary. It was the expected outcome of not having parents to check my mouth or schedule my dentist appointments, and then needing to pay out of pocket for surgery while making just over minimum wage. If the school couldn't even understand the basic facts of getting by when you weren't wealthy, how could I believe they'd know how to help me in any other way?

I broke down and agreed to take remedial writing.

DURING ORIENTATION WEEK, students flitted from classroom to classroom, deciding what extracurriculars to join, and—by extension—what we would do with our lives. At a jam-packed meeting of the Premedical Society, I scanned the room and determined that I would not be becoming a doctor: even with Harvard's rampant grade inflation, there was no way I could beat out the Intel Science Fair winners on the curve (let alone cough up five thousand dollars for an MCAT study course). Desperate for certainty that I'd one day have dental insurance, I set my sights on more accessible preprofessional organizations. I dashed from Smart Woman Securities, which offered a free trip to Omaha to lunch with Warren Buffett, to Black Diamond Capital, which required members to hand over a thousand bucks for the investment fund. In a conference room for the Financial Analysts Club, an upperclassman in an impressive-looking sweater presented a PowerPoint of the organization's structure.

You couldn't simply *join* the Financial Analysts Club. Instead, like almost all extracurriculars, it required a semester-long application process, inexplicably called a "comp." (No one knew what it stood for.) These drawn-out vetting processes were how students bonded. Only at the culmination of several rounds of cuts, forty hours of training, and trance-inducing amounts of alcohol and sleep deprivation could the culled group go around a circle, share their backstories, then never bring them up again. In subsequent semesters, one could comp various subcommittees, earning the privilege to choose stocks, organize conferences, or lead future comps. The diagram on the projector showed a pyramid. The point, as for every club at Harvard, was to reach the pinnacle, or at least join a board. Then, the director indicated, you, too, could purchase an embroidered Patagonia half zip and belong.

Of all the club's benefits, the sweater situation had me the most excited. Only tourists wore Harvard sweatshirts. My peers donned gear emblazoned with the logos of yet more exclusive organizations: polo team Lululemon jackets, squash team Nike backpacks, gold insects on skinny chains strung around the throats of Bee Club members. Cryptic crests graced the front of club-specific "casual hats" (which, to the untrained eye, strongly resembled baseball caps).

People saw my hair and assumed I was countercultural, the type of person who'd abscond from on-campus housing at the first chance to move to the cannabis-infused Dudley Co-Op, when in fact I was the opposite. I wanted to be emblazoned. I wanted to be claimed. Not being pulled in felt like being pushed out. I immediately enlisted in the Financial Analysts Club. Every Sunday morning for the rest of the fall, I was to report to the Adams House conservatory, where a junior named Amy would quiz her compers on that week's business news while we brunched, striving to be worthy of the Harvard crest embossed on our waffles.

AFTER THE INFO SESSIONS WERE OVER, the Poddies got ready in our shared bathroom, eager to go out. Alcohol was banned in the freshman dorms and heavily restricted in the upperclassman Houses, so social life took place at the all-male final clubs. They owned multimillion-dollar mansions around the Square. Rumor had it that if a member of the P.C. didn't make a million dollars by the time he turned forty, the club would give him the difference. Women weren't allowed in past the bike room. I was thrilled that my New Yorker hallmates knew guys in the Fox Club so that we could go out. I got as dressed up as I could in white-and-green-striped jeans and a tank top. My hallmates wore bandage dresses and stilettos, their long hair blow-dried and flouncy. A bouncer let us into the subterranean party room.

The only guys allowed inside were upperclassman club members. All of the girls were freshmen. It hewed to my concept of a typical party, except that the sticky floor was hardwood and the ceilings were ringed with molding. My friends dispersed into a sea of dudes who grinded on them and then went to retrieve red Solo cups of jungle juice. After a few songs soberly dancing on my own, I set out looking for a drink. No one would give me one. Eventually a guy danced with me. Burning with embarrassment about my awkwardly grown out colorful hair, I wondered if he had been dared. He pulled my hips to his crotch, but when I did not immediately indicate I'd hook up with him, he ditched me midsong.

I did not find this stupid in any way. Just to be close to power, even if it was not mine and could never be mine, was intoxicating. If any-thing, the absence of women only increased my assessment of the clubs' cachet.

A few days later, Victoria invited me to the Owl Club for a "jersey party." I asked what I should wear, having heard of a figure named Snooki from a television show called *Jersey Shore*. Victoria told me to wear a sports jersey; I scrounged up an intramural sports T-shirt. The gang of Victoria's high school friends left without me and I ran behind in my sneakers. When I got to the door, the tiny man in a tuxedo enforcing the list would not let me in. "Can my friend just come out and get me?" I asked. "She went in three minutes ago."

No, he explained: my friends were not members. They were just a guy's guests. He would have to come get me, not them.

"Next time!" Victoria texted me, but I knew better. I sat on the steps of the gym across the street, listening to the music blast from the walled courtyard, wondering what I'd do for the next four years of Saturday nights.

―――――

Instead of signing up for classes, Harvard offered "Shopping Week," a frantic rush of introductory-lectures-as-sales-pitches. Administrators told us this was the time to experiment and offered little guidance on choosing what to shop. I figured everyone just showed up.

The night before class started, I discovered three Poddies on the futon in our hallway comparing color-coded calendars, double- and triple-booked. Not only did they know what they'd take as freshmen, they were planning to shop advanced courses to help them narrow down which concentration they'd declare mid–sophomore year.

I studied the a cappella singer's agenda, filled with wonder. "How did you make this?"

She shrugged. "Oh, my parents helped me." The other girls nodded: everyone's parents had told them what classes to take.

Meanwhile, my mom emailed me every other day with dispatches from her adventures. After retiring from her job as a crime scene photographer during my gap year, she'd spent her time crafting cat faces out of polymer clay and hunting for discounted dog clothes that emaciated orphans could wear as shirts. She forwarded me advice about how to parent teenagers. Every few months, she sent a long diatribe urging me to avoid being raped (again).

I relied on my boyfriend, Leo, to help me navigate adulthood. He was the one who took me to the dentist and nursed me through horrific wisdom tooth removal complications. When I learned I needed $5,500 in root canals and crowns—decimating my savings—he dictated a pleading letter to Dr. Kat's friend the banker and another to the office of financial aid. Leo's apartment was the closest thing I had to a home. Even Annette said he was good for me, as a sort of parental figure.

And as the graduate of an elite college, Leo was the only one who could help me decipher the system. After the run-in with the Poddies, he told me to take economics, like he had. I was grateful for the advice, but I wanted my own color-coded calendar.

Harvard's hands-off approach might have been ideal if I wanted to "explore" and "find myself." But after everything, I mainly wanted to explore lucrative careers and find myself incredibly wealthy. Given my lack of parental guidance and ignorance of elite social norms, the freedom that Harvard offered didn't feel like freedom at all. Instead it felt like another way other people knew the rules and I was in the dark.

ON THE FIRST DAY OF CLASS, I trudged to Ec 10 as prescribed. At the end of the lackluster lecture, I was shoving my stuff into my backpack when electronic music started blasting through the speakers. The beat seemed to shake the chandelier. A sans serif logo replaced the Power-Point: CS50, Introduction to Computer Science. I had nowhere to be, so I stayed. At seven minutes after the hour ("on Harvard time") the lecturer, David Malan, tested the mic clipped to his black sweater and strode into the spotlight to teach us how to program.

He demonstrated our first algorithm—binary search—by looking for the name Mike Smith in a phone book. Malan flipped to a spot in the middle: too early in the alphabet. "So what do we do?" he asked. A row of teaching fellows onstage ripped tomes in half and threw them to the floor. The audience gasped. Malan's assistants picked new pages and repeated the procedure. Finally, the head fellow held up a single page, triumphant. The crowd applauded and hollered.

It took less than a minute, although Malan drew it out for dramatic effect. If the phone book had 1,000 pages, it only took an average of ten tearings to find the right one: 500 pages, then 250, 125, 62, 31, 16, 8, 4, 2, then 1. He said something about logs—1024 log base 2 is 10—but I couldn't think about math, only about magic. I stared at the resulting single page slack-jawed, transfixed.

I had never written a line of code, never even contemplated it. All I really knew about it was *The Social Network*: hackers staring at black terminal screens as unintelligible fixed-width text scrolled by. I doubted I had the necessary preparation. Despite all her encouragement to pursue art, when I'd begged my mom to let me test into a special math program in middle school, she wouldn't let me, saying, "But you're so verbal."

After the embarrassment of my placement essay, no one at Harvard would claim that I was "verbal." By the first day of class, I felt stripped down, laid bare. But the fact that I no longer felt particularly good at anything opened a door, because I felt no more out of place in the computer science lecture than anywhere else on campus. Malan assured us that most students had no prior experience. He promised that, if we could get into Harvard, we could pass his class. He made it sound so doable, though that night in the freshman dining hall, horror stories circulated about weekly problem sets taking forty hours each. Many would-be doctors had seen their GPAs destroyed and had to resort to consulting. Freshmen who were too scared to take CS50 swore up and down the long wooden tables that it was a cult. The naysayers only increased my excitement; I wanted to be told where to go and what to do. Although I'd chafed against institutional living, after so many years of it, I needed structure and clarity to feel at ease. And who cared if it sucked? Wasn't existence a parade of one ordeal after another?

The only problem was that I was in an application-only freshman seminar on "women's coming of age memoir" that met at the same time. All the adults urged us to take these special courses, so I petitioned my dean to simultaneously enroll. When that was denied, I had my answer. I'd already promised I wouldn't study English. And if CS50 made people so miserable, then maybe at least I'd have a reason for why I was struggling— a sticker on my laptop that said PROPERTY OF CS50, a symbol everyone could understand.

———

Two weeks into the semester, my mom emailed to announce that she was coming for Freshman Parents Weekend. I hadn't replied to her previous five emails, not since I'd sent a note asking her to ship me my comforter for my still-unfurnished room and she'd replied with her latest "sex talk." "Never let yourself be used," she'd written, ominously. "Don't think, 'I'll just give him a . . . (and get him off my back).' Very few guys will continue if you are objecting vehemently."

Detached from any reality about assault on campus—or the fact that I was in a relationship—it felt like a thinly veiled critique of my actions in Budapest. I wept, but I had nothing to say in my defense, so I just didn't reply. My mom's new dispatches floated in the detritus of my inbox, among irrelevant scholarship-contest notifications and the dozens of mailing lists I'd joined. Each note unacknowledged gave me a sense of strength, as if I were finally in control of my life.

But now she was coming in October and I couldn't stop her. She wrote, "I'm guessing you are not that keen on having me there and you'd prefer if I left as soon as possible," an accurate statement whose tone— like a spurned lover's—filled me with guilt. My mom wanted to stay in my room.

No, I wrote back, absolutely not. Harvard was my place, not hers. The idea of her presence on campus agitated me, as though she'd absorb the school's power through the ground under her feet, sucking it away from me.

Even if I couldn't stop my mom from coming, I promised myself I'd hardly have to see her. Exhausted and overwhelmed, which was quickly becoming my default state, I came home from CS50 and found my mom in my hallway. I froze. I wasn't sure how she'd learned my dorm assignment.

"How did you get here?" I asked.

"A very nice girl let me in!" she said, describing every Harvard female. I wanted to know everyone who'd seen her so that I could do damage control. I couldn't articulate it, but my mom felt dangerous. That night, when I was brushing my teeth, one of my hallmates said she'd met my mom in the hallway. "She told me all about her laser."

"Her what?" I asked, afraid it was a weird sex thing. It turned out it was about hair removal, which wasn't much better. I worried that if I upset my mom, she'd start dishing about my secret background to whoever was around. But I couldn't just tell my hallmates to avoid her—they all loved their families. What would they think of me?

The next day, feeling guilty, I called my mom and said I'd get in touch after doing homework so we could hang out. Instead, when I returned to the dorm, she was outside my room again. "Hi, honey! Do you want some food?" She extracted a red napkin from her pocket, filled with broken crackers and scraps of cheese she'd filched from an event.

"I told you I needed to study."

My mom followed me in when I went into my room to grab my laptop. "This is a pretty nice place! Big." She grunted and flexed, indicating the manly size of my accommodations. "Are you sure I can't stay here? There's plenty of room." She detailed exactly how far she had to commute to reach the home of the hospitable Quakers who'd agreed to put her up.

"Can you please leave?" I hated myself for being rude to my mom, yet I couldn't stand having her here, guilting me. I contemplated calling security. I wasn't sure if they'd remove her or if I even had a right to kick her out. "Please go," I begged.

She didn't budge. I grabbed my backpack and walked out, leaving my mom in my room. I stayed at the library until my head bobbed with fatigue. When I returned to my dorm, I worried I'd find her in my bed or passed out on the futon in the hallway. Worst case, she'd be dozing in a very nice girl's room. (Thankfully, she was nowhere to be found.)

After my mom had returned to Minnesota (and composed a poem

describing her lackluster trip to Cambridge), I went to the freshman dean's office to ask for her to be taken off the mailing lists. When Harvard had family events, I wanted to decide if my mom could come. In her attic office in an old house, the dean explained to me that all parents of Harvard students received these communications and asked me to really consider the implications of my request. Did I wish to alienate my one remaining parent? Did I really want to shut the door on a relationship with her?

"No," I said, shaky. I just wanted to have boundaries. I assumed the dean knew about my living situation in high school. She probably thought that my mom seemed like a good parent in a difficult situation. I wanted to believe this, too, despite the fact that the situation had improved, but our relationship had not.

If I told the dean about my mom's "sex talk" emails, I'd have to explain everything. Repeating my mom's words seemed like confessing that I had let myself be used. That I had not objected vehemently. That I had just given him a . . . It was impossible to describe abstractly what was wrong with my mom's guidance, so I didn't try, and she stayed on the mailing lists.

The adults at school treated me as if, despite all the extenuating circumstances I'd detailed in my application, enrollment had wiped my life clean of complications. In this context, the pain my mom caused me felt like my own failure: that despite getting into Harvard, I couldn't love my mom right.

THE MORNING AFTER a prestigious club held its initiations, a girl from my hall texted to see if I had any Plan B. She'd woken up to learn a fellow initiate had sex with her without a condom. I didn't know all of the details, but I had the impression that she had been incapacitated.

I was stunned, but not because I didn't know this happened. In fact, my boyfriend had a "fetish" for intoxicated girls. (He did not drink himself.) He said he'd never fucked a drunk girl he hadn't first fucked sober, although I didn't agree that was the same as consent. The first time he urged me to chug a bottle of wine, I'd had no idea what he was planning—I'd never even been drunk before. I got weak and blacked out and woke up filled with confusion. But I had excused that event, and all the times that followed it. Having been misunderstood myself, I was sympathetic to Leo's explanation that he was "kinky." He framed his predilections as being just as immutable and valid as sexual orientation or gender identity, and as harmless as dirty talk or neck biting, activities that seemed novel and exciting. Also, my mom made it sound as if a single beer invited savage violence, and society considered alcohol-facilitated rape a vast gray area. But when it happened to my friend, it seemed wrong and disturbing.

I wanted to help. I braced myself to accompany her to the police or the Office of Sexual Assault Prevention and Response. It didn't occur to me to share what had happened to me, with my boyfriend or in Budapest; I didn't want to make the situation about myself. I saw no reason she'd take solace in my disclosure. Besides Jane, the one time I'd opened up to a female friend, she'd replied, "That's not a big deal. It happened to me, too."

My friend replied that she was fine. The college pharmacy offered free Plan B, and she'd get it from them if I didn't have any. I dropped a box outside her door.

When I saw her a few days later, I asked if she was okay. She seemed not to know what I was talking about. "The initiation?" I asked.

"That? It's nothing. We talked about it." She said he was a good guy who had made a mistake.

I looked at her closely. She did seem fine. As always, she was vibrant, with poise I could strive for my whole life and never attain. No part of me considered that maybe this was a façade and that the same code of silence muzzled both of us. If she interpreted what happened to her as wrong, she'd face not only the stigma of being a victim but also the reality that this guy would always be in her club. They'd be guests at the same weddings, attendees of the same conferences, maybe parents of children at the same private schools. The only way to ensure she'd never see him again would be to cut off contact with everyone she knew. But all that I could see was her well-mannered perfection and, by contrast, how badly I was lacking.

As she left, I gritted my teeth so hard it hurt. A year and a half had passed since Budapest; what was wrong with me that I was still affected? All through high school, I'd fought against the idea that I was broken, instead subscribing to the notion that no matter what happened, I could remain the same radiant human who'd dominated the fourth-grade Bible-memorization circuit. I believed, in fact, that I should be better, improved by all the trials I had faced. That was the only way the past made sense.

THAT NOVEMBER, Occupy protesters took over Harvard Yard. They pitched their tents in photogenic locations in front of the John Harvard statue and propped up signs that declared WE ARE THE 99%. In response, the administration locked the gates so that no outsiders could join the camp. Every time I entered the space most of my classmates called home, I had to line up to show my ID. The guards sized me up. My new, Leo-approved magenta hair was marginally better than blue, but it regrettably matched my tie-dyed backpack and clashed with my polyester jeggings from Forever 21. I burned with self-consciousness but suspected that even if I dressed like my Manhattanite hallmates and had normal-colored hair, I still wouldn't look like I belonged.

This was despite the fact that Harvard went out of its way to provide for scholarship students. My $150 check from the Winter Coat Fund paid for my thin Uniqlo jacket. As I walked toward the Science Center, I passed a dozen girls in Canada Goose parkas. Each had a little patch on the shoulder that, inexplicably, depicted Antarctica. Each cost a thousand dollars. (When I learned this fact, I gasped.) The truly wealthy wore enormous Geese with seventeen unflattering pockets and a laminated spot for an ID—relics from family vacations to the South Pole.

I hated the Occupy protests because they reminded me of what I was supposed to do, but wasn't: giving back, right away. A girl in the year above me had, at twelve, founded America's second-largest eating disorder charity. Unlike me, she was a good survivor, a brave young woman from a respectable family whose trauma was a tragedy. She was a model citizen. What had I done? Nothing.

It didn't matter to me that starting a charity required capital I lacked. It didn't matter to me either that most of Occupy Harvard's demands seemed incoherent, formulated by people who weren't necessarily oppressed. My economics study partner was one of the organizers; both of his parents were college professors. These ideologically pristine late adolescents only seemed capable of agitating for their vision of utopia because of a certain kind of comfort, a confidence that their voices mattered. They weren't worried, like I was, that if they rocked the boat they'd get expelled. Despite my lived experience with inequality, I sensed that my perspective was less valuable than the average student's, because said experience had rendered me less educated: I thought hegemony was a cousin to the porcupine.

My critiques about the self-righteous activism at Harvard did nothing to dull the discomfort I felt about existing as a paradox. On one hand, I was privileged. As soon as I learned that word, it applied to me, and I would be frequently encouraged to "check it": I was white, straight-passing, able-bodied, intelligent, with parents who went to college, and I had a dorm room and an unlimited meal plan and was a student at the world's most famous university.

Yet I did not feel secure. After Freshman Parents Weekend, my mom emailed me to say she'd no longer provide any financial support. Because of Harvard's strict rules about outside scholarships, the money I'd won in high school would only help me by replacing the contribution the university would otherwise expect from a term-time job. Meanwhile, I had to buy my own health insurance and pay income tax on my twenty thousand dollars of aid for room and board. I did not buy textbooks. I relied on my boyfriend to house me during breaks, but that meant buying tickets to LA and acquiescing to his demands, which in turn meant I needed to drop out of my fall comps. I asked my cousin to access the remaining college money from my grandma, but she said no: I'd get it when I turned twenty-one, when I was a junior. After I took my gap year, Dr. Kat's friend no longer wanted to sponsor me.

If I was honest, I didn't want a revolution. I just wanted a job. An Ivy League degree in the liberal arts, without anyone to rely on, would, at best, provide me with a tenuous existence. But at the same time, a clique of vocal professors viewed "preprofessionalism" as a scourge brought in by the children of immigrants and students on financial aid. A former dean had even written a book about people like me. Every time I thought about the title, I shivered. It was called *Excellence without a Soul.*

## Twenty-one

Over winter break, Leo took me to meet his parents, two warm old people who lived in a lovely home filled with antiques. He called them "Mom" and "Pops," with no possessive pronouns, as if they were the platonic ideal of parents. I could imagine calling them that, too. Then I got my fall grades and wept. A semester of heroic all-nighters had earned me a paltry B+ in CS50, a devastating B in calculus, and a horrifying A− in remedial writing. It did not help that Leo had told me that each A was worth ten thousand dollars in additional lifetime earnings; I imagined a dumpster full of hundred-dollar bills in flames. Unconvinced that my sadness was just about my GPA, Leo questioned me until I admitted that I had doubts about our relationship. We almost broke up on Christmas morning, but I had no idea where I'd go if we did. He gave me a pair of knee-high black boots, so I could fit in with the girls in Cambridge, then took me to Mexico for the rest of break, where he threatened to leave me in a sleepy town hours south of Cancún.

When I got back to campus, housing hysteria was in full force. All the freshmen had to sort into "blocking groups" (Harvard's atomic social units) who would move into upperclassman Houses together. I feared no one would want to live with me. My conflicts with Leo, and the hours I spent either on mandatory Skype calls with him or agonizing about how he treated me, made it hard to make friends. Also, I didn't really know how to text. To my shock, I still got three invitations.

I went back and forth on the decision, reveling in the luxury of choice. I fantasized about a fresh start sophomore year. Like everyone, I hoped to live along the Charles River, ideally in Eliot House, which had a special endowment and was stocked with Nutella. Finally, I'd be in the center of things instead of on the outskirts, living in a suite with my lifelong friends. I pictured us all posing together in a Ferrari before the annual spring Fête.

I agreed to live with some Poddies. The night the form was due, I ran into my future blockmate as she ducked into the bathroom.

"Hey!" I asked her if she'd turned in the form.

"Yeah." She clutched her shower caddy. I waited. "But you're not in it."

"What?"

"I texted you."

"You didn't." I would have remembered being kicked out of my blocking group.

"We asked John and he said no, so we invited you. Then he changed his mind. We really wanted to live with you but we asked him first, so it was only fair."

*That's not how invitations work*, I thought, but felt I had no right to be angry. How had I expected this would work out?

"Yuqi or Anastasiya will be so excited to live with you." She flashed a giant smile. "Please don't be mad. We love you."

I hated the way that "we love you" melted me. Of course the Poddies wanted to block with a Kennedy or whoever. But why couldn't they just be honest? My classmates' social graces were so flawless that I never knew if they liked me or what I had done wrong. After years of reading people to get what I needed, the opacity left me on edge. My hallmate shuffled out of the bathroom, sticking one arm out as she held up her towel. When we hugged, I smelled the perfume on her nape. She kissed me on the cheek with an exaggerated smooching. I had to guard my heart. I was so susceptible to those sweet words, smooches that meant nothing.

The warmth of her embrace lingered as I texted everyone I knew. All their groups were full. Eventually, I found a random debutante to block with so I wouldn't have to be a dreaded "floater," though after fifteen minutes talking to her I knew we'd never be friends.

I was beginning to realize that any exclusive system was a system of exclusion. I chided myself for not realizing sooner. But the fact was, I'd wanted this—to go to school with celebrities' children who wore funny hats with their club crests—for so long, never contemplating how it would feel to be the one left out.

THE MORNING AFTER my blocking debacle, I woke up to a string of angry texts from Leo. No matter how hard I tried to be a good girlfriend, I upset him every ten days, with remarkable consistency. I was always finding new ways to err: missing his texts because I was studying, trying to get an on-campus job while he felt neglected, skipping too many runs in our marathon training plan, wanting to abandon the vegan diet that was supposed to remind me of his love with each dining hall Boca Burger.

This time, it was a listicle. For the *Crimson*'s spring comp, I'd been assigned a blog post about overrated activities. I included sex in the Widener Library stacks, a popular bucket-list item. Once, when Leo came to visit, we'd attempted this feat in a section, Ukrainian Literature, that I called out for having an extremely cold concrete floor. He interpreted my joke as a vicious critique of his sexual prowess.

I got an eight-page email followed by twelve hundred more words describing my other recent failures: I did not make him feel loved; my Skype produced subpar video; I hadn't upgraded my operating system in a timely manner; we still hadn't had a threesome, even though it would have been easy enough to get one of my hallmates alone and get her wasted (he made the sinister suggestion of the friend who'd needed Plan B). "I expect you'll do what you say," he wrote. "If you say that you're going to do something that you are not planning to do, that to me, is nothing other than a lie."

His reaction seemed a little extreme, but I had never learned to defend myself. Instead, I'd learned to take responsibility and apologize. "Sorry" gushed out of me. I set an alarm for 2:30 a.m. so that he could berate me over Skype at a convenient hour, Pacific time. He told me that he could not bear to speak to me for the time being, so I patiently waited for him to reach out at some indeterminate date, reloading my email every minute.

My mom was my main confidante when I fought with Leo. After our first argument, less than two months after we met, she urged me to "stay open to what will make things right." (I did not tell my mom what "making things right" meant to Leo—like pouring me a large glass of vodka at 10:00 a.m., then watching me drink it—because I knew how she disapproved of both alcohol and premarital sex.) When I almost broke things off before leaving for school, she convinced me otherwise. "What is three thousand miles if you love each other?" She said it was a very good thing I was so upset I'd hurt Leo, that it meant I cared, and that he got so angry because he loved me. My mom urged me to marry him.

I had been taught implicitly, but forcefully, that as long as I had needs, the people who met them were justified in treating me however they pleased. If I set boundaries, it would be my own fault if I wound up sleeping in my car.

And I loved Leo. When he held me, I felt safe, like I hadn't since sharing a bed with my mom. I thought I'd never feel that way again. Besides Annette, he was the only person to get me something for my birthday and Christmas. Before exams, he sent me care packages filled with Compartés truffles and Lush shampoo. After I got sick when he made me drink too much, he took me to Target and bought me a fuzzy blanket for my dorm room bed. I treasured these gifts as the sole comforts in my otherwise institutional existence. When I came to California to prove my devotion in the middle of a conflict, he took me to ride the Ferris wheel at the Santa Monica Pier and then to get vegan ice cream. He was handsome and charismatic—a former student body president— and when he shined his attention on me, I felt like the most treasured person in the world. He taught me that you couldn't merely apply for a class, you had to email the professor, advice that got me into courses I otherwise never could have taken. When my driver's license got suspended and no one would tell me where to go, Leo called on behalf of his "wife" and quickly resolved the situation. He knew about my past and helped me navigate my mom's intrusions. We messaged each other constantly: in the absence of normal parents, he was the only person interested in my day-to-day life.

Leo said he wouldn't have dated me if I hadn't gone to Harvard, which supposedly proved my maturity, so his affections felt like a fulfillment of my deepest wish: to work hard enough to finally be cherished. How many times had Dave and Jan and the others told me that life wasn't about success but about relationships and love? The more I floundered at Harvard, the more I agreed.

THAT YEAR, I did something I never thought I'd do: I tried to get therapy. The receptionist at the health center asked, "What do you want to discuss?"

I replied, "Um." There was too much to say, and I had no words for any of it, which was kind of the main problem.

After I coughed up a noncommittal answer, the receptionist read me a list of self-destructive acts. She asked me if I currently binged, purged, cut, abused substances, thought about killing myself, or had an imminent plan for ending my life. "No," I answered to each, proud of myself for abstaining. (Leo had helped by threatening to break up with me if I lost more than five pounds or ever hurt myself again.)

It did not occur to me to confess that I had previously indulged in all of those behaviors. But if disclosing those vices might have prevented my admission to Harvard, it seemed plausible they'd get me kicked out. Even though it was almost impossible to fail out academically, the school sent students home all the time on involuntary mental health leaves. If I got banished, where would I go? I held my breath, fearing that—just by asking for an appointment—I'd divulged too much already.

Instead, the receptionist said I didn't qualify for therapy through Mental Health Services and gave me the phone number for an office that offered time management training. Somehow, I had been too sick to get into Yale; now I was too well for therapy at Harvard. Part of me was pleased, as if the denial of services meant I no longer had a need.

My pride did not last long: everyone I knew who tried to go to Health Services for counseling instead received a prescription for Xanax. After a while, I started to wonder if the clinic offered therapy at all. Eventually, I met someone who'd received help after her mother died midsemester. They initially rejected her, too, but in response she refused to leave until they assigned her a clinician. At the end of her second day camped out in the waiting room, the supervisor came out and agreed to be her therapist. It was an extreme example, but it seemed to illustrate how the opportunities Harvard offered couldn't just be taken; they needed to be exercised, seized, claimed. But after omitting so much from my applications, I felt I had no right to insist the college help heal my wounds. No one owed me anything: not my mom, not Leo, not my friends, not Harvard.

As RAIN MELTED the gray snowbanks lining Mass Ave, and I found myself in trouble with Leo again, I started to panic. Soon, the dorms would shut for the summer. Leo's loft was the only place I could conceivably go, but my doubts became more and more serious. My drinking to the point of blackout seemed like a prerequisite of our relationship. After using my body, he often left me alone, and I'd wake up hours later in the same position. I feared I'd choke on my vomit and die. When I brought this up to him, he told me I was overreacting. Eventually, he promised that he'd consider my concerns even if they weren't "meritorious"—a word that would have impressed me if it wasn't so infuriating. Over spring break, he asked me if he could hit me until I cried, and then slapped me long after tears were running down my face. When I talked to him about the black eye that resulted, he said, sweetly, "I could hit you a lot harder."

If I wanted to break up with Leo, I had to do it ASAP. But I had no idea if I should: no matter what Leo did, there was always some justification. When he hit me after he said he'd stop, he pointed out that I hadn't safeworded. When I said I didn't believe I could consent in advance before passing out, he claimed that, as my boyfriend, he always had implied consent. When I expressed fear about the headaches I got after he slapped me, or about the dangers of him strangling me, he repeated that this was BDSM—but implied that I was just too immature to understand. These explanations seemed less improbable than the alternative: that I had gone from the neglect of my childhood, to the assaults of my adolescence, into the arms of an abusive older man. What were the odds?

My friends seemed ill-equipped to handle my crises. One night, I knocked on Victoria's door. She let me crawl under her duvet. "Long distance is so hard," she cooed, kissing my hair. All my seventeen-, eighteen-, and nineteen-year-old classmates echoed the same sentiment. I wished that Jane could help me, but we'd grown apart and she envied my apparent romantic success. I kept trying to meet with my dorm proctor, but our schedules never lined up. I called the number Health Services had given me and started meeting with a doctor of education at the Bureau of Study Counsel, which did not lead to any of the clarity I craved. After writing an essay about my boyfriend for my creative writing class, I went to my professor's office hours and asked him if he had any personal advice. He folded his hands on his wide wooden desk and declined to offer any. For years, my problems had been so intractable that I accepted that no one at school could help me. After moving from institution to institution, each lacking the resources to help, the possibilities of Harvard's thirty-two-billion-dollar endowment seemed irrelevant.

I even reached out to Michelle. I sent her another Facebook friend request and messaged her. I didn't mention Leo, but I did apologize. "I'm sorry for all the pain of the last decade," I wrote. "I love you and always have." She accepted my friend request but didn't reply.

GRASS SHOT UP. I sat in the rare books room of Lamont Library, staring at the Yard. I could not study. Instead, I left and worked out, trying to burn off the hot, sticky feeling that burrowed under my skin. I was grateful Leo had insisted I take up running. It was a wholesome, sporty hobby that allowed me to discreetly eviscerate myself.

One afternoon, I answered a listserv email for a running partner. I recognized Amy's name—she'd led my comp for the Financial Analysts Club before I had to drop out—and agreed to run with her. As we passed a boathouse, Amy asked me, "Hey, are you bisexual, too?"

"What?" I couldn't believe that she was so open about being bi. At Interlochen, I'd felt okay with being gay, but bisexuality still seemed so shameful I couldn't even think about it. I tried to pretend Charlotte never existed and that I wasn't attracted to girls, though I was. "How do you know?" I asked.

"It's the hair," Amy said. "I could tell right away." But she didn't seem bothered by it. It was just another thing we had in common, like vigorous exercise and our midwestern roots.

"So what are you doing this summer?" I gasped out as I trailed behind her. "Are you going to work in I-banking?" I still didn't know what an investment banker did, but I was pleased I could use the abbreviation in a sentence.

"No. I'm interning at Facebook."

"Facebook?" I was even more starstruck.

"Yeah, I'm a computer science concentrator."

I prayed she'd slow down so I could pepper her with questions. "Did you know how to code before?"

"No." She shrugged. "I just took CS50 freshman year. Did you take it?" I nodded as she dragged me along the Charles River Esplanade. "Oh, then you can definitely get an internship!" Amy started explaining to me how: every fall, there was an enormous conference for technical women where companies held interviews. Facebook handed out offers on the spot.

"But I don't have good grades," I admitted.

Amy shrugged. "No one cares." Because we were at Harvard, all the big companies wanted to hire us. If I chose computer science as my concentration, Amy promised, they'd talk to me. I just had to buy *Cracking the Coding Interview* and practice the problems. She was magnanimous and supportive. "We don't really learn anything useful in class anyway," she reassured me.


IN THE DAYS that followed my run with Amy, I couldn't stop thinking about what she said. I didn't buy her assurances that I could get a blue-chip internship: unlike me, she'd been valedictorian of her high school, captain of her track team, and had such low body fat she lost her period.

Meanwhile, I'd punted on taking the follow-up to CS50, instead taking fluffy courses in which I performed just as poorly. But the opportunities she laid out made it clear that Leo was holding me back. Even if I couldn't assert that he was mistreating me—or see that as justification to leave—keeping him happy was squandering my time at Harvard, the earth's most precious commodity.

I went to the career office and applied for an internship program in Korea for that summer, the only thing that was still open and had funding. When I got wait-listed, I did what Leo had taught me and sent a persuasive follow-up email.

I told my time management counselor I was going to break up with Leo, though there were dozens of logistical issues that I was trying not to consider. I was relieved when she didn't ask about them. "Do you feel like you have people you can talk to?" she inquired.

"Yes," I replied, thinking of the girls I hadn't blocked with. She gave me her blessing.

I Skyped Leo, ready. But as soon as I saw his face, doubt filled me. Even if I got into the program in Korea, I'd have weeks on either side where I'd need housing. My credit card had a four-hundred-dollar limit; I relied on Leo's Platinum Card for larger purchases, and on work Leo outsourced to me to pay him back. Realistically, I knew I wouldn't reach out to my hallmates or the Mormons I studied with at CS50 office hours; I didn't have a real blocking group. Harvard was set up for students with families and Leo was the closest thing I had. If I left him and then needed to come back, I felt sure he'd punish me for it.

As he looked at me, I could feel him rooting out my doubt. My lips opened and closed, wordless. His brow twisted in irritation at what he called "the fishy face," which I made when I was scared. This expression irritated him like nothing else.

"What's wrong?" he said. "Just tell me."

"No, no, no, nothing's wrong," I said. "It's fine." But he didn't believe me. By the end of the conversation, I was on relationship probation through the end of the semester.

THAT SUMMER, IN KOREA, the gym was my only outlet. On the Fourth of July, I lay on my back on the Astroturf in the middle of the track.

Staring at the sky, bright from the billboards of Seoul, I thought about how badly I'd longed to leave Minnesota. Now everywhere in the world felt foreign to me.

Almost exactly two years had passed since the assault in Budapest. I wondered where my rapist was. In a way, I missed him. He was the last person to see me back when I believed college would save me. Not even my boyfriend knew me like that.

When Leo arrived to visit me, the city glimmered around him. We bought matching couples' T-shirts. My roommate agreed he could stay with us and sleep in my twin-size bed. We went out with the other students. At the third club, after my third drink of the night, everything got hazy.

I woke up with Leo inside of me, midway through. I looked over and saw my roommate in her bed, five feet away.

"Stop," I hissed. When I hissed again, he did.

We talked in the street. I'd scrubbed my hair with laundry detergent, trying to get out the colored dye. I'd had it bleached as blonde as it would go. The stylist had snipped out all the purple strands. Still, when I caught my reflection in a car window, arms folded over my nipples, a halo of pink framed my face.

"You could have woken up my roommate," I said. Normally, Leo could argue that I would have had sex with him while I was awake, so it was fine to fuck me when I was unconscious, but I never would have agreed with her there.

"She wasn't going to wake up."

"How do you know?" Dawn lit up the alley where we stood. Gulls pecked at wrappers in the gutter.

"She just wasn't," he said.

"How could you possibly know that?" I said, shaking my head.

Eventually we went back to my room. He faced the wall and I lay on the edge of the mattress, as far away from him as I could get.

In the morning, he said he'd fly back to California that day. We were over.

Then I thought about the month left before school began. I didn't have any good enough friends to stay with. Annette would be on vacation again. Was I going to be homeless? Call the school, beg? Leo and I had tickets to Beijing, then flights back to LA. Even if everything went as planned, I'd have less than ten dollars in my bank account by the end of the summer.

"Don't go," I told him. "Don't leave."

Some part of me knew it wasn't all my fault—Leo, Budapest, high school—but it was easier to pretend it was. What recourse did I have if people had wronged me? None. All that knowledge did was leave me alone. At least if I'd fucked up, I could do better next time.

I swore to Leo that I would try harder to be a good girlfriend.

## Twenty-two

My sophomore year, I stopped trying to break up with Leo. I knew that he had hurt me, but I felt that I was so damaged that I needed him. There was no way I could leave, at least until circumstances changed. Instead, I asked him for more help, combing through the course catalog together and picking the classes both he and Amy recommended. As if sensing my submission, he loosened his grip, which was a good thing because I suddenly had eighty hours of homework a week.

On the first day of class, my computer systems professor announced we'd have partner problem sets. I squirmed, wondering who'd be dumb enough to work with me. As I trudged out of the auditorium, I heard someone calling my name. I recognized the girl waving at me from the Pforzheimer House welcome mixer. Like me, Erica had also been "Quaded" and assigned lodgings more than a mile away from the river. Perhaps because of our relative isolation, Erica asked, "Do you want to be partners?"

Soon, we were up until four in the morning together, fighting over who got to type. Like me, she'd also had an eating disorder, dated a girl at boarding school, and was currently seeing a man ten years her senior. Unlike me, Erica excelled academically. Everyone in class knew her as "that question girl." Whenever a nuance in a lecture eluded her, her hand popped up and waved in the air until the instructor stopped, backtracked, and forced one hundred students to listen to a personalized explanation.

When I wasn't implementing virtual memory with Erica, I camped out at economics and statistics office hours. Night after night in the Quad dining halls, the same people showed up and chugged cups of cold coffee. Although women were a minority in my technical classes, we were the majority of those lined up for help. We had more in common besides gender and desperation: we all needed gainful employment.

Once at 2:00 a.m., in the middle of a forty-hour problem set, I suggested, "We should do star jumps to wake up."

My classmate, a future Rhodes scholar, shot me a look. "What are star jumps?" she snapped.

"You jump up and at the top you spread your arms and legs, like a starfish." I stood up and demonstrated. "Come on. It's fun."

The girls I was working with stood up, tentatively, and hopped around the dining hall. After a few minutes, with my encouragement, they flung themselves into the air.

MY FAVORITE CLASS was Stat 110: Introduction to Probability. Even though I knew I wouldn't concentrate in statistics, I was drawn to the premise of the field: that truth exists and while we may never find it, with enough effort, we could get close. The professor, Joe Blitzstein, was endearingly awkward, like a tall teddy bear. He impressed me with his liberal use of the word "penultimate."

The class was proof-based, and I had never written a proof. Predictably, I got a C on the midterm and was, predictably, crushed. But at his next lecture, Blitzstein promised us "redemption": if we got a higher score on the final exam, he'd disregard our prior test scores.

Immediately, I leapt into action. In the Science Center library, I printed out all of the practice questions, prior years' midterms, and previous finals—every scrap of review material. The printer spit out warm sheaths smelling of toner. I stapled them into submission, my fingers stinging with paper cuts. I figured that if I repeated each problem until I grasped every subtlety—then I would be redeemed. I wasn't just looking to do over this midterm; I wanted to compensate for my whole first year at Harvard. Apart from the occasional thrill of my code compiling, I'd gotten bad grades in boring classes. I had learned little that changed me, in the ways a university education promised, and as I wanted to be changed. The next three years seemed at risk of progressing the same way, stumbling through homework in a sleep-deprived blur. I had to get an A.

When I went to stay with Leo for Thanksgiving break, four weeks before the final, I told him, "I'm going to study for Stat 110 six hours a day."

He put his hand on my shoulder. "That's not enough," he said. "Do ten." He wouldn't let me go to bed until I had put in my time. In those moments, I loved him the best.

I emailed the professor almost every day. Despite having hundreds of students, and thousands more who followed along online, he responded promptly and remembered every detail I'd shared; it was the only time I didn't feel alone. When I got back to campus, I got up before sunrise and studied while *The Nutcracker* repeated on my headphones. Snow drifted down outside. I accumulated cafeteria trays of mugs, teas that tasted like the color of their packets (red, orange, green).

Day by day, I felt like I was molting. I got a case of hiccups that didn't go away. One morning, I woke up with bruises under my eyes. As I struggled, I couldn't help but think about how Dave and Jan would have judged my all-out effort. I was sure they would have asked me why it mattered so much to get a good grade, that I was avoiding something that I should instead excavate. They would have urged me not to take Stat 110 in the first place, considering I'd learned algebra from *The*

*Princeton Review.* It seemed as if adults were always telling young people to think about what kind of person they were, and make the big life decisions from there. But what kind of a person was I? Who got to decide?

On the day of the final exam, I walked into the auditorium and did 110 push-ups (mostly on my knees) for good luck. Every few minutes, to the detriment of my fellow test takers, I hiccuped.

A few hours later, in the email thread where we'd wished each other a happy Thanksgiving, my professor wrote to me: "Just wanted to let you know that I posted solutions to the final. And that it looks like your score will be well above the mean!" My scream of joy echoed across the Pfoho dining hall. I had gotten my first A at Harvard.

WHEN IT CAME TIME to declare my concentration, I agonized. Leo advised me to pick economics so that I could work at a bank in LA. I knew ec was a solid choice. It led to the life I swore to Leo I wanted: us, reunited, in Southern California (he said he'd never move).

But all around me, I saw the fruits of engineering. The teaching fellows wore backpacks embroidered with Facebook logos. My crush, the impossibly cool Lexi Ross, sported a Google hoodie with TECH INTERN printed on the sleeve. I imagined how people would look at me if I donned one: envy mixed with respect, exactly what I'd wanted to feel when I got into Harvard. "What if I could get a job at Google?" I asked Leo, conjuring the best possible workplace (largely because of the sweatshirt).

"That seems pretty unrealistic," he replied. I agreed. I was pulling in B+'s, which would have been C−'s at schools with less aggressive grade inflation. At most universities, I never would have gotten past the weed-out classes. But at Harvard, tech was relatively inclusive. The Women in Computer Science club didn't even have a comp. I would never get a card slipped under my door inviting me to punch the Pleiades Society, but if I studied hard, I might be able to break into the tech slipstream and experience riches I couldn't yet imagine. I sensed that one day I might own so many free T-shirts that I'd only need to do laundry twice a semester; that for years, I would constantly be trying new seafood. A dream, I decided, didn't have to be realistic. It just needed to be a thread to hang on to, a fantasy to get me through.

I chose computer science.

My mom replied to the news, "What was appealing about computer science when there are so many choices and you have so many talents?" I felt spurned. My mom was in the flush of her second adolescence, training to become a certified life coach. That summer, she was taking a Harvard Summer School archaeology course. That fall, she was embarking on a cruise of the Yangtze River delta. That week, she'd asked to borrow $450. I'd recently gotten a check from Harvard, so I had the money. I loaned it to her without question, already assuming I'd need to support my mom financially. I was so aware of the freedom I didn't have, of how I needed to be so responsible, even as my peers flirted with self-sabotage (or at least literature classes).

THAT SUMMER, before my junior year, I interned at Yahoo! in Southern California. Leo's friend referred me. I pretended I knew what I was doing during the interview and somehow landed an internship. When I showed up after finishing my sophomore year, with four relevant classes under my belt, I was astonished by the reception I received. Marissa Mayer had recently taken the helm of the company and was widely adored for instituting free lunch. My boss took one look at me—my hair finally shoulder length and blonde instead of pink—and exclaimed, "You look *exactly* like her!" She even arranged for a day trip to the mother ship so that I could take a selfie with the head honcho. With all sincerity, she told me, "You are the next Marissa."

My boss told me all the time that I was doing a great job, even though

I knew I wasn't: I had no idea what I was doing, which I'd later learn is normal for software engineering. But getting the benefit of the doubt so explicitly illustrated what Harvard could give me. I looked like someone successful. I'd picked up the mannerisms and habits of my milieu, plus I possessed a nice-looking set of teeth (at least on top). It made me wonder how much people had gone out of their way to help me in the past because, looking at the poor girl I was, they could imagine the rich woman I could become.

Meanwhile, I was living with Leo. When I was asleep he forced himself inside of me, the pain splitting me open. Early on in our relationship, when he had trouble getting it up without making me drink, I told him that I was basically down to have sex whenever. I'd meant that he could always feel free to initiate, but he took it literally. Two years later, he reminded me of what I'd said then all the time, as though it were irrevocable; nothing I could do would make him stop penetrating me in the night. People acted like it was easy to leave that kind of situation, but it wasn't: the dorms were closed, my mom's house was worse than ever, my relationship with Leo had isolated me and prevented me from building a support system with my peers, and getting my own apartment would've eaten up my paychecks. So I stayed. I ran before work and lifted weights after, gathering strength. During my ninety-minute commutes on the city bus, I studied for interviews, *Cracking the Coding Interview* across one thigh, a marbled notebook on the other.

Sometimes a critical voice in my head questioned why I had eschewed my love of art and writing to study something practical, instead of being the ideal passionate liberal arts student while I was still on the hook for taking care of myself. But no matter my exhaustion, every day, I opened the book, flipped to the right page, clicked my pen open. I knew what I needed. I had known all along. And, in doing it, I felt like I was returned to myself.

———

I clung to my intern manager's faith, and her promise that I could always return, when I went to the Grace Hopper Celebration of Women in Computing that October. Nearly five thousand college students and engineers crowded into an auditorium to watch executives give keynotes before three days of parties, free swag, and interviews. "This is like a cattle call," I whispered to my friend. "And we are the cattle."

Everything about Grace Hopper said, "We want you." The convention center ballroom stretched out for several football fields. Recruiters hawked women's-cut T-shirts, thermoses, and laptop stickers. Booths offered free manicures and chair massages. LinkedIn sponsored professional headshots. Women only made up about 16 percent of engineers, due to what they called "a pipeline problem": girls didn't want to study STEM, or they weren't tough enough, or were too afraid to get B's in math instead of A's in English. I loved this story because it meant I was one of the intrepid few. I was not one to question the terms of being wanted. Instead, I reveled in the rewards: I won a scholarship to attend the conference, with my own bed in a nice hotel room and a preloaded card to pay for food. I had an interview scheduled with Facebook. And one afternoon at the career fair, I competed in a coding challenge and a recruiter called my name:

"Emi Nietfeld is the winner."

"What?" I screamed, heads turning. "Yes!" I cried, pumping my fist in the air. I knew that the competition was silly—I'd only beat out two other students—but winning something made me feel like my old self.

The recruiter handed me the prize, a backpack: gray with the Square corporate logo. I sat down on the carpeted floor and transferred my stuff from the pink-and-purple backpack I'd carted around everywhere since foster care, then stuffed it in the trash.

When I went to my Facebook internship interview, held in festival tents pitched at the other end of the ballroom, I strode in with purpose, wearing my new gear. My interviewer handed me a dry-erase marker and I explained how to balance a binary tree, writing my answers on a tiny whiteboard. The next day, I came back and solved another problem. That night, I was invited to a party for other candidates. Certain Leo wouldn't find out, I ate my first bacon-wrapped scallop, then another thirteen of them.

The day after, a Facebook recruiter handed me a blue folder and said, "Congratulations."

The din of the convention center fell away. It was just me, holding the letter that said I'd make $6,200 a month—an unthinkable sum— plus housing, round-trip airfare, and a stipend to buy a bike and a lock.

Here was the proof in my hand: I was going to be all right. I exhaled, as if I could expel the last seven years of uncertainty and inhale my fresh new life, as if it had always been mine.

LEO WASN'T HAPPY about Facebook, or the more appealing offer from Google that followed it. I flew to San Francisco to interview at a start-up and Leo flew up to see me. We stayed in his friend's guest room in the suburbs. Early in the morning the day after I bombed the interview, Leo and I broke up. I had just turned twenty-one; we'd been together for two and a half years. Both of us cried and held each other. Leo promised I would always be dear to him, that I could always reach out for his help.

After breakfast, he asked me, "Are you going to call the Uber?"

"My flight's not until nine-thirty p.m.," I replied.

He put his hands on my shoulder. "You should go now." Not breathing, I shoved my clothes and my homework into my backpack, as I had so many times before. Leo showed me the door. As he kicked me out, the weight bore down on me: I wasn't simply in a distant city with twelve hours to burn—I had no home. I got into the car with nowhere to go. I texted everyone I knew in the area until I reached someone who was awake; my friend let me spend the day sitting on her sofa. In the afternoon, I laced up my running shoes and headed out across her subdivision, over the freeway, through the empty office parking lots, and toward the bay. The map had shown the water as blue, like the lakes in Minnesota. But everything was brown, the color of scorched earth, and stank of fetid seaweed. I put my hands on my knees and gasped for air.

Loneliness squeezed me from all sides. *Someone loved me*, I thought. *And I gave that up. For what? For Silicon Valley?* I glared at the landscape, unimpressed. It seemed like my own fault that I was alone, because I had so many ambitions. That night at the airport, I called my mom to tell her about the breakup.

"But wasn't he a Rhodes scholar?" my mom asked.

"Almost," I admitted.

"Call him right now and make things right." She didn't know all the details of our relationship, but she'd always urged me to smooth things over. My mom told me to beg Leo to take me back if I had to.

"No," I told her. "I can't." In a way, it felt like breaking up with her, too. After we hung up, I turned off my phone and buried it in the bottom of my bag so that I wouldn't make any other ill-advised phone calls.

## Twenty-three

After the breakup, I woke up every morning feeling crushed. I couldn't think of a single person to text. No one would ask me how I slept, if I did my homework, when I had exams. The only thing that made me feel better was lacing up my sneakers and running laps around Fresh Pond. I ran until I was so sore the only way to shake it was to run again.

On the first day of class my junior year, filled with trepidation, I approached Weld Boathouse. For two years, I'd watched the slim shells glide down the Charles, filled with fit people in visors. I'd heard anyone could walk on, but I'd always assumed "anyone" didn't include me. Crew was the consummate prep sport, made up of everything I lacked: good breeding, money, and upper-body strength. But now I wanted to join the lightweight team, which would force me to lose fifteen pounds, back to my Lakeville weight. I wanted to be broken, transformed, changed—berated into shape. I longed for someone to push me harder than I could push myself.

Instead, on the first day, the Radcliffe novices' coach sent twenty freshmen, one sophomore, and me on a one-mile loop. We spent the first few weeks learning port from starboard and practicing placing a forty-thousand-dollar boat in the water without banging it on anything. (Free access to such an expensive vessel seemed like, in my mom's parlance, "the bargain of the century!") The coach fed us lore about the team, which was formed long before Harvard accepted women. The men's coaches, in fact, had tried to prevent women from rowing. Since then, they'd spurned Harvard's name. While I loved the origin story, I was tired of talking: I looked on with envy as the varsity squad swung down the river.

My pent-up desire to prove myself was ready to burst when the coach sent the walk-ons to an intramural running race. I thought I had a fighting chance to win: varsity track and cross-country couldn't compete and the best recreational runner was injured. When the referee called the start, I held nothing back. I saw no other ponytails in front of me. With half a mile to go, crossing the Weeks Footbridge, I felt home free.

Then I sensed a presence trailing me. Somehow, I knew it was a woman. I knew if I looked back, my rival would slip ahead of me. I focused forward, my legs moving in slow motion as we got closer to the finish line. A referee was handing out numbered index cards, determining the ranking of the runners. I decided that if my nemesis pulled ahead, I'd elbow her out of the way. If necessary, I'd shove her into Soldiers Field Road.

In the final steps, I felt my rival move forward. I lunged for the card, jumping forward so that I landed on the ground. I clutched the card close to my chest so no one could pry it out of my hands.

I'd won, at least against my shadow.

When I finally looked up, I saw one of the star rowers, Mary Carmack. "Hey, Emi!" she said, beaming, not even a little bit breathless. "You really picked up the pace at the end there!" Mary offered me a hand up and asked if I had dinner plans. She didn't seem to mind that I'd almost killed her.

When Thanksgiving break drew near and I had nowhere to go, I broke down. I wrote Leo a note parroting what I'd heard from Dave and

Jan, that my values were all confused. Influenced by Harvard's hollow, ladder-climbing culture, I'd chosen success over love and now regretted it. Leo took me back, on probation, and with the condition that I stop speaking to Amy, whom I blamed in my letter for leading me astray, down the path toward a blue-chip internship.

When I got back to California for break, we lay on one of the giant beanbag chairs in Leo's loft as he made a proposal: he wanted me to drop out of Harvard and transfer to a school in California.

A sharp pain replaced the ache in my chest. As disappointed as I sometimes was by Harvard's status-seeking bullshit, I'd finally found places on campus where I belonged, and I wasn't going to give it up. "I can't," I told Leo. It was over. I went back to campus. A few weeks later, during winter break, my plans fell through and I went back and let him fuck me so I had a place to stay. The tears pooled in my ears. But at least I knew I wouldn't miss him, that I was better off alone.

THANKFULLY, I had qualified for Radcliffe crew's winter training trip and could leave Leo and Los Angeles early. To my surprise, I was a good athlete, good enough that I would row heavyweight, not light-weight, and join the varsity squad. (The novices' coach encouraged me to gain ten pounds and fulfill my potential as a "big strong girl.") In Florida, the sun rose over a cove filled with manatees. The pink sky reflected in our wake as we glided under freeway bridges. We pushed and swung and feathered our blades, gasping for air. I had no idea what I was doing, so I treated each workout as if it were a round of the Hunger Games and I'd be killed off if I fucked up. In a sport that was all about suffering, I believed that I could take more punishment than the prep school recruits. My hands blistered and ripped open. I relished the wounds, as if every callus hardened me to the ways I had been hurt.

Despite all the Consequences I'd suffered, I'd never really been coached before. Left to my own devices, I assumed excellence was all about destroying yourself. As a new rower, I kept "catching crabs" and getting my oar stuck in the water. When the coach picked up her megaphone, I flinched. But no matter how many times they told me to keep my wrist flat or to sit up straight ("Emi, show off the girls!"), the coaches never said anything mean. On one bad day when I was sure I'd be removed from the boat because I was rowing so badly, a teammate pointed out the wind. As the shell rocked underneath me and water splashed over the gunwales, I felt viscerally for the first time that there were forces outside of human control that affected everyone, no matter how perfectly they behaved.

On the team, I felt taken care of. Whenever we'd miss a meal, the head coach reminded us three times to request a bagged lunch from the dining hall. We got assigned Nike parkas that came to our knees—my first truly warm jacket. Each of these acts made me love the coaches. Once the ice in the Charles thawed, I found myself in a four-person boat, coached by a woman named Cory. "Good, Radcliffe," she called as our white-and-black oars cut the surface of the river. Every word of encouragement melted me. I memorized her many inspirational speeches. In the pouring rain, Cory called into her microphone and advised us to repeat in our heads: "I am hard-core. I love this sport." When the lightning cracked above us, she pulled out her phone to take pictures.

For the first time, I saw that punishment was not the best, or only, way to compel change. The cheap way was to kick people out or exclude them in the first place and make them feel like they weren't good enough. The hard way was to ensure their success.

ROWING WAS A crash course in bodily awareness. I'd never been encouraged to think about my body in space. My family didn't exercise. Because of my eating disorder, I'd spend a year of gym time in CRTC standing in tree pose while the other Residents lifted weights and ellipticized. I felt baffled about where my skin began and ended. At times, authorities had strictly controlled my actions, but I'd never learned how specific choices made me feel.

In college, I stumbled across necessary skills accidentally—often due to self-destructive impulses. Trying a fad diet called Whole30 led me to realize that my customary six cans of Diet Coke a day had been giving me constant headaches. Beans, my longtime staple, had caused the stomach issues I'd struggled with for years. It seemed plausible that my dysfunctional relationship with food originated in my body rather than my mind. Throughout my adolescence, I'd had to roll with the punches, but I began realizing that I was extremely sensitive. When I decided to quit all-nighters and make sleep my first priority, I learned I needed nine hours—not five or even eight. After two restless nights off from my usual regimen, a voice emerged from nowhere, chanting, *I want to die, I want to die.* The constant mental refrain of the past decade had been, at least partially, the hum of sleep deprivation.

As an athlete, one who had made it into a championship-bound boat, I could be as precious as I wanted in the name of performance. My teammates' tall, strong bodies consoled me: it was completely normal to have fat below the belly button. In fact, everyone had it. I bundled up in leggings and a team sweatshirt and headed with my boat to eat six eggs and two English muffins. After so much self-denial, these felt like overwhelming pleasures.

THE NIGHT BEFORE RACING YALE, my boat gathered in our coxswain's hotel room, and Cory came in to go over the race plan and then read us a bedtime story. "Fast dreams," she said, patting the foot of the bed where no one was.

The next morning, I woke up at 4:45 as instructed, everything trembling. I couldn't believe that this was happening: I was a varsity athlete, wearing my uniform, borrowed Oakley sunglasses, and a nonironic visor. At the starting line, the referee called, "Yale, Radcliffe," and at the sound of our team's name, my chest seized.

The referee's horn blasted. Our coxswain, McKenna, called the starting strokes to get us up to speed, then we were flying. The first 500 meters vanished in a blaze. But by the halfway point, fire laced into my lungs, my arms, my throat. I gulped down air faster than I could exhale. I was going to have a heart attack. I couldn't keep going for four more minutes; it was impossible.

Then, McKenna called for a move for Radcliffe, and just that word gave me two more strokes, then two more. Not Harvard, not what I'd dreamed of and found lacking, but Radcliffe, the women before who were excluded and yet carved out a place for themselves and now for me.

At 700 meters to go, all I could see was a pin of light at the end of a tunnel, collapsing. I clung to the sound of our coxswain's voice. "Five strokes for Abba," she said. Abba, I loved Abba. I could no longer endure for myself, but I owed it to her. "Emi," she said, and I couldn't let them down. "Gen." Gen who saved me a seat on the bus. "Maura," the bow seat who kept the boat steady, even as my lack of technique shook us side to side. The sweetness of each name stung my eyes. I'd spent so long sacrificing myself on the altar of self-sufficiency, repressing the side of me that was sentimental and loyal. But, as my novice coach told me, "Sometimes emotion wins the race."

"Five for Cory," McKenna announced, and our boat shot ahead.

Then we were in the final 500 meters. In less than ninety seconds, I would be free to die. McKenna's voice called through the splashing and the screaming. "Yale has two seats on us," she said. "We have to sprint early. Go now. Don't wait." She counted down the final forty strokes. "We're moving!" she yelled. "Get me a seat!"

There was no world, just one inch of Abba's back and blur. "Eight. Nine. Paddle!"

After the finish line, I dropped my head onto my knees and heaved, shaking. After a few minutes, I opened my eyes. It took a while for my vision to focus. I stared at my calloused palms and the hem of my uni, white scars on my tan skin poking out underneath. My quads—I had quads. "We won!" McKenna announced. Still staring into my hands, I started to cry. There was a difference between being able to suffer and being able to emerge after the suffering, and it felt as if I had, or that I would. Abba tapped me, to give me a hug. I passed it back to Gen, straining to reach. Cory waved to us from the shore.

## Twenty-four

On my first day as a Google intern, the summer after my junior year, I beamed in front of a whiteboard covered in equations. After posing for my security photo, I put on a hat with a spinning top that said "Noogler." Then I got my backpack—navy blue Patagonia with a dozen tiny pockets and the company's name embroidered in white—marking me as part of the intern class of 2014. I cradled it on my lap. It smelled like waterproofing and belonging—what I'd studied so long for.

My internship manager came to collect me, wearing waxed jeans and a deep V-neck T-shirt that exposed tufts of chest hair. He led me to a row of primary-color bicycles, and we pedaled past sprawling office parks interspersed with wild grasses. I felt as if I were in a movie trailer for the previous summer's film *The Internship*. When we finally arrived at our building, my manager badged me in. "Are you thirsty?" He pointed me to the barista, who made drinks at one side of the café. Beyond were pizza ovens, a fish station, and two rows of salad bars. I had arrived at the center of the universe.

"Do you eat here every day?"

"Pfft. This is not the good café." He preferred the barbecue joint that smoked brisket all weekend to serve it on Mondays. Or Kitchen Sync, which offered sushi and homemade pasta on handcrafted plates. There were two dozen cafeterias serving breakfast, lunch, and dinner, not including the ubiquitous micro kitchens stocked with almonds, dried seaweed, and multiple types of sparkling water—everything included in our compensation. There were on-site health clinics and subsidized massages and vans providing bike repairs and haircuts. Someone had considered every detail of our lives, in a way no one had ever done for me, and it felt like love.

In the weeks that followed, I enjoyed software engineering a lot more than I expected. I'd worried my background would set me apart, but most of my colleagues came from other countries where, as teenagers, they'd taken exams that determined their paths. Very few people seemed truly passionate about coding—engineering was just the best job. This made me feel less guilty about majoring in something practical, ignoring the voices telling me to "do what you love." The work required deep focus, like studying for standardized tests. Sometimes, it made me want to go outside and scream in the parking lot. Other times, I felt like the luckiest human to have a job that stimulated my brain all day.

It didn't bother me that I wouldn't interact with another woman at work all summer—let alone anyone who wasn't white, East Asian, or Indian. All that I saw was this sparkling new world, with its promise of purpose and fulfillment. Google felt familiar to me as an all-encompassing institution: I got on the 7:15 a.m. shuttle and returned home at dusk. If I got a full-time job, my years would be split into two halves, each one graded, like school. I would spend my years climbing up the ladder, going from Level 3 to Level 4 to Level 5, racking up stock grants. I didn't know what more I could ever want.

THAT SUMMER, I was constantly busy since I'd joined Harvard's Women in Computer Science board. As the head of sponsorships, I called companies and shook them down for cash, which we used to hold a five-hundred-person conference. This is what rich people did for fun, I learned: they joined boards and organized things. At Harvard, we practiced.

I never went out, except when my roommates invited me. One Friday in June, I skipped a workout to get dinner with one of them, Ren, who'd lived with Amy at Harvard.

As we left the restaurant, she invited me to get a drink at a friend's apartment. "I don't drink," I told her.

"Have water."

"I have to get up early to row."

Ren checked her phone. "It's eight p.m. My friend's house is on the way back."

I relented.

I sat in the living room with my glass of water when a guy ducked out of the kitchen, holding a plate heaped with bare white rice.

"Byron!" our host called out. The guy stopped, looking startled. He was very thin with messed-up blond hair. His roommate teased him, "Be a good host and say hello to our guests."

Byron acquiesced and sat down next to me. "Please excuse my food," he said. "I just biked a hundred and thirty miles."

"Really? How long did that take?"

"I started at six a.m."

We ignored Ren and her friend and the other guests who arrived and talked about sports. Byron had gone to Harvard, graduating the year before with a degree in computer science. He spent his free time alone, riding his bicycle.

He asked me where I was from. "I went to boarding school," I said, automatically, "but I grew up in Minnesota."

"I'm from Virginia," he said. "But not the hick part."

My eyes narrowed. "You went to that high school, didn't you? 'The best public high school in America'?"

"Thomas Jefferson." He blushed. "How did you know?"

"Everyone knows." I felt pleased with myself. I was learning the landscape of my new world. "'Not the hick part of Virginia . . .' Way to downplay the richest county in the United States."

It was nearly 10:00 p.m. when he stood up and said, "If you'll excuse me, it's past my bedtime."

As we walked up Bernal Hill to our rented house, Ren teased me. "He's so into you."

I rolled my eyes. "I'm too busy," I told her. But that night as I lay on my futon, my back ached, longing to be held. I scolded myself: *You have to be okay. You have to be okay being alone.* Needing anyone felt like inviting a lifetime of abuse. The only solution was to protect myself with ceaseless productivity.

ALL SUMMER, I kept running into Byron. One evening, I found him in my kitchen, wearing an apron and politely explaining to his roommates how to chop an onion: Ren had invited them over to cook for us. A few weeks later, I followed Ren to a party at some start-up guys' condo. In a sea of men in black T-shirts, Byron's blond hair popped out of the crowd.

"Hey!" I said. To my surprise, I was happy to see him. Ren was off talking to some founders; I had nothing in common with anyone else there. I asked Byron if he wanted a beer.

"You know that drinking impairs workout recovery." He wasn't scolding me, but he wasn't joking either.

I brought us each a red Solo cup full of water. At 9:00 p.m., Byron said he had to go to bed and called an Uber.

"Do you want to share?" I asked.

We went to his building first. "Do you want me to put in your address?" he offered.

"No, that's fine, I'll just get out here."

Standing beside his door, he said, "Well, it was good bumping into you."

"You, too." I turned, disappointed, although I wasn't exactly sure about what.

"Wait. Can I have your number?"

"Sure." I smiled, despite myself, and gave it to him. I trudged up the street, the sidewalk turning into stairs before I reached my house. My phone buzzed and warmth flowed over me: I was going to be normal, in spite of everything, with friends and plans and maybe even a date.

I unlocked my phone and found a Venmo request for my half of the Uber.

HALFWAY THROUGH THE SUMMER, my manager told me, "Don't be surprised if you don't get a return offer."

The conference room around us fell away. I'd known a full-time job wasn't a given—I'd still need to do interviews and pass through the Hiring Committee—but my boss's warning made it seem like I wouldn't even have his vote of confidence, the most basic requirement.

After our conversation, I wandered through the parking lot, stunned. I passed the outdoor gym and the experimental coffee lab and the sand volleyball courts. I went into another building, where they had fresh-baked cookies. I stared at my reflection in the door of a refrigerator full of beverages. I ran my hands over the bottles of sparkling water, the plastic cups full of diced turkey breast, the cans of Diet Coke at the bottom shielded by an opaque panel to dissuade us from choosing a sweetened drink.

I felt as though I were being cast out of Eden. I sensed that if I could just get a job there, Google would become a place that felt like family, that felt like home. It seemed possible that everything I'd lacked was right on campus, that somewhere in the cubicles were my surrogate parents, the people who would make up for my real parents' failures. Just like Harvard, the institution invited this kind of magical thinking. But unlike Harvard, you could stay for decades.

I had come all this way, I feared, just to lose it all. The adrenaline ran hot in my arms. My teeth gritted together with determination that I would get a full-time offer, whatever it took.

Perhaps, after everything I'd gone through, outsiders would expect me to keep things in perspective, to reassure myself that there were other jobs. But I could not; my hopes for Google were just as high as my hopes for college had once been. Even the small problems of my new life took on outsize importance: As I organized the Women in Computer Science conference, I started having night terrors about boxed lunches. I woke up at 2:00 a.m., clammy in the darkness, panicking that attendees would somehow not get their Panera turkey sandwiches.

The old patterns were ingrained into my nervous system. Everything was life or death. I knew people would tell me that things were different now, but it hadn't been that long—just six months earlier I'd been lying under my ex-boyfriend during winter break. My body and brain could not change as quickly as my circumstances had.

I paced an empty women's restroom, trying not to hyperventilate. All it took was the threat of security being stripped away, and I would re-double my efforts.

A MONTH LATER, after I'd turned in my intern project, I finally got a text from Byron, inviting me on a run. "Perfect," I wrote, Sunday afternoon no longer gaping empty ahead of me, even though my quads were already screaming from three hours of rowing that morning.

I met him in front of his apartment. His bangs were cut across the middle of his forehead and he wore a white mesh T-shirt from his high school cross-country team.

"I'm supposed to go nine miles today, but my calf hurts. So maybe it'll be shorter," he told me. I gulped and followed him up a hill and over to the Castro.

At Market Street, we paused for the light. He looked at me. Coming straight from rowing by myself, I'd worn shorts instead of leggings. "What's on your legs?"

"Scars."

"How did you get them?"

"I gave them to myself."

"Oh. I'm sorry." Byron winced at his faux pas. He started jogging again.

"It's fine." We were quiet for a while, as he led me up Twin Peaks, a mountain I didn't know existed because of the fog.

By the time we got back to his house, we'd run almost fourteen miles. My roommates had come over and were eating steak and drinking wine. Byron and I each had a glass, which made me just a little giddy. It didn't even seem to impair my recovery.

We ran again on Tuesday and on Thursday after work. When we finally got to my door, Byron hugged me goodbye, quickly. His body felt light and stiff, like a bicycle. It seemed like if I nudged him, he'd tip over.

I drew a cold bath and dumped in all the ice from our freezer.

"What is Byron doing?" I asked Ren, explaining how he had taken me on another detour up a mountain. "I think he's trying to kill me."

"He's trying to impress you. It's clear he likes you."

"Ugh, I don't know," I said. I had a plan. I was going to go to graduate school or else get a full-time job in Silicon Valley. If I ever fell in love again, it would be when my life was over, so in my midthirties.

I climbed into my ice bath, ready to read a book on rowing techniques. But I kept getting distracted. I thought about Byron's blue eyes, his heart-shaped face, his earnestness. I even found his old T-shirts charming. Imagining how good it would feel to have those skinny arms wrapped around me, I felt myself melt as cubes clinked against the side of the tub.

I woke up the next morning thinking about Byron. We were supposed to ride bikes that weekend, but that felt so far away. Who knew how much could change in twenty-four hours, or if he'd even make a move. I couldn't just hope that things would happen. Life never worked like that. Besides, I only had two weeks left before my internship ended and senior year at Harvard began.

I texted Byron and told him to come over that night.

When he rang my doorbell, I found him dripping in sweat, bicycle in front of his body. He reached out, took my face in his hands, and kissed me.

We went up to my room. I'd already decided that I'd set the pace. We'd do it quickly, that way Byron wouldn't have a chance to hurt me on any level.

"Wait," he said, wanting to slow down.

We lay side by side. He traced the scars on my legs.

When Byron ran his hand across my face, I teared up and looked away. The way he touched me made me feel like he cared, even though we came from such different backgrounds. If I'd ever had a chance to really date him, I was sure I'd blown it by making the first move, or taking him to my futon.

"Can I ask you a question?" he asked.

I wiped the moisture out of my eyes. I regained my composure and turned to him.

"What was the biggest compliment you've ever gotten?"

I thought about it for a while. I told him about how when I interned at Yahoo!, people called me "the next Marissa Mayer." "It's probably just because we're both blonde."

Byron stroked my cheek again. "Of course you're the next Marissa."

*I love this guy*, I thought, then immediately corrected myself. It was way too early to love someone. If I ever committed myself to him, it would only be after extensive observation and testing.

When the sky brightened, peeking through the window in the attic where I slept, I offered Byron an eye mask. The next day, we slept in, something I could never manage on my own. "There's a food truck festival," I offered. As soon as we left my house, Byron reached over and took my hand. I was alarmed: Wasn't he worried that anyone would see us? That they might think that this was serious? But I let him thread his fingers through mine.

At the fair, he agreed that all the prices were ridiculous. We split a single crêpe.

That week, our only one together, we spent each night asking each other questions. I wanted to be close to Byron, but I felt held apart from him. I felt this way with almost everyone I met, as if my past rendered me incapable of connection, ineligible for the normal joys of life. "Tell me a secret," I asked him. I held his chin in my hands.

He told me about his shame, that he probably wouldn't have gotten into Harvard if his mother and his grandfather hadn't also attended. His gap year was the loneliest time of his life, in a childhood that was already lonely without knowing why. He turned to his stuffed animals whenever he needed solace. "I never feel like I belong," he said. "I feel like there's some language everyone else speaks, but I don't."

"I'm weird," he continued, and I laughed because he appeared to be the epitome of normal, an archetype of a privileged white boy. But in our circles, even the smallest failure to conform made someone an outsider. Byron was skinnier than me, with a smooth, flat chest and shaved legs that he claimed helped him cycle 2 percent faster. He spent his free time playing online chess, reading about World War II, and watching television shows about witches.

"I like the ways you're weird," I told him, and he nestled against my chest. I bit my lip, waiting for him to ask me for a secret in return. When he did, the words flowed—I told him that my mom and I had a tense relationship and that I hadn't seen my other parent in a decade. My ex-boyfriend had been bad to me and, when I was a teenager, a man in a hostel hurt me.

I turned away from Byron. He rested his chin on the back of my shoulder. It felt so sweet, sweeter still because I feared I'd shared too much, revealed too much baggage, and that this was the last secret we'd share.

"How do you feel about me now?" I asked. If he was going to reject me, I needed him to do it right away, before I got attached.

"I respected you a lot before, but I respect you even more now."

I turned and kissed him. I willed myself to imagine that Byron could be good, that I could have one thing in my life that didn't have a sharp edge. I couldn't make myself believe, but if I put in enough effort, I could hold on to the hope.

At the end of the summer, Ren invited me to Yosemite. We went with her ex-boyfriend and a Thiel Fellow who had received one hundred thousand dollars for dropping out of Brown (and would be a billionaire two years later). While we hiked, I kept checking my phone for messages from Byron, eventually dropping my phone and shattering the screen when he sent a photo of himself wearing my Radcliffe casual hat. "You are in love!" Ren declared, pleased with her matchmaking.

We headed back through the Sierra Nevada in the early evening. From the passenger seat, Ren summarized a book about a former child soldier from Sudan. "It really had me wondering: Could someone like that ever be in a relationship with someone who just had, like, a normal life?"

"That's a good question," Ren's ex started, ready for a big philosophical discussion.

I squirmed. Of course the question wasn't theoretical to me. The fact that this debate was happening at all only underscored my isolation. With the exception of one rower who knew I'd been in foster care and a treatment center, none of my friends knew my backstory. The others in the car assumed that we were all spectators to tragedy—never victims of it.

"I think they definitely can," I said, convincing myself as I said it. If the answer was no, where would that leave me?

I wasn't going to claim any special authority on suffering, especially compared with a child soldier. I was too ashamed. Besides, I thought Ren's opinion or the Thiel Fellow's was just as valid as mine. Instead, I said, "Everybody's been through something." I brought up the rowing teammate whose dad died just before her freshman year, then an athlete-heiress with a degenerative disease that meant she'd be in a wheelchair by age thirty. I thought about, but didn't mention, the girls from Methodist, whose troubles I'd never taken seriously because I couldn't comprehend them.

I needed to believe that people were never broken. That any wound could be redeemed. That eventually, with enough work, I'd become mentally like Ren, whose life wasn't perfect but who'd never had someone ejaculate on her while she cried.

"Yeah, I disagree," Ren replied. "I just don't see how it's possible. When you've been through something like that? How can someone understand?"

"You don't have to understand everything to love someone," I replied. No one in the car agreed. Conversation moved on to Larry Ellison's yacht, but I kept contemplating the question that Ren had raised. It would define my early adulthood. After everything I'd been through, could I still be normal? Could I ever really love? Could anyone normal, like Byron, love me? How much would someone need to know about my past to understand me? And if the answer was anything more than my desired quantity of absolutely nothing, how would I ever bear to share it?

*Twenty-five*

B ack on campus, I waited to hear back from Google. I wouldn't know if I had a full-time offer for six nerve-racking weeks as I sent my résumé to forty companies, did dozens of first-round interviews, and tallied as many rejections.

When I was crying after my Facebook interviewer advised me that "I don't know what you were coding, but it's not Java," my phone rang again. It was my Google recruiter, telling me I had a full-time offer. "Thank God," I gasped. "Thank God." I would make six figures, with health insurance and dental care and a 401(k)—everything that defined adult stability.

Immediately, I Skyped Byron. We'd made no promises when I left San Francisco, but we talked every day and he'd already come to visit. I slept with his small plush penguin in the crook of my neck. Byron was elated about my job offer, hopeful we might live in the same city.

"Yeah, but I might still go to grad school," I said, testing him to see if he'd try to stop me. My classmates were flocking to Oxford and Cambridge. I loved flirting with the idea that I, too, had the luxury of simply skipping across the pond, money be damned, and continuing to row.

But, truthfully, I no longer wanted an itinerant life. I craved a home, with things on the walls, a suitcase buried in the closet, furniture I wouldn't throw away when I left. That desire felt so essential and so dangerous that I kept it at arm's length, swearing to myself that I would break up with Byron at the first sign of trouble. I reminded myself constantly that the odds of us staying together long term were very low. But that didn't make me less delighted to find his handwritten letters in my mail slot, or less thrilled to share my good news. I held our penguin up to the camera and flapped his wings. Even he was happy for me, too.

EVERY DAY IN OCTOBER, as my deadline to sign with Google drew nearer, I said a prayer of gratitude that I'd passed the hiring bar, especially because it seemed as if I'd just barely made it. Google offered me $130,000 a year, an impressive sum, especially for a twenty-two-year-old, but I had peers who would be earning twice as much. When I asked about roles in New York City, where I desperately wanted to live, I learned that that office was reserved for stronger candidates. By the end of the month, I had no other offers.

The night before the Google deadline, I got an email from Yahoo!: they had lost my résumé weeks prior. The recruiter all but guaranteed me a job if I came to California to interview. I flew out the next day. By the end of the week, Google matched Yahoo!'s offer to pay me $200,000 a year straight out of school—more than six times what my mom had made. I was stunned, less ecstatic than in shock. The massive difference in money confirmed my long-held paranoia that one wrong move could materially alter my future. I had not been Catastrophizing—the reality of our winner-take-all world meant that the difference between the top and the next tier down was hundreds of thousands of dollars. With my increased compensation from Google, even after taxes, I figured I could save $100,000 my first year and have a safety net for the first time ever.

Still, part of me couldn't stop thinking about how, in so many other versions of my life, I'd spend the next who-knows-how-many years struggling to pay off debt. As I'd come of age, the world around me had become even harsher. To supplement her pension, my mom worked for just over minimum wage as a receptionist at a strip mall storefront. She graded standardized tests in a shuttered Bloomingdale's, rows of folding tables and chairs next to garment racks under the fluorescent lights. Her third job was working as a personal care attendant to a woman she despised. If her job while I was growing up hadn't been union, that could have been how she made a living my whole childhood. If I hadn't had the support to get into college and graduate into a lucrative career, I likely would have found myself in the gig economy, too. Anthony from photo camp was doing the best of anyone I knew from before: after getting full rides to college and grad school, he was working at a newspaper in Beijing. But when I tracked down people from residential treatment on Facebook, they were single moms, hairstylists, working low-paid health industry jobs. Given what we'd been through, they were doing well, but their lives looked hard, the margins for error razor thin. I heard through the grapevine about other former Residents in jail; another died in his sleep (apparently from side effects of his medications).

Harvard had changed my life. But the fates I narrowly avoided haunted me.


ONCE I SIGNED WITH GOOGLE, despite my existential anxieties, I had the idyllic college experience. No longer worried about getting a job, my course load consisted of The Meaning of Life, Mommy Wars, and Chocolate. I spent hours in brick buildings with grad students, debating whether free will was an illusion.

My teammates and I ate our meals in a pack. Athletes with wet hair came and went during hours-long breakfasts. I made my social debut at the talent show, when I applied my best Gollum impression to recite Cory's five-minute speech, verbatim, on how there are no ties in rowing. When I felt accepted, I became loud and confident and outgoing.

One spring morning in the locker room, one of the girls in my boat said, "I always knew I was going to an Ivy."

"No way," I replied.

She shrugged. "Dartmouth was my safety."

The girls with lockers near ours nodded in agreement. My mouth fell open in shock, though I knew it wasn't that surprising: many of my teammates were legacies who'd attended feeder schools. My wildest dream was their destiny.

At that moment, I pitied them: they would never know what it was like to have such a far-fetched dream come true. In the Yard the trees were exploding into blossom and I walked around slack-jawed, staring at the light on bricks. How could my peers ever appreciate how lucky they were? That morning, it felt as if suffering had sharpened me and made all the good things lovelier. I was grateful for it.

When my good fortune caught me off guard, I felt the best about myself. I was supposed to feel this way, always: endless, stupid gratitude. I heard stories about people who survived near-death experiences and came back transformed, ready to seize their lives, endowed with wisdom. I thought I should be able to hold on to my astonishment, too, to bask in it perpetually. But it didn't always come naturally. To feel such unconflicted joy, I had to forget about the bad things. I needed to decide that everything had been for the better and that my reality was, in fact, the best possible outcome.

I felt grateful that I had adapted. I had become a Harvard person, with a special voice that I used on the phone. But it was easier for me than for many, because campus could be horribly racist (under a façade of liberal wokeness with tokenized diversity). Meanwhile, I'd entered college a relatively disadvantaged white girl and would graduate a rich white woman. Though my classmates who'd grown up wealthy would always spot my charade, to the rest of the world, I passed. I hoped that I could take the good from Harvard and sidestep the bad, perhaps naively underestimating how much the place, and my quest to get in, had shaped me.

I HAD TO MISS GRADUATION. Radcliffe crew made it to the national championships again, and I was rowing. My mom begged me to skip the regatta and stay on campus, even recruiting a cousin to email me and tell me I'd regret it, but I could not be persuaded. The last time she'd tried to see me was during a race in Indiana, when she'd threatened to drive ten hours, though I begged her not to come. I had cried in my coach's hotel room, unable to explain why I didn't want to see her, feeling powerless to keep her away. My mom stayed home, but I still rowed badly.

I was grateful to skip the rigmarole. I didn't want to pose beside my mom for pictures, dressed in my cap and gown, as she gushed about how my Harvard diploma was her biggest accomplishment. Worse, I didn't want to see my classmates wearing white dresses under their regalia like pristine virgins, kissing their dads while wearing their Cartier Tank Française graduation gift watches. Instead, I would attend half of one event, then wait until the last minute to pack, shoving all of my stuff into the two boxes I'd take with me when I moved to California.

After our races, I clung to my teammates and threw my arms around the coaches. We derigged the boats and loaded up the trailer. Byron was waiting for me with keys to a rental car, ready to drive us to San Francisco, where I'd start my new life.

Three weeks before, on Mother's Day, I called Grandma Edna, as I did on every holiday. Usually she only wanted to talk for five minutes. But this time, when she finished her standard questions—"Are you going to graduate?" "Do you have a job?" "How much will you make?" "Do you have a boyfriend?" "How old is he?"—she looped back to the start and began again. She couldn't remember my answers. She was ninety-seven and dying. The sadness of that fact faded compared with the joy of telling her what she wanted to hear, again and again. Each question had the same meaning: Are you okay?

And my answer to each was the same: I'm okay now.

*Epilogue*

Three months after I got married, I sat in a windowless room, fiddling with my ring. The office in Manhattan was smaller and darker than the ones from my childhood, but the psychiatrist sat on an expensive chair.

"Do you have trouble sleeping?" she asked me. Dr. Bougie wore a wrap dress with poufy sleeves and Salvatore Ferragamo flats with the little bows.

Clutching the side of the couch, I nodded.

"How often, would you say?"

"Every night," I croaked.

She went down the checklist of symptoms for post-traumatic stress disorder. Did I feel guilt, shame, horror? Yes, yes, yes. Did I believe the things that had happened to me wouldn't have happened to someone else? I fought back tears and nodded.

"Are you angry?" I shook my head. I was never angry, because I never imagined things could have been any different. Outrage required believing there was a better alternative, but wasn't my life the best-case scenario? I called that resignation acceptance.

But I was deeply unsettled. Even after Byron passed a battery of relationship tests—including moving across the country for me when I transferred to Google's New York office—I panicked every time he didn't immediately respond to my texts, sure he had died. After we married, I feared he'd divorce me. In my nightmares, I was chased, kidnapped, and institutionalized, or I had to fuck a row of men for cash. Even though Byron and I were both fully employed software engineers, I was too nervous to spend money, insisting we live in a fourth-floor walk-up studio with a shower so small I couldn't lift my elbows and had to wash my hair at the office. I couldn't relax even for fifteen minutes. I never forgot that only three highly correlated things had to happen for me to be out on the street: becoming disabled, getting sued, and having Byron leave me. My friends thought I was crazy, but they had families.

I'd pretended these anxieties comprised the human condition until, in the spring of 2018, I stumbled across emails my mom had sent me in Budapest, which flooded me with details I'd managed to forget. Meanwhile, the Me Too movement was in full swing and I'd recently had to file an HR report at Google detailing a mentor's harassment. Each headline about assault made my skin hot and my lungs contract. The only way to burn off the feeling was to work out, until I was exercising three hours a day. A few weeks after I found the emails, a premarital counselor asked Byron and me, "Is there anything you don't feel comfortable discussing with each other?" "Nope," Byron said, tapping his sneaker against mine. I burst into tears.

But even with resources, getting help wasn't easy. I was terrified of therapists. When I found my first psychologist in New York, I came in eager to tell the story of my life, starting with that night in the hostel that had come to stand for all of the vulnerability and humiliation that came before. The therapist stopped me. "It will just retraumatize you," she said. She suggested I could discuss it in five or ten years, when I was no longer upset.

"You don't understand," I told her. "I don't have five or ten years." Every time I tried to share a detail, she gasped and recoiled.

Byron didn't know how to respond either. Stone-faced, I told him what I couldn't stop remembering. In response, he smiled, seemingly unable to make any other facial expression. "How does that make you feel?" I asked, wanting him to express sadness or anger or horror, even disgust. Instead, he answered in a robot voice, "Emotion not found."

I'd done what I was supposed to do and tried to move on, but instead of the past shrinking behind me, it just loomed larger. I realized that if I didn't get help I was going to kill myself, either quickly or slowly. I cursed myself for marrying Byron because my wedding vows seemed to prohibit suicide. After I had exhibited so much resilience and self-sufficiency, the ongoing consequences felt like moral failures. In my desperation, I decided to submit myself to brutally painful prolonged exposure therapy, going through the worst moments of my life again and again, until I could form them into a cohesive narrative that could be filed away and thus stop terrorizing the present.

"How much time would you say you spend thinking about these events?" Dr. Bougie asked, pen poised, face in a twist of rich-woman pity.

I stared at the corner of the wall, white-noise machine whirring in the corner. "Seventy-five percent?"

REALIZING I WAS SICK DEVASTATED ME, because throughout my life sickness was often conflated with badness. I saw evidence of this everywhere when, in the years after graduating from college, I started tracking down documentation and interviewing people from my adolescence. The 246 pages of medical records from Methodist described a homicidal, psychotic fourteen-year-old "young woman" who didn't speak so much as "claim" and "deny." When I went back to Dr. Woods to ask what she remembered about me, she said, "You were a manipulative liar." ("It's okay," she added, chuckling, after I flinched. "All teenagers are.")

Sitting across from Dr. Woods in her office, I took pride in being "good" now, but I knew I was only good because I'd changed. In my psychiatrist's notes, I'd found extensive commentary on my appearance. I asked Dr. Woods why she wrote so much about my hair. "Is that some kind of shrink thing?"

"It's a commonsense thing. Anyone could see you today and then see someone with blue hair and know you are a totally different person."

*But I'm the same person*, I thought. And then I realized Dr. Woods's timing was all off: in high school, my hair was always blonde. I only dyed it bright colors once I was already on my way to Harvard.

Dr. Woods wanted to hear all about my new life, and I was happy to give her the satisfaction of one patient achieving the stability that eluded many young adults with similar backgrounds. But I couldn't help but feel she was especially pleased that I had a corporate job and was partnered with a man. Even though I loved Google and Byron, the pressure to conform felt crushing. It left me feeling guilty for wanting to write and ashamed of my attraction to women. When I'd called Jan a few weeks prior, she was eager to recall my sexuality. "You were so rigid," Jan said, laughing. "You were always so sure you liked girls!" I didn't exactly respect Jan's opinion on the matter, but not conforming had real consequences, too. As I got older, I feared that looking queer—in my men's jeans, sports bra, and Birkenstocks—had motivated the attack in Budapest. I lived in fear of being reprimanded, scolded for minor things, afraid that I'd get in trouble, that if anyone didn't like me, they would hurt me. My rich white millennial persona was a defense.

Despite the expectations she imposed on me, I couldn't deny that Dr. Woods had been one of my strongest advocates. When I asked her what the hardest part of treating me was, she replied, "When you got back from Europe." The answer caught me off guard: I'd expected her to cite something that I'd done, a character flaw I needed to amend. And after six years without a word, I assumed everyone had forgotten. But Dr. Woods remembered, and she cared.

Twenty minutes later, she told me, "You were promiscuous."

"How was I promiscuous?" I asked.

Dr. Woods said she couldn't remember any specifics. "But it was clear. You said certain things."

When I worked up the courage to tell Byron, he shook his head and said, "Wow, I just lost all respect for her."

"No," I started, ready to jump in and defend my old psychiatrist. But then I asked myself why. Maybe when I felt ashamed of my younger self, I was just reflecting back how adults had seen me. Maybe I was the one who needed defending, not them.

THE MORE I RESEARCHED, the more I realized how little I understood about my own adolescence. As a teenager, I'd only known what I was told, and many things had been kept from me. In the absence of all the facts—and any larger context in which to understand them—I felt responsible for everything that transpired.

After Michelle moved away, I wondered what I had done wrong to alienate her. In high school, she told me I'd refused to speak to her or see her. Though I recognized that she was blurring the truth and I had been a child at the time, I felt at fault for our ongoing estrangement. Only in my midtwenties did I see the family court records and learn that, in sixth grade, I was scheduled to travel to visit Michelle. Before my cross-country trip, her lawyer argued that because Michelle was in the throes of a mental health episode, she needed extra time with me. Rather than put an eleven-year-old on suicide watch duty, the judge canceled the trip completely and ordered Michelle to go through mediation before making further contact. My mom didn't explain that an adult had made a decision to protect me. Instead, she let me believe Michelle didn't reach out because she no longer loved me.

I saw in the records that from my very first therapy appointment after my parents' divorce, discussions of my mom's diagnosis and potential treatment took up as much space as my own. Professionals knew she was sick, but they didn't hesitate to medicate me rather than her. When I found my descriptions of our living situation, I wondered why no one had investigated. A decade after Ingrid first showed up at our front door, she told me she was glad I hadn't let her inside. She knew Child Protective Services would've taken me away: "It would have made a bad situation worse." One downside of a broken child welfare system is that no one wants to use it. While some families, largely those of color, have their kids taken away because they're poor, other families who need interventions, like mine, do not get them. Much later, Annette told me she'd filed at least one maltreatment report. They told her there was nothing they could do since I wasn't in immediate danger. As far as she could tell, no action was taken.

Instead, I was told I had a social worker not because my parents had issues, but because I was troubled. Confinement at CRTC was presented as the natural consequence of my actions. But from my research, I learned that in fact Ingrid's initial plan was foster care. After a meeting in which the care team, my mother, and I had already agreed I should go to a therapeutic home, I was mysteriously labeled "not a candidate" in the records—probably because Ingrid couldn't find a family. Only later did I learn that residential treatment centers are often holding cells for adolescents no one wants. The emphasis on accepting responsibility we had been subjected to is completely unscientific: it's normal for teenagers to reject authority, to not want to conform, to act out and make mistakes. Usually, the cure is growing up. But institutional living changes kids in ways that harm them in the wider world—when they are lucky enough to avoid flat-out abuse. When another former Resident found me on

Instagram, I learned about a fourteen-year-old who had recently been raped by a Staff in one of the classrooms. According to the news story, the security cameras trained on the adolescents, waiting for us to mess up, conveniently didn't work when an adult attacked her. The police found a beverage bottle containing tissues with her rapist's semen on them. I wondered if they only believed the victim because she could furnish evidence.

Meanwhile, when I wasn't conceptualizing my own rape as an accident, a punishment, or something my own sick mind had conjured into existence, it took on the inevitability of fate. I was on my own for so long, of course someone was bound to hurt me. I knew I couldn't have lived with Dave and Jan and gotten into Harvard, and my alma mater was the one thing I wouldn't bargain away, even hypothetically. There were no other homes, Ingrid had told me. So, my destiny inevitably included the night a man in Eastern Europe called me a bitch and told me to swallow his cock and I got lucky the other man didn't join in, that they didn't kill me.

But then I learned that Annette had tried to take me in but was thwarted by the strict rules. My mom might not know what country I was in, but foster parents couldn't let me out of their sight. Annette would have had to quit her job, which wasn't an option. Learning this devastated me at first, then made me more confident that there really had been no easier way.

Shortly after, my brother told me that he'd also tried to take me in. He and his wife lived across the street from my first high school, with two young sons, and had an extra bedroom. When they heard I was going to foster care, they'd called my mom and said I shouldn't live with strangers. Then she ghosted them. The next time they heard from her, I was already in Lakeville.

When I heard this, I burned with anger at my mom. She had thwarted my chance to grow up in a family, with a home, knowing my brother's kids. But it wasn't only her fault. Everyone involved in my case knew I had an older brother who lived less than two miles away. He called me "Sis" and had only ever been kind. Yet no one reached out to him. While federal and state laws dictate that children live with relatives whenever possible, that mandate is all too often overlooked.

No one else supported my relationships with other family members. I wasn't even allowed to call my brother from CRTC. Later, when I was out, I was scared to get in touch. Our infrequent contact remained superficial, usually planning visits with their kids in public locations. I worried they thought I was nuts. But I never questioned why they might have thought that until my sister-in-law told me that when I returned from Budapest, my mom explained that I had been "detained as a potential terrorist and sent back by the State Department." I laughed at the absurdity of my mom's explanation, until I realized that they had believed her. For eight years.

In 2019, Hennepin County settled a federal class-action lawsuit on behalf of children who were in foster care or were the subjects of maltreatment complaints since 2011. I'll never know what happened in my case: my records from CRTC were destroyed by the time I thought to request them when I was twenty-six. Even with the help of expert attorneys, I could not get access to my foster care file. But the lawsuit allegations sounded eerily familiar: failing to investigate reports of abuse and neglect, not providing services, placing kids in overly restrictive institutions, and making interventions voluntary in cases where that wasn't enough to protect kids or help families. When I learned about the suit, I felt envy and bewilderment—how did the plaintiffs know they deserved better? Who told them that the system was flawed? I was jealous of them, because I wished so badly that someone had leveled with me. I needed someone to say, "Your mom has a problem and she can't take care of you," acknowledge that there were very few options, and make it clear that despite everything, I did not deserve punishment, not at CRTC, not in Budapest, not at the hands of my boyfriend.

Instead, I was left trying to please my mom. Shortly after exposure therapy, I asked her what happened, starting with my time at Methodist Hospital. Her version was simple: "I think you did it all to make me look bad."

I'D TRIED HARD to fix my relationship with my mom, believing it was the one thing I still needed to be a true success. During college I had tried to reconcile with her, seriously considering attending a weeklong "Brain Skills" seminar for "bonded partners" (a term that made me shiver). The program sounded like a cult, especially because it was held in rural Illinois with no hope for escape, but I was willing to take the risk, hopeful that if we finally learned to "return to joy in each other's presence" we could have the connection that eluded us. But in the end, it conflicted with a trip to Romania to meet Byron's grandparents. When I told her I couldn't make it, my mom got upset; she'd already paid for both of us before inviting me.

A year after I graduated from college, I brought Byron out to meet her. At the end of our visit, she dug in her trunk and extracted a plush baby penguin, its matted fur speckled with mouse pee. She held the chick out in her palms, eyes gleaming. The gift was so touching: she'd remembered that Byron gave me a penguin stuffed animal, then thought of me at Target, and held it for me for months until our visit. On the other hand, it made me sick to see the tiny bird, neglected and filthy. No healthy person would allow it in their home.

I wept in my rental car. The next day, I invited my mom for brunch at her favorite restaurant, IKEA, and asked what she remembered about the summer before my senior year of high school. She said, "You went to camp."

I saw myself standing outside of the Bridge, with greasy hair and bandaged legs, wounds searing. "Do you remember anything else?"

My mom took a sip of her lingonberry soda. "No, I think you were at camp for almost the entire summer."

I studied my mom as she sliced her Swedish meatball into tiny pieces. But I saw nothing on her face that indicated she was lying. I felt like I was going nuts. How could you forget picking up your daughter at a shelter and sleeping with her in your backyard on a tarp?

For another two years, we didn't speak about the past, until I started therapy in earnest. When I worked up the courage to call and ask what she remembered about my ill-fated trip to Europe, I expected to hear her sunny voice tell me I'd had a fun time backpacking. Instead, she said, "Oh. The creepy situation."

"The creepy situation?"

"The creepy, *creepy* situation." When pressed, she told me I'd been drinking, then said, "He forced you down and held you down."

The specificity shocked me: she knew. It really had happened. Without realizing it, I'd been waiting eight years for my mom to confirm my experience. It felt as if nothing existed without her acknowledgment.

That conversation renewed my belief that the truth lay somewhere in between our two perspectives, that we could agree on a version of my teenage years that we both could live with. In the weeks that followed, I called and asked her about Methodist. But the things I remembered most vividly, she denied. She insisted there was no therapy at Methodist, no remark about my breasts, that the records were wrong and she was right. When I broached the topic of Budapest again, she told me I'd taken shots with the two men, then denied that there was force. When I brought up what she had told me about my rapist holding me down, she replied, "I never would have said that." She sounded almost angry. "That's not what happened at all. You agreed. You just didn't like it when he got aggressive."

I recognized my mom's words from the worst thoughts in my head. For years, I'd feared that everyone would believe that I had invited the attack—that I had agreed to deep-throat a man's dirty penis and then suggested he come first in my mouth, then on my clothing. But was I afraid that *everyone* thought that or was I just afraid of my mom?

*What am I supposed to do?* I wondered. What are you supposed to do when your mom tells you that you agreed to your rape but just didn't like it?

My first psychologist in New York suggested that I just needed empathy. "It must have been traumatic to hear something like that happened to her daughter." She acted as if my mom's generational norms of silence and shame should be respected instead of challenged. Even my exposure therapist responded to my mom's insistence that I'd been drinking, and her comment that I'd agreed and just didn't like it, with an attempt at justification: "Sometimes people say things to try and help make you feel better, but they don't come out the way they intended."

"I don't think that's what's happening here," I replied.

I knew how it looked: I was a Googler with visible biceps and a *New York Times* wedding announcement. My mom was a poor, sick woman. She hadn't showered at home in years. She slept in four pairs of socks and didn't have heat. A mysterious stomach illness meant she could no longer eat vegetables. She kept falling asleep at the wheel and getting into accidents until her insurance dropped her. When she landed her dream job, she couldn't wake up on time and got fired after a few months. No one believed she was capable of deliberate manipulation; much of the time it wasn't clear she was even cognizant of what she was saying.

And my mom was the only parent I had left. During college, I tried to meet up with Michelle, but she said it wasn't possible. After Grandma Edna died, I sent my condolences and mailed her a Mother's Day card. I never heard back. Despite these being our only interactions, I reached out in the flush of my engagement, hopeful I could invite her to the wedding. She'd replied, "Congratulations." After so many failed attempts to get back in touch, the period at the end somehow felt final.

"Do you really want to make your mom's life harder?" Annette asked, when I said I was going to confront her, gently, and tell her how her hoarding affected me, how her words made me feel (using all the "I" statements I'd learned in treatment). "Leave the past in the past."

But it wasn't in the past for me. As I went from bad to worse, my mom's comments tortured me. It wasn't as if I were holding a grudge for something she had said years ago and then recanted. She was still telling me I had agreed to the rape. Every time she texted me to see if I needed a thousand votive candles, I felt ill knowing that she had this cheap way to hurt me.

Despite the urging to the contrary, I decided to tell my mom how I felt. Six months after I got married, I flew to Minneapolis, rehearsed, and then told her, "Your hoarding has definitely placed a big wedge in our relationship." Immediately, I added a caveat: "And I know it's an illness."

"Well, I think they put it in the diagnostic manual so they can charge for it," my mom started. I was ready for her to deny being sick; that was part of the disorder. She claimed that doctors had been out to get her and that I'd only gone to foster care "to get out my angries" on strangers. That, too, I was prepared for.

I brought up the emails I'd found, the harmful things she said.

"Well, you were drinking," she replied, insisting I'd accepted shots from the men at the hostel. She had made this a question of fact—had I been drinking or not?—a question that would consume me for six months of research through old emails and journals, even though I knew it didn't matter.

"I don't understand why it's really relevant."

"Well, you said you had a good, stiff drink to kind of steel you for what was ahead." She denied holding me responsible, but she said I'd "willingly participated." She said she was sorry I felt blamed and told me I'd expected performing oral sex in a kitchen to be "sweet and nice and gentle."

All through the conversation, I pleaded with her: Why couldn't she let me off the hook? Wasn't my rapist the easiest scapegoat in the world? He was a nameless, faceless stranger half the world away, the stereotype of a monster who preyed on her daughter. Yet again and again, she turned to my supposed drinking and to the fact that I did not object vehemently, to the idea that I had, in fact, consented. It didn't matter what this grown man did or that the crime had the elements of ritual (like the perfectly accented commands from porn). All that mattered was what I had done: drank (or not), decided to comply, opened my mouth.

In that way, it was the same old story, where outside forces did not matter, only my own actions. No wonder that all these years later, I was still telling my therapist about the rape that "a good person, a moral person, would die before letting that happen." Of course my mom could not absolve me: if this one thing wasn't my fault, then other things might not be my fault either. That would contradict the story that we both believed in, that I'd once endorsed more than anyone: that I was the master of my fate, that I was the one in control.

IN THE YEARS after I graduated from college, it made me squirm to watch the gospel of "grit" make its way into the mainstream. In a viral TED talk, the psychologist Angela Duckworth proselytized that youth in crisis needed mental toughness. From the way she talked about it, grit was more important than food, shelter, or safety. Others seemed to agree: in 2015, when a cover-up of contaminated water in Flint, Michigan, was exposed, behavioral scientists flocked to the city. Combating the effects of lead poisoning required unrealistic efforts, like funding for maternal health care, pediatric nutrition, and early-childhood education. Instead, The New Yorker reported, before many homes even had safe drinking water, behavioral scientists were on the ground figuring out how to teach children "a growth mindset."

This doctrine was supposed to be for young people's own good. Society's constant problems—poverty, racism, violence—seemed intractable. Others, like inequality, were only becoming worse. Even in a country as rich as America, there seemed to be simply no hope of all youth having a fair chance. I recognized the emphasis on "grit" as a final throwing up of hands. Kids too young to speak would be held responsible for their own problems. It didn't matter how they were wronged, or how preventable the harm; their job was to contain the damage, making the blast zone smaller by absorbing all the impact.

When flagrant affronts drew the ire of society—like migrant children separated from their families and detained in tent cities, oil fields, and a converted Walmart—I found myself numb. *Maybe it's for the better*, I thought. *Maybe the adversity will make them stronger.* The doctrine of "anything bad can be alchemized into something good" had been so drilled into me that it seemed to apply even in this extreme situation. I was horrified by the logic I'd internalized.

The whole song and dance of resilience chipped away at my humanity. It required a profound lack of empathy. It erased any pain, no matter how great, as long as it resulted in productivity. And when I was not productive—when I cried for hours every night for months, when I screamed when people came up behind me, when I never felt at ease, even in my home with my partner—it made me feel like a failure. I told Byron I wished I had not lived, that the world would be better without me: "What have I even done with my life?" He teased me for not starting a charity. I took this as a serious critique.

I was supposed to smile in Harvard Yard, not sob in bathroom stalls. I was supposed to be happy and grateful for all I'd been given. I was supposed to exemplify post-traumatic growth, not post-traumatic stress disorder. When people asked me, "Was it worth it?"—did an Ivy League diploma compensate for the ways I'd been mistreated?—I was supposed to respond, unequivocally, "Yes." All the other lives that could have been mine—lost to incarceration, addiction, lethal violence—were supposed to make my success shine in bright relief. Yet these alternative fates weighed on me. It didn't make me feel better that my generation was poorer than their parents, largely because of the crushing student loans I'd avoided. The suspicion that I would have gotten put into the justice system instead of the mental health system if I were Black or Latina gave me no relief, to put it mildly. It did not console me that I had worked hard: in hindsight, my adolescence felt like buying every lottery ticket I could afford.

As MUCH AS I struggled with attitudes toward overcoming and resilience, society also changed in very welcome ways as I went through my twenties. The Me Too movement meant my mom no longer had a monopoly on my understanding of what had happened in Budapest. Thanks to reality television, people understood that "hoarding" didn't just mean my mom had a lot of stuff. Generation Z embraced the word "queer"—the label I needed when I knew I wasn't straight—and ushered in a new era of body positivity. Cultural awareness around trans identities exploded, and the terminology became infinitely less jarring than phrases like "sex change," "transsexual," and "sexual reassignment surgery," which I'd grown up using. Discussing Michelle no longer required an informational lecture. For years, I had avoided talking about Michelle at all, ashamed of the mistakes I'd made in discussing her in the past, and because I didn't want people to think I was blaming her transition for the pain she caused. I wonder, all the time, how things would be different if I'd been born even a decade later.

Meanwhile, the progress made by activists has been countered by anti-trans legislation that specifically targets children, who are easier to police and control. Texas began investigating gender-affirming care as abuse; Florida proposed mandating that schools disclose any "noncon-forming" identities to parents. Advocates of these measures frame them as issues of "parental rights"—once again placing the preferences of adults above the needs of children. These laws weaponize the very systems that are supposed to protect kids, turning our society's most vulnerable into pawns of the culture war.

The consequences of anti-trans discrimination are dire. The 2015 U.S. Transgender Survey found that 40 percent of transgender respondents had attempted suicide—nearly ten times the rate of the general population. Nearly one third of the trans respondents experienced homelessness; almost half reported having experienced at least one sexual assault. Many of the most devastating aspects of my experience are par for the course for trans kids, who need not just awareness but protection.

As I struggled in my midtwenties, I wondered if I had "survivor's guilt"—the persistent questioning "Why me?" of someone who makes it out of a situation that others don't escape. But the more I saw of our increasingly unequal world, the more it seemed like "thinking person's guilt." The deal I'd struck made me feel sick. My role in the system was to smile and to show that the status quo was not that bad, because some people—including me—supposedly transcended.

AFTER I TOLD MY MOM her hoarding affected me, I'd promised myself I wouldn't contact her first. I was no longer willing to let her call the shots and pretend everything was okay. But four months later, on Mother's Day, I broke down. Her texts resumed, but she stopped saying she was proud of me or that she loved me. I ached like a child to return to her good graces.

Ten months after our talk, just after I turned twenty-seven, she wrote me, "It's forty-seven degrees and a star-filled sky in New York." She added the star emoji. The sweetness of her words made me think of myself staring at the sky, hoping for a better life—not to be treated like she was treating me.

Byron held me as I dialed. With each ring, I wanted to hang up, but that would only make it harder. My mom picked up as she was walking into Hobby Lobby. I said, sniffling, that we couldn't have a relationship while she denied the things she'd done that had hurt me and held me responsible for the rape.

"The what?" she asked.

"The assault."

"Oh." Cash registers clicked behind her. I was ready for my mom to apologize, for her to hear me, and finally realize what I'd been saying since I was a child. My mom sighed. "I just feel like you are an endless well of mea culpa. I just don't know what I can say to make you think that I don't think it's your fault."

"You can say, 'It's not your fault.'"

She wouldn't say it. Items beeped in the background as they scanned. Four beeps, five, six. I knew I'd done the right thing.

I said "I love you" again and again, as if all of the "I love yous" I had left had to be compressed into one fifteen-minute conversation, although my mom didn't seem to register what was happening. She probably thought I was premenstrual.

When I clarified that she shouldn't call me again, she said: "Look, the hoarding is not your responsibility, except for the hole in my heart. And I don't blame you for the assault."

*Except for the hole in my heart.* Who was the parent here? Whose heart got to have holes? And "I don't blame you" was a world away from "It's not your fault."

"I love you," I said, one more time, my eyelashes matted together with tears. "Goodbye." My hand shook as I pressed the button to hang up.

Without my mom, I waited for my life to fall apart. I expected a void to open inside of me that would torment me for the rest of my life. But

I realized that I'd already experienced my mom as an absence. I'd already suffered so much when she'd taken her love for me, and her faith in me—as true as it was—and used it as a weapon.

Sometimes I lie in bed and ache, wishing for a parent who loved me regardless of what I achieved. I think of my mom's idiosyncratic truisms—the way she'd finish a task and say, "Good enough for government work!"—her generosity and strength, the ways she's a remarkable human, someone who made the best out of bad situations and carved her own version of happiness out of her disorder.

But I never miss the way she treated me.

MY EXPOSURE THERAPIST told me that the purpose of my treatment was to accept what happened. Not accept it in the sense of the final stage of grief—that would come later, if ever—but merely to acknowledge reality. To do that, I combed through all the details (touch, smell, taste, thoughts, bodily sensations) until a coherent story emerged. That was the same goal I had while writing this book, which consumed seven years of my twenties.

One big part of the process was tracking down the man from Budapest who raped me. People told me I had to make peace with everything I'd never know, but through the years, I was haunted by the fact that he knew my name, but I didn't know his. The hostel had since closed, the owner impossible to find. With the help of an investigator, I looked through hundreds of photos taken on the premises and posted online, wondering if I would even recognize his face. After a few weeks, when the cause seemed hopeless, the investigator tracked down a former hostel employee on Instagram; she identified my rapist from the picture I couldn't remember taking. I learned that he was forty-two or forty-three when he attacked me, and he wasn't Serbian. Growing up during the war was a lie. Perhaps most chilling was the time stamp on the photograph. It was taken at least two hours after I entered the hostel to get my things, a time I have no memory of. Together, these facts painted a very different picture of what happened than either the story my mom told or the one that I'd clung to. I wanted so badly to believe in human goodness, and to minimize the situation, that I'd justified what he did. But the more I learned about this person, the more I realized that believing in the good of humanity means acknowledging that some people are bad.

The sad and enraging things I found in my research mostly did not surprise me, but again and again, I was shocked by the acts of kindness. When I called Jane and asked if she understood what happened to me in Budapest, she replied, "Oh my God, Emi, I should have known." She swore it was okay to be mad at her. But I wasn't. We had been teenagers constrained by different norms. After our conversation we started Facebook messaging again constantly, picking up where we'd left off.

Even imperfect people changed my life for the better. As a girl, Ingrid had dreamed of attending Interlochen, so she advocated hard for me to go. The more time I spent with Harvard people, the more I respected Dave and Jan for opening their home to me. By the time we spoke years later, they'd fostered many other children and become adoptive parents. Dave asked me what my time was like with them, acting like he expected frankness. "It was important," I replied, telling the truth. I gained new empathy for Annette and forgave her imperfections for good when my oldest nephew came back into my life. He was a nineteen-year-old community college student, realizing for the first time how my mom had impacted his dad, and moving out on his own. I was terrified for him. Every time we spoke, I couldn't sleep. Even though his circumstances were better than mine had been, I worried about every detail of his life: Would he get a bachelor's degree? Would his job include health insurance? What if he got injured or had a mental health crisis? For years, Annette had had those fears about me. Without her, I would not have made it.

Each bit of information I learned gave me a piece of myself back. It helped me create a story independent from the one I'd believed, the one where the trouble started with me. When I was in a dark place, I got an unexpected email from the man from the embassy in Budapest. A month earlier, I'd written him and received a notification that began "I have completed my time . . ." and said the address would no longer be monitored.

"Of course I remember you," he wrote. "How could I forget?" He said he could tell that something was seriously wrong when I came in; he even noted how little I had with me. His description of the day was so clear that I could see the framed photos of President Obama and Secretary Clinton on the wall. His witnessing was a gift I'd struggled to give myself.

"I remember that you were shattered but not destroyed, if that makes sense," he told me. "I had the feeling you would find some way to salvage a life for yourself."

*My salvaged life*, I thought in wonder.

I had spent my young adulthood desperate for redemption, striving to make everything that happened "for the best." It would only be a good story, I believed, if it had the happiest ending. I had to take tragedy and twist it into triumph. Otherwise, I would be pathetic, if not forever broken. But the man's email revealed a third option: I was allowed to be affected. I was allowed to be changed.

With that understanding, I built scaffolding to support myself. The year I turned twenty-eight, my insurance paid out fifty thousand dollars for therapy and acupuncture, plus chiropractic and physical therapy to treat chronic physical pain. Without guilt, I warned people that I screamed when approached from behind. When I couldn't sleep, Byron tucked me back in, handing me a plush penguin and telling me a story about a family full of mischievous birds.

Instead of making a life that would redeem the past—an impossible feat—I sought out a life that I could live with. For the first time, I felt lucky for the little things: to wake up in the morning in my own bed, to eat breakfast, to do my work. It was no longer so important to me to achieve something great, because I was happy to be alive, which had seemed impossible and tenuous. I became grateful for the passing of time, each milestone that brings me away from then, into now: my marriage, buying an apartment, changing jobs, each new baby penguin, one day a child of our own, for whom I swear I will not make the same mistakes, though I know I'll fall short in some regard.

On my wall, I have a poster that always reminds me of when I was growing up. A girl stares out the window at a city while a plane crosses in front of the moon. Every time I see it, I say a prayer of gratitude to my younger self for delivering me here, into adulthood, where I can make my own peace with what I learned along the way.

AUTHOR'S NOTE

Memory is the primary source of the material in this book, supplemented by interviews, emails, journal entries, and medical records. Dialogue has been reconstructed, to the best of my recollection and with the help of documentation where available. Some names have been changed and certain identifying characteristics have been omitted—for example, to protect the privacy of people who were minors at the time.

# ACKNOWLEDGMENTS

This book would not be what it is without my editor, Mia Council, who found a very early version of this manuscript in an agency slush pile and, over two jobs and four years, shepherded it into what it is today. Mia, I wrote every draft (from the seventh onward) for you. Thank you for pushing me to unite the two halves of my life, when I thought the story ended after high school.

I'm deeply indebted to everyone who helped me reconcile my past with my present, starting with Michael and the team at the Weill Cornell Medicine Program for Anxiety and Traumatic Stress. Without your witnessing, I would still be silent. To my therapist, Aditi, and to countless early readers, especially Cory Bosworth, Lea Page, professor Margo Seltzer, Dr. Adrienne Carmack, and Adrian Nicole Leblanc, all of whom explained my life to me so I could understand it. Dianne Heins helped me understand my rights as a foster child and tried to track down my file. My endless gratitude to the dozens of folks who sat for hundreds of hours of interviews, especially Noah and Savanna G. from CRTC.

This book would not exist without the kindness of the people in it. Thank you to everyone who helped me as an adolescent, including the therapists and treatment workers who did the best they could. Special thanks to Dr. Woods, Ingrid, Dave and Jan, Dan at the embassy in Budapest, and my friends' moms. Dr. Kat, I strive to emulate your eternal youth and vibrancy. Annette— I don't know who I'd be without you.

ACKNOWLEDGMENTS

Time and time again, my teachers saved me. Huge thank-you to Miss J., Kurt, Mrs. Z., and to the writing faculty at Interlochen for teaching me coherence. To my French teachers—I hope this book is not an abomination.

Thank you to Alexandra Franklin and Vicky Bijur for finding this project an ideal home. I could not have asked for a better team at Penguin Press, including my incomparable editor, Mia Council, Sarah Hutson, Stephanie Ross for the arresting cover, Colleen McGarvey, Shina Patel, Randee Marullo, Maureen Clark, and Karen Mayer for your wise counsel. My sincerest gratitude to the Sales Department for helping this book find its readers and to Ann Godoff and Scott Moyers for their support.

I owe a huge debt to the Scholastic Art & Writing Awards for making me believe I could start, Hedgebrook for powering me through the middle, and the Blue Mountain Center for taking away the internet when I needed to finish. My writing group, led by Hillary Frey, provided tremendous camaraderie, as did the friendship and feedback of Savannah Carlin. Caroline Bleeke, Donna Freitas, and Qian Julie Wang each provided crucial support as I navigated the publishing process. Shane Tan's overall read was very helpful, and Lily Moss and Ryan McDaniel provided thoughtful notes on writing about trans issues; any mistakes are mine alone. My research assistants, Julia Fay, Sam McCue, Elizabeth Gassman, and Rose Escandon helped me ungaslight myself. Thank you to the YoungArts Foundation for providing a grant to support fact-checking this work and to Nikki Shaner-Bradford for your relentless search for truth (and caring as much as I do about the makes and models of long-scrapped cars). My endless gratitude to the activists who changed the world with the Me Too movement, especially Tarana Burke, Chessy Prout, Chanel Miller, and Lacy Crawford. Melissa Chadburn's writing about resilience shaped this book. A huge thank-you to my attorney, Katherine Conkey, for your sound advice and for being my biggest fan. Nina Kossoff took the cover photo at summer camp and kept it safe through ten moves over fourteen years.

I will forever be grateful to Cory, Wendy, Liz, and all the athletes of Weld Boathouse—past, present, and future. To my admissions officer, Elizabeth

Pabst, who wrote me a handwritten note so I would know my acceptance wasn't a typo. To Joe Blitzstein, Radhika Nagpal, and the Women in Computer Science crew. To my friends Victoria, Amy, Ren, Mary, and Gen, and too many others to name. To professor Anne Harrington, the Pforzheimer Pfaculty Dean, whose Madness and Medicine class made me wonder if maybe I hadn't been crazy.

Thank you to Jane, for your sisterhood, and to Charlotte, for teaching me to double-check my work. To my in-laws, thank you for accepting me (and teaching me how to ski). Thank you to my parents, for urging me to work hard and making me believe I was special, and to my brother and sister-in-law for standing by me over the years. To my nieces and nephews, my Girls Write Now mentee Marion, and the youth of the world going through impossible things—thank you for your light. You inspire me.

And finally, to Byron, who read at least twenty drafts, asked me "What's the point?" until I found it, and held me while I cried night after night, month after month, until I didn't need to anymore. Thank you for your steadfast love and devotion. Our family is the great miracle of my life.